A Look Through My Eyes

by

Everard Knights

PRESS

A Look Through my Eyes
by Everard Knights

Printed in the United States of America

ISBN 9781612157856

www.xulonpress.com

Table of Contents

Dedication

As I read over the information that I've written about myself, I quickly realized how sad of a person I've been. For my entire life, I've lived a life of an imposter who lives from within me. Human beings in general are conditioned to follow as a youngster from the day of birth. Our emotions are usually customaries by what we are fed through the digestion of food, but the majority of the time it's through the power of verbal dialogue and what we're told.

We live in a world where there is a double standard for what we believe in our confused society. There are those of us that live our life in an introverted manner, and those that are extroverts. I believe that the reason for those of us that have the mechanical build up of an introvert is due to what we felt from within the womb of our mother before entering this universe. The chemical that is released from carrying the fetus decides on the disposition of the person.

To put it into a clearer light, it's like a car being assembled at a plant. If the person that is in charge of putting the engine together is working with people that portray an unhealthy attitude, then this type of behavior is transcended to the mechanic, causing him or her to work in a lackadaisical way or frustrating manner. I guess by now we've all heard the saying, "pay me now or pay me later." So basically it's what you put into, it will decide on what you get out of it.

The type of behavior that I had been exposed to as an adolescent was totally and extremely atypical for a child to be exposed to. Such demented unhealthy behavior that may have carved me into the person that I've become. I know that the professionals have done their researches to try and assist people who may be similar to me by injecting them with poisons that we call prescriptions. Now that we can see what we've been taught that a person that is looked at as being a professional must be important and needed in this world.

In a world that everything is visual to our eyes, but has anyone ever stopped and asked themselves the old question. How does a blind man see? Well, the answer to that is from within. Our heart and soul are clearer than any eye that is wide open. Most of us walk around on a daily basis with a transparent mask to feel accepted in this world. The truth is that the average person that is walking around on the planet we call Earth, is usually not what you see. The way to survival is to live as if you belong among the creatures on this planet. Until we find an avenue that we can feel like we belong, I say that the only hope we have, other than removing our selves without permission, we must seek the help through our divine Alpha and Omega.

Acknowledgments

I am extremely grateful to have such a strong force around me. The entire Ross family has been a blessing to be around. I must thank God for all of His blessings, for delivering me into this world through His daughter Doreen.

First I would like to thank my family in no particular order. I would like to convey my deepest appreciation to my Aunt Winifred for all her support and having the skill to listen and not being judgmental.

Her wisdom and her heart felt love for me would never go unfounded. She's been more than an aunt to me and if at a mere mention of any need, God knows, I'll be there. My Aunt Winifred has spent tireless moments encouraging me and guiding me through my rough times. Understanding that my aunt has had her own misfortunes, she's tried to use some reference from her life to show me that there is a light. I know that whatever happens to me, no one will ever stop me from being there for her. I say to the entire family that Aunt Winifred has been like a mother to me and knowing that she's only a phone call away from me gives me peace from within. I love you.

My Aunt Monica has always been a sensitive and loving human being. She wears her heart and soul on her sleeve and searches for peace love and tranquility in all of our lives. Her eyes always have the sparkle of joy and happiness, even if she's going through her own trials. Aunt Monica was the closest to my mother and therefore, shared many secrets that probably have never been revealed. She has supported me in numerous ways that it would be difficult to list them all. She believes in me and truly wishes the best for me at all times. I know without a doubt that I'm very near to her, and she sees me not only as a nephew, but as a brother and a friend. The relationship that I share with her is different and can't be compared with anyone else's relationship. I say this to her: "It's better to say thank you and not mean it than for me to mean it and not say it at all." To her I say "who loves you baby?"

I can recall the first time that I met my Aunt Cita. She had a genuine smile on her face and was cut from an expensive material we know as happiness. She carried herself as smooth as silk, and she was blessed with wonderful features. Aunt Cita had the ability to draw you in because of her personality. Her biggest asset was her addictive laughter. It comes from deep within. Time has been a factor in our lives, so it has prevented us from speaking with each other on a regular basis. However; whenever we do speak, the conversation has always been filled with laughter and thoughtfulness. Aunt Cita has been an inspirational to me with each conversation we've had. She continues to motivate me in staying strong and having me believing in myself, telling me that this is the only way that God would provide for me. I know that there will come a time before we all move on from this world, and that I'll be able to fulfill her wishes and thank her for being my aunt. "Bella" I say.

From the moment I had set my eyes upon this particular aunt, I knew that there was something peculiar about her. She had the disposition of a person that can be whatever you pushed her to be. Although she carried the title of aunt, I found it extremely difficult to take orders from a woman who wasn't that much older than I was. As with anything in this world, time is the deciding factor. Gradually, as time passed, I realized how wonderful of an aunt I had, and that I wished for nothing more than to see her happy and for her to be proud of me.

Aunt Merle will always have a special spot in my heart, not because of the time that I spent at home in Grenada, but because of her genuine ways and non-hypocritical values. She has never stopped caring about me, and she showed her divine love and thoughtfulness of my son and me when we all traveled as a family to Grenada. Merle I say to you, "a lot of good could be accomplished in the world if nobody cared who got the credit." However, at this time in my life, I want the world to know how wonderful of a person you are, so that you can receive the credit. "May the stars shine brightly every night over your head."

I couldn't thank or speak about this person without mentioning his other half. This family prays together and always plays together. Jude at one time in his life saw the world as an open door. He felt that he could take whatever he wanted when he wanted and wouldn't care about the wreck he left behind as he focused on his trail ahead. As with everything in life, age brings wisdom and usually by the force of God, we have no other choice but to change or to prepare ourselves for destruction.

Fortunately, for Jude he had an option just a one-time opportunity to change his life. This remarkable woman who happened to enter his life at the right time, played a huge role in converting him into the person he is today. Uncle Jude has played his cards right in the sight of the Lord and since then, has been blessed with a beautiful wife and two adorable children. Uncle Jude and Aunt Eileen have been in my corner so many times, that it reminds me of a boxer and his trainer. They both have done their best in directing me on a path that is clear and safe.

It's always better to walk the path that you know than to improvise without research. They've seen me through so many moments that I had thought all had been lost. The amazing thing about having a Christian believer is that they never forsake you; and even when you're flourishing, they continue to support you. I believe that Uncle Jude, Aunt Eileen and others have a purpose, and one of their missions is to help me in continuing to seek Jesus.

I know that they will be blessed and rewarding them with health, strength and prosperity has already marked their future. God knows that if there was ever to be a time that I can repay them, I would. So I've decided to educate those around me and to speak to whomever I believe needs my care.

How can anyone not notice this gentleman when he enters the room? He has the disposition of a teenager but the mannerism of an adult. His smile is radiant and the energy that flows from within him is effortless. Uncle Thomas has always been a jovial person, and anyone within ten feet of him would catch this infectious delight of being in his company. As a child I had many opportunities to see this gentle man show his love and devotion for his family. Uncle Thomas really convinced me when an altercation took place at our home, and how quickly he was willing to put his well being on the line for his beloved sister.

I knew that this sister, in particular, being my mother, was extremely close to him, but I didn't know to what extent he would go out of his way for his family. As a result of the numerous episodes that have taken place in his life, I've come to have the utmost of respect for him. Family is something we can never be without, so he's thought me in his own way that sometimes you don't have to say much, but it's your action around you what means the most. I will always remember what he has done, and hopefully one day I'll touch him in a way as he did to me.

As a small child, I always wanted to be as big and as tall as this Uncle. He carried himself without fear and believed in whatever he decided on. He spoke with a gentle voice, and he tried his best to see that everyone around him was always happy. He's extremely giving, especially around the holiday season. The kids all love him, and we all look forward to hearing his jokes. Uncle Winston has always treated me with respect and has always wished me the best. There have been times when I've been down, and he may not have had the financial means to help me, but he always inspired me to be a man and stand strong.

Sometimes we all see money as our escape to our problems, but if we would take the time, we would see that to spend the money wisely, we first have to have responsibility, and that means being a man. Uncle Winston has thought me that "Courage is not the absence of fear, and it's the master of it."

As a child I really didn't have an opportunity to spend much time with this uncle. I do recall an incident that took place at my grandparents' home. This was the opportunity when I observed a man who never spoke too much, deal with a matter that could have been explosive distinguished by pure brilliancy. Yes.

Uncle Walter was a man of brains rather than bronze. By having a good head on your shoulders didn't mean that once confronted with danger you had to the option of standing and fighting or walking away. What it meant was, if possible you should try your best to outsmart your opponent with your wealth of knowledge. Uncle Walter has shown his keen senses on many occasions to deliver his stern message. He's advised me on a plethora of subjects, giving me the advantage on whatever the subject or situation may be.

Uncle Walter and his wife Aunt Theresa have shown their love for me and Austin. There were times when we had virtually nothing and had taken us in. I knew that the sight of seeing myself and Austin in a destitute situation weighed heavily on both their shoulders. At times, I could see the hurt through their eyes for us as he probably thought about his sister. For whatever the reason, they were ready to see us back on our feet and neither of them was going to stop until they saw me returning on the saddle again. If there was ever a moment in their lives they needed me, I would like them to know that I've not forgotten and I'll be there without a moment's notice. I believe that this quotation describes the thought process of my Uncle Walter. "Always keep your head up, but be careful to keep your nose on a friendly level."

Many years ago I had the honor of meeting one of the nicest uncles whom anyone can ever ask for. His face had a shine on it that magnified the rays of the sun. He stood with poise and had a smile that had you thinking, that this man must have been as smooth as silk in his younger days. His voice was clear and powerful to ratify his existence. As I walked beside him, I knew that someday, this uncle and myself will become near and dear to each other. He showed his concern for me as he educated me on the simple things about Grenada and life.

After leaving Grenada to venture on a new beginning for prosperity, I knew that one day in the very near future, we would see each other again. Uncle Fitzroy has been nothing short of being a fantastic uncle, and if I may say, a brother to me. His generosity over the past years cannot go untold. He's assisted me with shelter to protect my son from the harsh elements; he's assisted me without having to see me in an uncomfortable position, by offering to help in a monitory way. Uncle Fitzroy has spent endless hours speaking to me about having the strength and teaching my son and me the ways of being a man.

His sincere devotion to seeing that I conquer whatever obstacles that I'm faced with in my life, has given me the discipline to be a shadow in his footsteps. Uncle Fitzroy I take my hat off to you, and I can only hope that one day I'll be able to make you smile by seeing that all your hard work and tiresome nights have paid off.

I want you to know that, no matter where I go. I'll always give credit to you for being the step dad that I never had. "Who loves you baby?" My hope is that, everyone who reads this book will find it enjoyable and find its reading difficult to forget.

I wrote this book to show the world that just because a

person walks around with a smile on their face, it doesn't necessarily mean that person is happy. I've worn a mask for a great part of my life, and one day I would love to take it off and have a chance to be a normal person of this world we live in. I hope by writing this book and releasing some of the hidden demons that crowd me daily, will help me to at least loosen, the knot to start the procedure.

I would love to thank my one and only son Austin for being such a great son. I know that being a youth in this life that we live in can be extremely difficult and tempting with all different kinds of poisons. So I'm grateful that you've been strong and blessed to shun the vice that you're confronted with. Austin I've always wanted to tell you thank you for allowing me to be your father and for having the faith in me to be your guiding parent. I love you and I'll always love you my son. I hope your life is filled with love and happiness and that whenever you're in need that you can come to me or any of your aunts and uncles.

Continue to strive towards the sky and settle for nothing less than self fulfillment.

Love daddy,

Everard Knights

INTRODUCTION

I would like to notify all readers that this book has been written to advise and help anyone who has lived a similar life, in fear and need for a little admiration as I have. Some of the names in the book have been changed to protect them from their true identity. I must present you with the facts of the book before you decide to read it.

The book has been written through the eyes of a young person who was subject to violence, emotional stress and physical and mental abuse as a young child, up to his adult years.

Every word that has been written is true and for some, might be difficult to digest. I am obligated to warn you about some of the events that took place in my life are very graphic and sometimes disturbing, but the only purpose is to give the reader an insight, so that you will have a better understanding of what I went through.

I hope the book shows you the journey and struggles that I was faced with and how I had to make a choice of either dying through the hands of our judicial system or receiving the help to feel the freedom and peace through Jesus Christ.

Thank you, please enjoy.

Chapter 1

My name is Everard Knights; I was born in Trinidad and Tobago. My mother was originally from Grenada and traveled to Trinidad where she met her husband by the name of Lionel Knights. I'm one of six children, and as you'll come to see soon, a child with a dark past. As I take you on this never before told journey, some of the events that are covered, have been mentioned before. However, never in depth like now. Information that has never been mentioned before will be an eye opener to many, and hopefully, will bring change to those involved in this reading. I suggest to my readers, that the information within, may at times be explicit and probably not enjoyable to digest.

As a child I guess I was always very intuitive and felt that I should know as much as possible about my family and reason for certain behaviors.

Doreen Ross, my mother, came from a family of fourteen children. She was the second oldest child. Technically speaking she was the third child because her brother and sister before her were twins. From what I was told by my aunt and uncles, my mother was highly regarded. She was the one that assisted her mother in the care of her brothers and sisters. Being from a family with so many children, it was certainly difficult for my grandmother to do it all on her own. My mother was soon placed in an acting position of motherhood at a very young age. The entire family referred to her as "Sister Doreen" not just "Doreen." By then, she now had rank on them, but never abused her position.

As in any family of this size, there will always be ups and downs within the household. My grandfather apparently had a drinking problem which brought unsettledness at times within the household. With so many children (having more boys than girls), the probability of physical abuse was under control. My mother was adored by her entire family and also loved by the community she lived in. She was certainly a beautiful woman. She stood 5ft 6 in tall with an olive complexion. She had straight black hair and sparkling brown eyes. She walked like a tiger that was in no hurry to go anywhere. Her smile was addictive, which left a mark in your mind. She had a laugh that was infectious that would leave you forgetting all about your troubles, leaving you to laugh along with her.

Doreen was the type of person that always placed herself last, so that she could help those who were less fortunate than her. She would always sacrifice her needs in order to accommodate others with whatever their concerns were. One thing that stood out about my mother was that she was a no-nonsense person. Doreen was never afraid to speak her mind, whatever the topic was, she spoke how she felt. She would refer to "this is just her feelings and it may not be what everyone else felt." She always felt that, what good would it be to come home and complain when you had the opportunity to speak your mind and chose not to do so because of fear.

Doreen had so many paraphrases that at times I wondered if she sat with the disciples. She said to me one day, "Courage is not the absence of fear; it's the mastery of it." I can testify to her words that she was definitely not a coward. From what I was told, my mother felt that it was time to start a life of her own, and although her mother was against her decision, she traveled to Trinidad.

Her oldest sister had traveled at an early age to Trinidad also, so she embarked on a short visit to the beautiful island. One day while walking along the water front of down town Port of Spain, she heard the whistle of a man. Being the lady that she is, she ignored his attempt by his impoliteness. Such an attempt to speak with her was not appropriate, so she continued on her way. Suddenly there was a man who stood approximately 5ft 8in tall, dark and handsome with a Fedora, and dressed like a man who owned the world. She was mesmerized by his charm, but acted as if she wasn't taken aback.

He had her attention and asked for an opportunity to have dinner with her. She agreed and met with him for dinner in a beautiful upscale restaurant in the town area. Lionel was a man of high taste and always got what he wanted. He was a ladies' man, and a vast part of the cities women had been fell to his charm. Lionel enjoyed the finer things in life. He loved to dress well and never went anywhere without one of his hats. He drove one of the Island's nicest cars and ran his own construction business. He knew that he was the town's biggest catch.

Within a short period of time, Doreen Ross would become Doreen Knights, and the eligible bachelor was no longer a free man. Lionel bought a home in an area that is looked at as being rich with a picturesque setting. In that house, my sister Maureen and I would be born. My father provided my mother with a maid and the services of one of his workmen to drive her wherever she needed to go. In today's world, we see this type of living as posh. Wilma was extremely good with us and also a great friend to my mother. Being granted all the glamour usually meant it came as a result of loneliness. My dad worked long hours and when he wasn't working he spent a lot of time away from the house.

Being the wife that my mother was, she always looked at her marriage and my father as being good. Regardless of what anyone said to her about her husband, she dismissed whatever comment was mentioned to her. I think my father knew she would believe whatever he told her; especially that he always brought home a gift for her.
He knew in so doing, this would erase all ideas of him as being the player whom her friends and family were saying he was. After a while, of being lonely and not having the experience of how to deal with such a lifestyle, she summoned for her closest sister to come and live with her. Monica arrived in Trinidad and took on the role of second mother to my sister and I. Life had become much better for her, seeing that she had someone whom she knew as family.

As a child I was always left by myself to entertain myself. My brother was much older than me and my sisters were busy building
their own lives. My sister Maureen spent her time with my aunt Monica and Wilma, the Nanny, doing girl things, so I had to make my own fun. The neighbor beside us had two boy children. One boy I didn't like, because he always bullied me and lied when asked about what he had done. The other boy I didn't know that well, but every time I had a chance to speak with him, I did it. This boy was disabled and deformed.

His deformity was unappealing to the eye and one would have to be strong from within. He had a severe arch to his back, along with a disfigured face. One of his eyes was much smaller than the other and half closed and his lips were extremely large with deep groves. His body was extremely frail, and he had very large hands and feet. He spent most of his time sitting in a hunched over position and had problems talking. At times he would grunt as if he was either in pain or was trying to say something.

The mother and father would keep him in this large cage during the daytime and would have him in his room during the evening and night time. Almost daily, you would hear the screams and groaning of this boy. His body was always scared, and his eyes were filled with tears of pain and sorrow. My heart always broke for him, and I wished that I could have done something for him. I decided that regularly, I would bring little snacks and candy, along with water for him. I began sitting with him and telling him stories and jokes. Soon I developed a friendship with him, and little by little he started smiling and enjoying the bright blue skies.

His younger brother was a wicked minded little devil. He had no care or sorrow for whatever happened to his elder brother. I referred to his brother at times as "the monster." I believe that the boy they called "monster" was transformed as a result of the brutality through the beatings that his parents applied to him. This angered me every time I heard him yell or bugged by his brother. I promised the older brother that as long as I was around, I would always be there for him. I continued to regularly bring him food from my plate. I would bring my toys out and to try make him smile. As I developed a trust with him, I even got him to allow me to touch his hands and face, which was very difficult for him to accept even from his own family.

I knew in my heart that at the rate that the parents were harming him, he would not survive a long life. One day while I was out in the back yard, the younger brother was outside teasing his brother and laughing at him. I walked over to him and asked him to stop. He looked at me, as if I was crazy and continued to tease and berate his defenseless brother. As I stood there, I wished for God to punish him. I told him he was stupid and a coward, so he decided to be confrontational. He walked up to me, called me a few names and pushed me. This was the opportunity that I was waiting for, to show no mercy for someone who enjoys taking advantage of a defenseless person. That day I was out of mercy!

As I ran inside of the house I asked for him not to go anywhere. I assured him that I'll be right back and to be patient for a brief second. I looked at the back of my brother's closet and found his 22 caliber rifle pilot gun. I placed one pilot inside the chamber, and kept two in my pocket. I have this saying that "when dealing with hard headed bullies, you never know what they can take, so be prepared." Casually, I walked out the back door and walked right up to him with the gun in my hand. Knowing fully that I was going against the wishes of God, but I strongly felt that God would understand. I asked him if he would like to try pushing me again. He stood there with his eyes wide open like a deer in the night with head lights on it. His mouth seemed to have been glued shut, or maybe he had lost his tongue.

I looked over my shoulder at his helpless brother as he looked on. His brother bowed his head and turned his back as if he was saying to me, "Just do it." I looked at him and said: "maybe you'll understand what it's like to pick on someone that's helpless. I pointed the gun first at his stomach, and changed my mind and shot him in his foot. He screamed loud enough to wake the dead. He dropped to the ground and twirled around like a dog trying to catch his tale. I looked over at the cage, and I could see a slight smile on his brothers' face, feeling that it was time that someone felt what he'd been feeling his whole life. I walked back into the house, placed the gun back into the closet and had a cold drink of orange juice while I sat at the table. As my mother entered the kitchen, she enquired about the noise she heard. I told her that the noise was coming from the next-door neighbor, as she was punishing the boy again.

My mother was sick and tired of the ill treatment of the young boy, and wished that the police would do something about it. I had to prepare my mind for what was to come, because I knew that they would be filing a complaint against me. My father wasn't at home yet, so I had an opportunity to think. Later that evening, the boys' parents came over with their son. His mom showed my mom and dad their sons' foot. It had a huge hole and was extremely swollen. They wanted to speak to them about the situation, and what should be done about it. My father looked at me and suggested to them that he will be willing to pay for any medical expenses, if they could work it out without calling the police. They agreed with hesitation and took their son to the hospital. The wound was visible enough, but wasn't life threatening.

After they left, I was questioned about what caused me to do such a thing. I explained that he was taking advantage of his brother, and that I had promised his brother that as long as I was around, I'd never let his younger brother hurt him. I told them that I had asked him to stop teasing his brother and to stop poking him.

He walked over to our property and stood in front of me and pushed me. I felt he had pushed me once too many times, and this was going to be the last time that he shoved me.

Seeing that I was passionate about my devotion towards my friend, they cautioned me and asked me to stay away from their son. Every so often, I could hear my friend, who I will refer to as "Caged," moaning and often even trying to talk, for me to be able to hear him. Sometimes I'd pay him a short visit, just to let him know that I had not forgotten him. Caged's brother seized poking and making fun of him. I think the incident between us sent him a hearty message.

Robert was the oldest of our siblings. We shared the same bedroom with double beds on either side of the room. Since Robert was the eldest, he always felt that I should acknowledge and do as he requested. One would think by now, that I didn't take orders very well. Being much younger than him, it's obvious that I was not in the position to fight with him. Whenever we got into an argument, he'd walk over and rough me up. In my defense, I'll wait until he fell asleep and repay the abuse. My normal course of action was to cover his head with the pillow while striking him with a bat to his body. The tremendous rush that you felt as you got revenge puts you on a high. The satisfaction that I felt as he yelled like a coyote was worth any trouble that was to come. At a young age, I had to make it known that I'll never be a pushed over.

I truly believe that at times I felt as if I was reenacting the scriptures from the Bible. God gave David the knowledge, strength and heart to do what was right for the people. God also gave Samson the strength through his hair to have the power over all men and to do what was right through the eyes of God. Sometimes we're left with no choice but to destroy whatever evil stood before us.

Once I stopped with the blows because of the screams, I knew that the worse was about to come. It didn't matter because I knew that Robert would always remember that I wasn't going to allow anyone to push me around. My father walked into the room half sleepy with a concerned look on his face. He soon realized that the only danger that was occurring was Robert being taught a lesson. Being awakened in the middle of the night to pull your younger son away from his older brother, because of fear of losing an eye or having a broken leg wasn't what he was expecting. He looked at me without any hesitation and began to slap and hit me all over my body.

The slaps were loud and forceful. Being as angry as he was, I really didn't think he was going to stop. My mother was awakened to the commotion and intervened before my father sent me to the hospital. I guess that the few extra shots he applied to my body, really were for the expense I caused him for shooting the neighbor. My father warned me not to try this again or next time I'd really feel it. "Listen, I got news for you, it did hurt, and it'll probably happen again. So what?" I said.

Sure I went to bed all battered up and miserable, but I knew my brother was also beaten up. Knowing that he wouldn't mess with me anymore was worth a few bruises.

I think a couple of weeks passed when we had another argument over his knife. He had a very shiny knife that he kept in his cupboard. He used this knife to make tops and slingshots. He found out that I used his knife because my mother saw me using it to carve out a few pieces of sculptures. Fearing that I may cut myself, she asked that I return the knife to where I got it. I was confident that once Robert returned from his round about, she'd probably be speaking to him about his safety habits. Now that he found out that I was poking around in his cupboard again, I knew it would cause him to freak out all over again.

My brother can be very nice, but he can be a total meathead at the same time. He quoted that he didn't have the time to give me a pounding, but once he returned from his matters he was going to teach me a lesson that I wouldn't forget. I acted based on his comment, as if I was terrified. This situation annoyed him even more. I knew that I was no match for him, so I decided that I'd do my best in an attempt not to be beaten up too badly.

As promised, later that evening he arrived home. He spent some time in the kitchen, as usual, with my mom feeding his big trap. After devouring the food like a lion in a safari, he made his entrance into the bedroom. Thinking that I would be afraid, I sat there with a slight grin on my face waiting for him to say something. The only thing he said was: "I'll deal with you later" as I pretended to act as if I were scared by shaking and showing fear in my eyes. I knew that he had to be steaming like an old ferry, making its way through the rough waters.

Nighttime was upon us, and I was tired of waiting for this, so I retired to bed. I think it must have been around 11:30 pm, when I felt myself being dragged off the bed by force. My head was hazy due to the deep sleep that I was in. Robert began to slap me like a newborn. He threw me back on the bed and smothered me with the pillow. Gasping for air and being claustrophobic, I began to scream and yell. Knowing that either our dad or mother would tend to what the problem might be, he slapped me one more time and walked away. Crying and upset like King Kong being provoked, I picked up the same switch blade that he had told me to never touch again, and threw it at him as he was about to exit the room. To the unknown that my dad would be entering the room at precisely the same time that Robert was exiting, was beyond me. The look on both of their faces as the knife stuck into the frame of the door, narrowly missing my dad's face was stunning. I knew right then that the episode that I just had with Robert was going to seem like two puppies play fighting.

The beating I took that night taught me a big lesson. The lesson was that my father was nuts when it came to beatings, especially to me. I decided that night that it would be in my best interest to stay away from Robert. Avoiding any violent interaction with Robert should keep me out of my dad's line of fire.

Chapter 2

As I mentioned earlier, my father owned his own construction company, and had many employees who worked for him. One, in particular, was his cousin, whose name I still don't know to this day. He went by the nickname "Throat." I think they called him "Throat" because of his long neck and huge Adam's apple. In my opinion, he had a neck as long as a giraffe.

The other individual was a man by the name of Samson. Samson was my friend and protector. Samson was a close friend of my dad. He worked alongside my father, and he also assisted my mother with the day-to-day errands.

My father owned a number of dump trucks pertaining to his business, for whatever the reason. I had an addiction to motor vehicles and the speed they possessed. From a very young age, I felt that if given the chance, I'd probably be able to drive anything with wheels. In the evening time, I would sit on our balcony and envision myself driving the truck. Being the fearless kid that I was, I decided that I'd take the keys off the board in the hall way and try starting the truck. I waited for my mom and dad to go for their usual walk to burn off the delicious meal that we always had.

Making sure that they were out of view of the house, I climbed up into the truck. As a young kid I can tell you that climbing up the truck felt as if I was rock climbing. Sitting in the driver's seat felt like sitting on top of a mountain. I felt that I could see everything and felt virtually untouchable. Knowing that time was running out, I decided to try starting it, but it would only jerk forward. I couldn't understand why it would only jerk forward and not start fully. I was disappointed that I couldn't get it to move. Before I decided to get out, I shifted a steel shaft that sat to the left of my leg by accident. I tried turning the ignition one more time, and to my amazement the truck started. "Holy Mack," I said to myself. Should I also mention that as I looked at the dash of the truck, it also said Mack Truck? The pedals were out of my reach, but the truck sure was shaking! For a brief moment, I felt like a tough guy with a cigar in my mouth. Suddenly, the truck started to move forward gradually. At first I thought it was going to stop, but it just moved forward even faster. My heart was pounding, yet I felt that it was so cool. The pedals couldn't be reached to stop the truck, and for a short moment I began to panic. Shaking, rocking and rolling down the street, all I could hope for was to steer into a gully when possible. I'm not sure if the words "thank God" were the correct ones that I should be using, but there was my dad walking towards me. He had this shocked look on his face, as if to say "what in the blazing saddles is happening here?" As I yelled at him to help me stop it, he ran beside the truck, opened the door, pushed me aside and brought the truck to a stop. As phony as this may sound, I was so happy to see my dad at that moment. After the truck came to a halt, I realized that I probably wasn't seeing right. I decided that I would look at my mothers' face first so that I can remember her eyes smiling at me.

Indeed she had a slight smile on her face as she shook her head. Turning my head to the right I saw a different picture. I saw a man that had the nostril of a raging bull. "What do you think you were doing?" He asked.

"Well," I said, "I thought I would take it for a drive."
"Joking," I said. "I just wanted to see what it felt like to be sitting up that high while driving.."

Before my father could say anything else, I asked for forgiveness, and if he was going to punish me, that he gave it to me now. "I mean right here dad and now." This puzzled him and had him speechless. You see, what I was trying to do was either bluff my way out of a beating or for him to actually beat me in a public place where everyone would see. By beating me in a public place, he couldn't beat me as severe and as long. He looked at me and said, "You're lucky. Next time you get in trouble you'll pay for this time also." Before I got out of the truck I asked, "How am I supposed to handle such a beating when the time comes?"

As usual, the same comment, "No trouble, no licks."

As I walked along the street with no shoes on my feet, my mother would sing to me. She stopped and said "Everard, when are you going to stop being so inquisitive?" "Mommy," I said. "How am I supposed to learn if I don't snoop?" My usual kiss on the cheeks and a tap on the bum usually meant, "I love you." Driving that big machine really felt cool as I struggled with steering that big wheel. Although I got caught, I must say it was well worth every moment of it. Now I could say to my friends at school that I actually drove a Mack truck.

My mother had a friend who would come around almost every Sunday. He carried a guitar and played Calypso music for my mother in return for a plate of food in fun. He ate lunch with us as often as possible to keep in touch with my mother. I was told that this is a running joke that they had between them for many years. Sparrow would place me on his lap and then would play a melody of songs as he waited until lunch was ready. One would think, how could a man dressed as well as he did and carried an expensive guitar, be homeless? This is what I thought at first until the truth was told to me. That's what I thought at the time, but I was told that he's an entertainer and a good friend of the family.

Sparrow was originally from the Island of Grenada and traveled to Trinidad to promote his music. After many years of producing and writing his own music, he became an international Calypso singer. The normal routine after a hearty meal was to play a few songs and my mother and Sparrow would take a stroll to walk off the food. In the meantime, my father was busy building and promoting his business.

One of my mother's brothers arrived from Grenada to spend time with her and hopefully to work alongside my dad. From his arrival, I could see that the spirit between my dad and my Uncle Jonathan wasn't going to be easily accepted.

I think my father felt that my mother sent for her brother to keep a watchful eye over him. After many days of sitting at home doing nothing, my mom had a discussion with my dad before turning in for bed. My father wasn't very receptive, but he agreed to give my uncle some work. Honestly speaking, I can't say that I ever saw my uncle doing any actual work, but he was an employee. I learned that my uncle was supposed to protect my dad from other independent contractors.

Business was very competitive and the word among

the other contractors was that my father was receiving too much of the market. My dad couldn't stand the idea that my mother's brother was living at home with us, and that made him very irritable. To be fair to my dad, my mother had a discussion with my uncle Jonathan about his living arrangements. Before my mother could bring the subject up, he told her not to worry that he had already found a place to live, that wasn't too far from our home. He understood perfectly well the spot he had left my mother in and felt that it would be better for all.

For me to bring to you the entire story of what took place in Trinidad with regards to the event that took place in Trinidad while my uncle lived and worked for my dad, I had to go straight to the author himself. On a sunny day during a beautiful summer weekend, I had the opportunity to speak with my Uncle Jonathan.

One of my relatives decided to have a family barbecue to welcome my uncle from New York City after not seeing him for quite some time. This is where I got to question him about the events that took place in Trinidad. Uncle Jonathan was more than willing to entertain me with the events that took place. He suggested that he would like to visit with my father regardless of whatever happened because he still admired my father. Some of the other siblings did not echo the same feelings, but he didn't care too much about their beliefs.

Uncle Jonathan went on to explain to me the events that took place and how they came to be. He went on to explain how the events unraveled and why things felt the way they did. As he sat and spoke with my father, some of the events came to light as they laughed about the past. As they chuckled about the past and teased each other about who was really afraid of whom. I could see that my father truly had a soft spot for my uncle, and the feeling was mutual from my uncle.

Wilma would assist my mother with the day-to-day chores and with any assistance she needed with us. Wilma was a wonderful person. My mother and Wilma were very close and at times would sit and talk about each other's problems. I guess Wilma was like the hidden agent among us. Any time my mom would have an argument with my dad who left her either bruised or upset, for some reason, my uncle was always aware of the problem. The assumption was that my mom's sister, Monica, was the news carrier, but it was difficult to tell because they were all so close. It wasn't very long before my mother figured out who was actually leaking the information out of the house. She kept the secret between herself and Wilma, fearing that if my dad found out, he would probably have made sure that she would leave.

I think our home was becoming a bit like a cat and mouse story. Who was out smarting whom? Apparently, one evening on his way home from work with my dad, he was confronted by three men wearing balaclavas. They jumped out of their car and tried to stop my uncle from going home. A fight began where my uncle had to fight for his life. He broke one of the suspects' arms, while putting the boots to the other culprits. At the end of it, my uncle was left pretty bruised up but alive, while the other culprits were left with some serious injuries to remember him by.

Apparently, once my father had got word of his faith,

he wasn't very pleased to know that my uncle had survived. My uncle could not have hidden his bruises from my mother. He left my mother with the idea that someone attacked him on his way home, but he was alright. Meanwhile, my father was sitting just ear distance away from my uncle as he told his story. My father had a poker face on and inquired nothing about my uncle's safety. Suspicion was in the air by my mother, Aunt Monica and Wilma. Uncle Jonathan knew in his heart that my dad had sent those men after him, but he wasn't about to let the cat out of the bag just yet.

A week or two would pass before another confrontation would take place again. This time my father waited for my uncle after dropping him off approximately ten minutes away from our home. My dad had two men in the car with him and was prepared to see the job done properly. Little did they know that Uncle Jonathan wasn't any ordinary man. He had the heart of a lion, and he walked in God's shadow. Suddenly, as he got half way down the street, he could see the lights of a car traveling at a high rate of speed towards him.

The car was heading directly to his path, and he had nowhere to run. Uncle Jonathan began to run so that he could find an open area where he could jump. He jumped into a gully along the roadside, causing the car to lose control and stall. That was the moment when he confronted the men. Realizing that it was my dad, they began to fight along with my dad's bullies. The fight between my uncle and my dad was vicious as the two men stood by and watched on. There were a lot of grunting from blows to the body and face, along with any weapon that could have been used to injure each other. My uncle said that at that moment he felt like his life was on the line. He said that out of nowhere he felt the strength of ten men and found himself having the strength of Samson.

After getting the upper hand on my father, he turned to the bullies, but they ran seeing that my dad had jumped into the car and drove off. Bruised and battered, he made his way home to tend to his wounds. Uncle Jonathan didn't turn out to work for an entire week, and my mom was worried about him. As for my dad, he wasn't in any better shape himself either. He had no choice but to go to work, but his days were short.

The following week my uncle appeared at our home as if nothing had happened. When asked about his whereabouts, he told my mother he had an encounter with the same men, and that he had put a stop to it for sure. Uncle Jonathan was back to work and neither my dad nor Uncle Jonathan spoke about the incident. Weeks would go by before my father, and my uncle would butt heads. The threat would finally come out of my dad's mouth as to what he would do if he stuck his nose once more in his business.

Uncle Jonathan felt that he had to know why my dad disliked him so much, so he confronted him at home right after work. I never did learn the reason for the dislike, but what I assumed was that my dad felt threatened with my uncle being around. He felt that if he were to attempt any harm against my mother, my uncle would intervene. So I was thinking to myself, "Which brother wouldn't stand firm for his sister?" As the months passed, my uncle and my dad settled their differences and became friends. Just like anything else, if your heart is pure, your enemy eventually will have no choice but to become gentle.

One Saturday after we had lunch, I decided that I'd like to go along for a drive with my dad. Can you imagine that I was taking a chance by going for a drive with my dad while he tends to a business meeting without anyone to save me? I figured that it was a beautiful sunny Saturday and even if I got into trouble for doing nothing that was bad, at least I'd be in the public eye. So he took his nice fancy blue car, and we were off. We arrived at the address of the person who he was supposed to visit, but I guess we were a bit early. My father knew that no one was home because he didn't see the vehicles outside. Luckily, I always carried my baseball glove and ball with me, so I asked if he would like to play catch with me while we waited. The house was of a decent size and was fenced completely around by chain links. I had my back towards the client's house, and my dad was facing me. We stood a good distance apart from each other so that I could practice throwing the ball with accuracy. We were out in the street throwing the ball, partly shaded by the branches of a tree, so it kept the heat off us. My dad was throwing the ball fairly well at me, some a bit off and some really well.

As I stood prepared for the next ball, suddenly the ball was thrown over my head. The ball was thrown so high, that, even if I had a fireman's ladder with me, I couldn't have caught it. I looked at him and asked, "What was all that about?"

Knowing what the answer would be, he said "Sorry." I ran down the front path to where I saw the ball roll. Not aware of any danger, I proceeded around the side of the house, only to notice a dog that was as large as a wolf. I tiptoed towards my ball, bending over slowly. With my heart beating to the rhythm of a drum I slowly picked up the ball. Suddenly, the eyes of the dog appeared open. I could see the ears of the dog perk up into the upright position, and his sparkling white Chiclets sharpened just for my behind. Knowing that it's now or never, I figured the only chance I had was to run for it. The race was on and there could only be one winner. As I got almost to the fence another monster of a dog was coming, not to my rescue, but to share in the feast. I made a leap to the fence and so did the dogs. While yelling for help, the dogs were having their way with my butt. My father eventually ran around and scared them off with one of his tools from the trunk of his car.

Dropping to the ground like an injured bird with no wings, he quickly picked me up and hustled me to the car. As I lay on the chair at the back, all I felt was the pulsation on my butt. We arrived at the hospital in quick time, and were attended to by a doctor expeditiously. I hoped that he wouldn't ask me that ridiculous question about "What happened to you?" Obviously he could have seen the pain that I was in, so he tried his best to calm me. I remembered being given a needle or two and being cared for by a nurse while she prepared my dressing. The doctor spoke directly to my father in privacy in the hallway, so I had no idea what was said.

The drive home was very quiet, seeing that I had nothing much to say. My father didn't say sorry for throwing the ball that high, and I was not about to ask him to say sorry. I believe that he wanted to have a laugh at my expense, so he did it to see what would happen. I knew that once we arrived home, he would hear it from my mother. She was furious with him and that alone in my eyes was retribution. I know he felt that I loved every moment when my mom was yelling at him, especially when she told him she believed that he's much too hard on me. That was a good thing for me, but at the same time, I knew that those words would come back and haunt me.

For the next few days I felt like I was the king of the castle. Any and everything I desired, I received. Life was good and I was enjoying every bit of it. At times, I would even fake that Robert
was bothering my wound so that I could hear my mother yell at him. Payback couldn't be sweeter. Having my brother drive me wherever I needed to go was a blast. Even if I wanted to go to my friend's house, three blocks away, he would have to drive me. Watching television was the best part of it all. Because of my injury, I couldn't play with my friends, so I would sit inside and read or watch television. I had full control of the television. Robert had no say in what he wanted to watch because he didn't have any of his freedom, which had been temporarily stricken.

With all good things, everything comes to an end. My injury was healing and I couldn't have faked it much longer. Finding a way to be "buddy buddy" with Robert would have to be high on my agenda. I played my role perfectly by being extremely nice to Robert so that I'd stay out of my dad's line of sight. For a short while I felt as though I could have been the most perfect child in the neighborhood. My dad's business was beginning to thrive and with any success comes misery.

Apparently, some of the competitors were upset that my father had a firm hold on the industry. Threats were being made, and accusations of undercutting the market were an issue among the competitors. At the beginning, I mentioned that my father had a friend and also a worker who was very close to him. Samson feared no one and if necessary he would confront the individual that was making the threats. If Samson was to initiate any type of verbal confrontation, that would only be adding fuel to the fire. Samson understood that under no circumstances he's to show himself as being a protector or what we would call "muscle."

Things were beginning to heat up to the point where my father's trucks and materials were being tampered with. His truck was found with a flat tire and a fair amount of his supplies had gone missing. We all knew that no matter what you do to keep the lid on boiling water, eventually it will overflow. Well, this is exactly what happened to Samson. After listening to the threats and seeing our supplies vanish, it was just a matter of time before he said something. Words were exchanged and threats were probably made by the opposition. I say opposition because Samson was not the type to initiate threats. Realizing that things were getting out of hand, my father decided that maybe it was about time he started looking at an alternative.

After a month or two of throwing words at each other, a shadow was caste upon our family. One evening after work, my father dropped Samson off at his usual spot so that he could take his usual stroll home. That day they had finished work late and decided to stay back and chat about my father's plans to travel. After dropping Samson home, he came home and prepared for dinner while chatting with my mother. As we sat at the table talking, he chatted a bit with Maureen and Robert while giving me his, "I'm going to get you" look.

Once dinner was finished he got up from the table and walked towards the window and casually looked out. He was in shock at what he saw.

He yelled out in a manner that showed that there was some urgency that needed his immediate attention. "Samson" he said, "Samson!" Running out the front door in a mad rush only meant trouble. As he got to the front gate, there laid Samson on his back bleeding from head to toe. Samson had a wound in his stomach and on his forearm. Blood was pouring from him like a fountain without a valve. My dad had me stay with him while he went for the car. We picked up Samson and placed him in the back seat with his head resting on my lap. I tried my best to comfort Samson by talking to him and pressing gently on his wound with a towel to stop the blood. Samson's eyes had closed and I could barely hear him breathe. My dad was in a panic and all he kept on saying is "you'll make it my friend, just hang on my friend."

My father must have gone through every stop light, barely stopping at the stop signs. Finally, we were at the hospital and thank God for our luck, because as faith would have it, there were a couple of nurses standing outside of the emergency entrance. We yelled for their assistance, although my dad had driven the car almost inside the emergency room. Samson was in the emergency room while we were taken to an area to be washed up. Nervous was not the word to use at a time like this. I couldn't talk and my dad's eyes looked like they had a fire in them.

He paced the hospital floor for almost half an hour. The doors had opened as if we were trapped in a tunnel for days. There he was, the man who can break your heart or mend your heart. The word wasn't good. Samson had passed away, due to the severity of the injury in his abdomen. My dad was completely speechless at first, and then he started to cry like an ordinary person. This was a complete different side to see of the man that I thought was as tough as nails. The doctor stayed with us for a brief moment and then said his sympathies and walked away as if he had another person that needed his assistance urgently. After my dad had regained his composure, he told me to make sure I didn't say anything to my mother. He would be the one to tell her the fate of Samson.

We arrived quite late in the morning, tired and drained. I walked in the front and looked at my mom, and immediately I could sense that she already knew the outcome. As I sat in my room with ears pierced against the door, I could hear the nervousness in my father's voice as he attempted to explain what had happened to Samson. As he began to talk, I could hear the crying from her voice. She wept and wept as my dad tried to tell her how hard he tried, and the valiant effort of the doctors for trying. Samson was almost like a brother to my mother. They had many happy moments together, talking about the future and everyday moments.

The following morning at the breakfast table was extremely quiet. Everyone ate with their head down with absolutely nothing to say. Mornings would pass. Afternoons would pass and nights would come and go for weeks without much being said. The night before the funeral for Samson, my dad had mentioned to my mother to try her best and control her emotions at the funeral. Samson had a large turn out to pay respect to him and his family. The service was nice and reflected on the memory of Samson. The gentle giant has gone to meet his father. Almost everyone attended the cemetery to say their final goodbye to the gentle giant. I think my mother and father did extremely well until the moment had reached for Samson to be lowered into his final resting spot. As they sang the hymns while the casket was lowering, my father finally burst into tears and required the strength of my mother to keep him together. He cried uncontrollably and swore for justice to Samson. By his actions, it was almost like a domino effect, everyone started to yell and cry and was seeking justice. Surprisingly, to me, my mother was strong, but cried a minimum amount and controlled her actions.

On the drive home, I continued to ask myself, "What am I going to do now without my friend Samson?" My heart was filled with hurt and my head felt as if I were floating into another world. All my father could concentrate on was seeing to it that Samson's criminals were going to be punished severely. Surprisingly enough, the culprits were caught within days of their crime. My dad went to the courthouse every day so that he could give his statement and to make sure the criminals got what was coming to them. Years ago the tribunal system was much different than it is now. The case didn't take very long in court and to the best of my knowledge, they were found guilty.

Within a month, all three of the convicted men were sentenced to death to be hung by the neck 'till death. The entire courtroom was elated with the outcome. Personally, I don't think the three men had a chance to begin with. Their fate was written on the wall before they entered the courtroom. Any verdict other than death would have been a complete disrespect for the law. One week later, the bells at the prison could be heard ringing, indicating that the three convicted men were put to death. Justice in the hearts of the people was demonstrated on behalf for their old friend Samson.

My dad had the task now of preparing to leave Trinidad for the safety of his family. Work was being cut back, and he started to gradually sell some of his dump trucks. Throat had agreed to travel along to Canada with my family, seeing that most of his family had either passed or had already traveled abroad. As luck would have it, another stressful moment would plague our home and community. My father's relative had been stabbed to death. Apparently, Throat was on his way home from visiting with a few of his friends. He was attacked by two men who wanted to teach him a lesson and to provoke my dad into retaliating. Their intention was to rough him up sufficiently that my father would be scared and leave the city altogether. Throat wasn't about to be roughed up without putting up a good fight. Knives were used and Throat was slashed in the abdomen and arms, but the fatal wound was the one near his windpipe. By the time help had got to him, he had already lost too much blood. He fought for his life on the operating table but couldn't survive the attack. Fortunately for Throat at the time he was being attacked, an elderly person had seen what was taken place and had a good description of the culprits. Within a few days, they were apprehended and placed in custody to stand trial.

This time the country was tired of innocent people being killed unnecessarily. The pressure was on the government, and the trial Judge. No jury was going to allow these men to walk free. Within a week, the case was over and their fate was sealed. Their penalty was death, to be hung by their neck until pronounced dead. We're all sorry after the fact, after they'd committed an offence, but the courts had heard their plea, but their plea wasn't sufficient enough for the crime they committed.

A week or so would pass and one can hear the bells of death being rung again. The two men had been hung. My father had absolutely no reason to stay in Trinidad now, seeing that everyone close to him had been killed. Arrangements had been made for Maureen and me to be looked after by my mother's parents. We were about to meet our Grandparents for the first time. All that was left was to say our goodbyes to family and close friends and whatever financial issues that needed to be addressed.

We were off and the plane ride was quite short. Within a few hours, we were in the land of the spice and everything that's nice, Grenada. The house that we were about to spend our time in was quite small. I couldn't believe that fourteen kids had lived in this house together. My grandmother was pretty and had a beautiful smile. She looked as if she had been mixed with some other heritage. My grandfather was of a decent height, handsome with a light complexion but serious. To her left stood a young woman of light complexion, average height with a smile of concern on her face. Already I knew we weren't going to get along, and she would try to boss me around, but it wasn't going to work out. Maureen
had already established herself as the neighborhood pet. Everything to them was "She's so sweet." It made me sick.

My mom and dad took a trip into town with my grandparents and a few of her siblings. I was now alone with the dragon lady. An hour hadn't passed before we would get into an argument. She wanted to send the message that she was my aunt, and that meant I had to listen to her at all times. Did I mention to you that her name was Merle? Yes, she was about to find out that I didn't take orders very well. She tried to hold onto my arm as she spoke to me, so I pulled my shoulder away from her. The battle that I thought would take place came sooner than I thought. I ran out into the street and gathered some stones. My pocket was filled with stones like a machine gun with bullets. I hid behind a tree and began to throw the stones at her like a marine casting hang grenades. Rocks were flying by each other's head like rockets flying over the head. With great accuracy, I waited for her to step out from behind the wall and bombarded her with stones, finally striking her on her shoulder. I knew she felt the blow by the noise she made and by the lack of stones being thrown back at me.

I knew she was injured, and it was just a matter of time before she stopped, so I just waited for her to give up. Merle was not the type that was going to give up easily. Within a short while she was back at it again, throwing rocks and yelling at me. The fight came to a stop as a result of my parents returning from down town. My father was out of his mind, and my grandfather wanted to drop a quick beating on me. That was not to be, because my parents were still in charge so any punishment would be done by them. A warning was what I received and an apology to my aunt. The weekend had arrived and my parents were on their way to the airport. The frustration and anger that covered my face, that my mom was leaving me behind, was quite visible.

My mother sat and spoke with me at the airport before

boarding the plane and reassured me that as soon as it was possible, she would be sending for us. The tears flowed from both of our eyes as we embraced each other for the last time. My father looked at me and asked that I behave and that he looked forward to seeing us soon. In the conversation that we had, no hugs or kisses were given; nevertheless I was confident that Maureen got all the hugs and kisses for the both of us.

The drive back home from the airport seemed like I was going to a military school. Silence was the order of the day, and Merle sat with her hands under her chin, glancing at me from time to time. As I sat in the car I started thinking of a way to defeat my aunt and have her at the mercy of my mouth. I had to find her weakness, and I had to find it quickly.

Once we arrived, our grandmother prepared us a lovely meal and a treat at the end of the meal. That evening my uncle Fitzroy took me for a walk with him. He was kind and well spoken. He made me feel really comfortable around him, and that was the best feeling I had since I had been at their home. We walked in a northerly direction, and as we walked, he pointed out where some of my relatives lived. A song was playing on his little pocket radio that he had. As the song played, he sang along to the words, as if he wrote the song himself.

He was really cool. The night was clear, and the sky was shinning with stars. After a lengthy walk, we arrived back home and I headed to bed. The next morning after I had my breakfast, some of our cousins came by to meet us. I didn't know that I had that many cousins. I had a good feeling with all of them except one. His name was Crompton, and he acted strange. He never looked at me in the eye, and he didn't really have much to say either.

My female cousin Jaclyn and I took to each other right away. She was friendly, pretty, funny and she seemed as if she had a bit off tomboy in her. My aunt Monica had this ingenious idea that I should attend her school and be a part of her classroom. The following Monday, bright and early, I was off to school with her. First day of school in Grenada and the only people I knew were my cousins and none of them was in my class. She taught math on this particular day and I had no clue as to what she was teaching.

The lessons were hard and I had to get my mind in shape so that I could spend quality time with my cousins. I had to learn all the timetables and be able to spell rather well for me to have any chance of
seeing daylight after school.

With great effort and tutoring from her and my cousin Jaclyn, we began to see improvement. Months turned into a year, and I hadn't heard any news about my parents sending for us. I was missing my parents, especially my mother and my time in Grenada was growing weary on me. I started writing letters to my mother and asking my grandmother to mail them to Canada for me. I even attempted to run away a few times, but I didn't get too far because I didn't know where to go.

As time passed, I grew closer to my grandmother, and we would sit and have some great conversations. She liked me and I knew it by the things she would do for me, and by the way she would look at me. My grandmother would speak to me about life and what it has to offer. She always insisted that I have to make my own way, or I would be left behind. She wanted to see that we did well, and all she ever asked was that we respected our family and respected other people, and God would do the rest. To this day, I live by her code of ethics, and I truly believe that her words were absolutely true.

My grandfather didn't say much so I really didn't have an opportunity to get close to him. Talking about my grandfather, one of the tasks I had was to accompany him from time to time to his garden. Did I say that the garden was in the mountains? We had to wear our garden boots and older clothes so that it wouldn't be ruined. My grandfather carried a big mesh bag with a sharp cutlass. As we made our way through the bushes he would cut whatever branches or weeds that were in our way. The path was narrow and hilly. There were areas that you would have to take your time to get around, fearing that at any time you could fall and never be seen again. The scenery was amazing and as far as your eyes could see, fruits were everywhere.

Once we got to the area where the garden was, he explained to me how much of the area he owned. Let me tell you, it's a hell of a lot of land. We sat for a while and ate mangoes along with drinking fresh coconut water. The water tasted as if we were drinking it straight from a fresh stream that poured from the mountain. My grandfather picked a large quantity of coco and dug up lots off yams. We traveled just a bit further where there was an endless supply of banana trees. I packed my garden bag until it was full of bananas, and then we proceeded on our way back home. The trip to the mountain was fantastic, and it gave me a chance to see the other side of my grandfather.

Once we returned home, the job was to clean the fruits off with water and prepare them for sale in the market. My grandmother would go into town and sell the fruits and vegetables to the people in the market. Now that I was becoming more familiar with the area, I would venture out on my own to visit with family. My cousin Raphael told me that he would meet me in the mornings for the next little while and escort me to school.

My grandmother was big on church, so I had to attend the services almost every Sunday. Having to wear a tie and shirt was the most uncomfortable thing I had to do. My aunt Merle would wake us up quite early and have us prepare ourselves and go along to church with her. The church was huge and a lot of people attended. They were hoping that I would participate in becoming a choirboy or something in the church, but I declined. Remember when I said I had to find a way to beat my aunt? Well, I did.

My aunty Merle had a guy, who was interested in her and after church they would walk and talk. I wasn't sure if my grandmother knew that she was speaking with someone, but I was about to find out. On our way home, I realized that Merle and her friend would walk a short distance behind us and talk and giggle the entire time. Although I felt some type of anger towards her, I felt that it wasn't any of my business. Seeing how happy she felt, I knew that I couldn't do anything to come between her happiness.

I remembered what my grandmother said to me about being honest and straight with people. Fearing what can come back to haunt me by the doings of our savior, I felt that it was best for me to be the nephew and not a boy possessed by the Devil. After looking over my shoulder numerous times, Merle finally had enough and asked me to behave otherwise she would have no choice to complain to my grandmother. I told her she had nothing to worry about, and that I was happy with whatever she did. She was taken back, slightly smiled and continued to make our way home. I no longer felt like blackmailing her, and we both changed our attitude towards each other.

Things were about to heat up with my choice of friends and cousins. I had to learn that not all of the time I had to be a follower, but that it's good to be independent. Monday morning, Raphael did indeed arrive at my house for school. We walked a short distance away from the house and stopped at the next bus stop. Raphael explained to me that we were about to hop a ride to school by the bus.

At first I was confused about how we were going to do this. He explained that once the bus stopped, you walk slowly away from it, and once the bus picks up its speed, we were to jump on. The idea of jumping off was different. To get off, you wait until the bus slows down a little then jump and keep running. Everything was a go. The bus arrived as planned, and we waited for a while and then jumped on. The bus was traveling at a pretty fast speed, and I was a bit scared. This was my first time trying anything like this, so I had no idea what the outcome was going to be. It was time for us to get off as we were nearing our school.

Raphael jumped off first and now it was my turn. I jumped off
as he explained but things didn't go as expected. I jumped but

I forgot to run at the same time. I jumped and stood still causing my body to jerk backwards. I landed on my head, splitting my head open and losing consciousness. I woke up in the hospital after a day of being completely out. My head was pounding and I felt extremely sore all over. The laugh was on me and everybody at my school now knew that I was uncoordinated. The punishment to me was a lecture that my grandparents felt would be sufficient.

Out of the hospital and ready to have fun, I attempted the same thing all over, although I had been warned not to do it again. This time I was prepared and better informed, and I prayed that there wouldn't be a repeat. The jump was successful and I felt that I had beaten the demons.

Hanging out with my cousins seemed to be a dangerous thing, because they seemed to be extremely street smart, so I had a lot to learn. An elderly man had died in the community that everyone had known. They had a different way at the time of keeping the dead from rotting. I visited the home of the person where everyone was paying their respect. I observed that the person was in a casket and with ice below him and around him. This had a strange effect on me to see such a thing. Raphael and my other cousins and friends decided between themselves that they would play a joke on me. Obviously, I wasn't informed about the joke, so I had no idea of what they were up to. As I stood beside the casket looking at the body, the guys decided to pick me up and try to place me on top of the deceased. Panic took over my mind and body. I became like a wild cat that's been cornered and had to fight for his life. I remembered twisting and kicking until they couldn't hold me anymore.

Once I was let go, I attacked the first person in my site. Punching and screaming at my cousin with the others trying to get me off him, and then turning my anger towards the others. I became a wild person that had blacked out. Finally, when one of the elders intervened, I settled myself down only to break down into tears. The guys realized quickly that there are some pranks that aren't suited for me.

Since I wasn't speaking to any of them, they apologized to me the day after. For a short part of the day, I stayed away from them because I didn't trust them anymore. Realizing that I had kept my distance from them, they confronted me and asked if I would be willing to put it behind me. I felt that they were sincere, so I was back in the gang again. Raphael had a way of convincing me to do things that I shouldn't do. On this school day, he suggested that we take the day off and went into the mountains and fly our kites. It wouldn't be possible for me to take my kite out of the house because my grandmother would be suspicious. I decided that I would take turns flying his kite. The adventure was on and we were off.

Raphael took us through a heavily bushed area. There were snakes in the trees and wild animals running around. We found an area that had mangoes, bananas and coconuts to drink. The sky was blue and the wind was perfect but with all that beauty, there was a dry heat. Raphael and I took turns flying the kite as it roared in the sky. We had a great time performing tricks with the kite as we entertained each other. Suddenly, the kite started to pull strongly to the point where it felt as if the kite was trying to lift us of the ground. Raphael and I were doing everything possible to keep the kite from breaking from the line. Unfortunately, the inevitable happened, the line broke and the kite started to drift away at a fast pace. Raphael was off and running like a deer in the forest. Not used to the woods like he was, it was difficult for me to keep up. I asked him to slow down a bit, but he was only concerned about his precious kite. Slowly, but slowly I started to lose sight of him. Before you knew it, he was no longer in my view. I shouted out to him as loud as I could but Raphael was nowhere to be seen or heard.

Now the task of finding my way out of the woods was on my shoulder. With the sun beating down on me and no water to drink, I felt as if everything was about to collapse. I soon focused and tried my best to find the right direction of getting out of the woods. I decided that I would walk towards the sun but in a North West direction. Hopefully, by following that path it would lead me to a road, and I would be able to make my way home from there. As I walked and ran through the woods, I could feel that the heat was affecting me. Along with not having any water to drink, I began to feel nauseous.

The closer I got to the road, I could hear the sound of vehicles. I knew I was close, but I didn't know exactly where it would lead me to. Finally, I could see the road, and I could hear the vehicles as well as the voices of people. I burst out of the woods like a man who had just escaped from prison. Standing on the side of the road with my head tilted over I began to puke from feeling ill. After I threw up, I dusted my clothes off and gathered myself together. As my luck would have it, a friend of my grandparents had noticed me and approached me and inquired why I was not in school. I told him that we had gone on a school trip, but because I wasn't feeling well I decided to leave the trip early and go home.

Thinking that I may be lying, he told me to hurry and make my way home.

Wondering if I was successful in convincing him, I made my way home. Along the way, I began to think of an excuse, in case I was questioned of my whereabouts. The entrance was clear when I arrived home, so I made a dash for my bedroom. Changing into a fresh set of school clothes and making my way back outside to act as if I had just arrived from school, my grandmother greeted me as usual in the same friendly manner. Everything seemed alright until after supper. It took them three hours of having me relax as if nothing was wrong before confronting me. So she asked: "How was your day at school today? Learned anything interesting? Your teacher sent us a message through a friend inquiring on whether you were ok or not." I tried to come up with a lie, but based on her abrupt comment about lying, I became confused. I had no choice but to tell the truth about what I did for the day. My grandfather looked at me, as if he had been waiting for this moment. I wondered if he wanted to whip me because of the first day when we arrived, and he never got a chance to deliver. He suggested that I should find myself a tree, and pick my own branch to be whipped with. As I was picking the branch that was supposed to crucify me, I decided that if I was going to be whipped, then I may as well be whipped gently. I returned with a small branch that I thought would be proper for the beating. Looking at the branch made my grandfather so angry that he went into the bushes and picked his own branch. "Wow" I said to him, "that's a tree, not a branch" I said to him. Without talking, he started to swing the branch like he's done this before.

Every blow that landed left a mark along with causing

some parts of my body to bleed. To add insult to injury, he had me sit on the front balcony with just my shirt on and no pants and underwear on. This was the most humiliating thing that they could have done to me. Some of my friends would be walking by, and they would be able to see that I had no clothes on. As they smiled and laughed, all I could think of was hurting my grandparents. I actually thought of burning their bedroom down and seeing how they felt not to be able to sleep for a while, but that was the Devil in me.

A week would pass before I would say anything to either of them. My cousins never said too much about the incident and neither did I. I knew that hanging out with Raphael was not in my best interest, so I had to start doing my own thing. We still spoke but I just started hanging out with my other cousin.

One morning at recess, one of the kids asked if she could go to the store across the street. On this day, and since we weren't doing anything important in our class, we had a few extra minutes for a break. Her name has faded from my memory but what happened next hasn't. As she ran from the top of the hill towards the store, all the children were asking for a favor. She got to the bottom of the hill and proceeded to cross the street under extremely busy traffic. As the teacher yelled at her to be careful as she crossed, she appeared to turn her attention to what the teacher was trying to say. At that moment, she had stepped into the traffic. Thinking that the traffic had given a break, she stood in the middle of the street and was struck by a dump truck. The truck had applied its break but could not stop in time. She was struck dead on. Her head had been run over so she literally didn't have a chance of survival. This was a horrific and sad day to remember. The entire school was shocked by what they had heard or seen. The teacher was literally in shock, and decided to take a leave to overcome what had happened. To the day that I left Grenada, that teacher had never returned to her teaching duties. Some say that she should not have allowed the child to cross the street, and at the same token, others said that it wasn't her fault. I had no comments to give. The entire school attended her funeral and paid their final respect to a young and beautiful school mate.

Approximately two weeks from the horrific incident, a young classmate took a chance by going to the field on his own without permission. He had asked to go to the washroom. After ten minutes had passed, the teacher inquired of his whereabouts. One of our classmates told her that he had gone to the field to either get a mango or a piece of cane. The adventure into the field was on. The principal and our entire class traveled together in search for our classmate. We searched between the canes. We searched around the mango trees and shouted his name out.

We came upon an outhouse and entered it, as we all continued to shout his name out. There he was about six feet down, covered in human waste up to his shoulders. The fire truck was called seeing that we had no way of reaching him. The fire department attended along with a few police officers. They had him tie a rope around his body and pulled him out gently. The smell was intolerable. They sprayed him down with the hose first before checking him over. He had nothing more than scratches and bruises, only his ego was damaged.

Some lessons are better felt than learned. I should have learned from my mistake of skipping school with my cousin Raphael. I decided to have my lunch hour at home, rather than staying at school. What a mistake this was going to be. After my lunch, I gave my granny a hug for a wonderful lunch that she prepared for me and started on my way back to school. On my way to the bus stop, I ran into my cousin Ali. Ali suggested that we take the remainder of the day off and hang out in the trees eating plums and mangoes. That sounded like a fantastic idea; however, the last time I did that, I paid dearly for my mistake. I decided that I'd do it anyway and went a little further back into the woods. We climbed a really high tree and sat in it and ate plumbs and told jokes.

There was a long rod with a knife at the end of it that was used for picking plumbs from the ground. We saw the rod that was a few branches below us that was left by someone, but paid no mind to it. We were laughing and having a great time. Suddenly, Ali lost his balance and fell from the top of the tree, smashing his body against the branches along the way. I could hear him yelling on the way down but figured it was the branches that were spanking him.

Once on the ground I saw all the blood pouring from his upper part of his body. Because his hand was lying on his chest it made me believe that he had an injury to his chest. Fearing the worst I tried to move his hand and realized that it wasn't his chest that was injured, but it was a severe knife wound to his wrist and forearm. Panicking and not knowing what to do, I had no choice but to run for help. First I ran to his home and told his parents what had happened, and then I ran to my grandparents and told them what had happened.

Chaos was in the area to get Ali the help that he desperately needed. With the help of my grandmother along with Ali's mother, we managed to secure the wound until we were able to get him to the hospital. Ali's hand was in a critical state, and I believed once this was all over with, we would have to answer for our deeds. Personally, I believed that I was already dealing with my own conscience. If only I had gone to school like I should have, Ali wouldn't have been in the state that he was in. Here's a prime example of how the Lord takes things into His own hands. I'm quite sure the Lord didn't intend for Ali to harm himself, but it was our dishonesty, we paid for.

My grandmother had nothing to say the entire time we were tending to Ali. I knew she was really upset and disappointed in me for not being resilient when confronted by temptation. If I ever needed a wake up call in my short life, I felt as if this was the moment that taught me a lesson. Ali spent a few days in the hospital to be treated for infection and to make sure that he had proper movement in his hand. My grandmother finally approached me about what had happened. She asked me if I had learned from this situation. Still fresh in my memory of that terrible moment, I shook my head and stood still without saying a word. I think she felt that I had punished myself, and that, just maybe it affected me enough to set me straight.

Ali was released from the hospital, and nobody knew how happy I was to see him walking and smiling once again. I told him that I was not going to do anything stupid anymore, "so please, don't ask me to run off anywhere when it's school time."

Weeks would go by and none of the guys had got themselves into any type of trouble. One Saturday just after midday, Ali, my cousin Jaclyn and I decided to walk down to the river and set traps for the shrimps. We all had our own style and idea of what was the best way to catch a shrimp. After the traps were set, we sat around and told stories to each other. Maybe the right word is a bunch of lies. Setting traps take patience and sometimes you may not catch anything until the following day. In the meantime, we climbed a mango tree that was filled with huge ripe mangoes. Jaclyn was like one of the guys, just prettier and fun to be around. We climbed at least half way up to the tree and sat on our own individual branches. The sun was bright, but the branches shaded us as the wind blew softly. The mangoes were juicy and every bite spouted juices like water out of a hose. We licked our fingers like we were eating Granny's fried chicken.

Only the mangoes left little furs in between your teeth. Sometimes that can be aggravating enough to drive you nuts. We were having a blast as we sat up high in the tree and not a care to worry about. What a day to be alive. I decided that I would turn over and lay on my stomach, as if I were about to take a nap. As I turned over and got into a comfortable position, I observed a huge snake twirled around a branch a few feet from me. I panicked and lost my balance as I tried my best to hold on to the branch. I swung for a moment before I lost my grip and fell through the branches, hitting almost every branch on my way down. As I smashed my body against the branches while I fell to the ground, the pain I felt was out of this world, but not as much as the pain caused by a rock, which was penetrating my shin. As I lay there screaming in pain, I could still see the nasty snake still wrapped around the branch.

My leg felt as if it was about to fall off. My cousin

summoned my grandmother and aunt to assist with trying to get me to stand. Standing was an impossible task, so they had to have other men assist with taking me out of the woods. The pain was so unbearable, that the next thing I knew, I had awoken in the hospital. They had to inject me with something to stop me from going into shock. I spent approximately four or five days resting my leg and doing certain exercises with the nurse. That had to be the strangest thing, because I wasn't breaking any rules, but I still found myself in trouble. I had asked God to protect me from injuries and any temptation that I might be confronted with.

I guess in His own way he did protect me because the injury could've been far worse. As the days went by, I began to think more and more of my mother. I wondered if she would ever send for me. I thought to myself that maybe they were having it difficult to settle. Seeing that it took me some time to get used to being in Grenada, I could only assume that they were finding it the same. Friday and Saturday nights, the men would sit around a table and smoke and drink while playing cards. Playing cards and dominos were a favorite among the fellows. Almost every weekend a fight would break out because of someone cheating. Once this started, it would take one of the more sober men to calm the situation down. Usually a few fists are thrown and a little bit of horse play on the ground. Amazingly at the end of the night, everyone is laughing and usually too drunk out of their mind to be angry. I believe anywhere there is money and alcohol, the Devil waits.

One afternoon as I sat in front of the house, I observed an argument. Two men had started to curse to each other and neither of them seemed to be willing to back down. A crowd grew as if they knew it would be just a matter of time before all hell would break out. My grandmother told me that I should stay away from the crowd and not to enter the street. Suddenly, one of the men drew their cutlass causing the other to draw his own also. At first they pointed it at each other in a threatening manner, and then within a blink, their cutlasses clashed. They swung at each other almost like a sword fight. You could hear the metal from both cutlasses banging against each other. With every swing from the cutlass, the irons would ignite a spark sending a spark to the ground. The crowd had grown even larger and some of the elders were asking them to stop.

We knew that someone was going to be injured severely. As my words would say so, you could hear the cry out loud as one of the men was struck on his chest with the cutlass. This blow angered the man, and he began to fight as if he wanted to kill his opponent. The blow was swift and smooth. The man with the chest wound maneuvered his cutlass well enough to slice off the other man's hand. The hand lay on the ground while blood fell from his wrist. He was definitely in pain as he lunged over and picked up his hand. Both parties were injured severely, and yet neither was about to forgive. They stood and looked at each other briefly and then walked away.

Someone had asked if they could find a way to get the police up here. The man who had lost his hand made his way up to the hill towards his home. The other man was stopped by the police and questioned about what had happened. None of the residents revealed any information about either party. Watching this fight right before my eyes made me feel as if I were in the Wild West. Both men stood their ground and never ran to talk another day. They said: "a man that runs from a fight today, lives to talk about it the next day." Fortunately, they both did, only with scars to remind them. Being around all the blood that I've seen, for some reason, it didn't affect me the way it would someone else. I started to wonder if I was becoming desensitized to all the blood and gore around me. I believe what has happened to me, was that I'd developed a tolerance for danger around me.

As we approached the topic about tolerance and danger, here's a situation that I had no tolerance for or was able to desensitize. My uncle Thomas lived and owned his own tailor shop in the basement of their home. His skill was in making pants, but he also made jackets. People came from various areas to place an order to either have him prepare a pant or to fix or alter their pant or jacket. He seemed to enjoy his work and worked to please his customers. One day while visiting his shop an unwanted act took place. I enjoyed being in his shop to pretend that I was making the clothes and to watch him put together a pant from start.

One of his old friends decided to pay him a visit. He hadn't seen this friend in quite some time and was happy to see him again. Uncle Thomas and his friend sat and talked for some time while I made myself busy with the sewing machine. Uncle Thomas had run out of some materials that he required for finishing some of his orders. He asked his old friend if he would mine watching the store for a little, while he ran to the store to buy the goods that he needed. His friend was more than happy to assist.

Shortly after Uncle Thomas left, the man approached me and suggested that I pull my pants down. I found this to be very odd. I asked him why, and he suggested that I just do what he said or else. Being afraid of this huge man who stood well over six feet and carried a cutlass in his boots, I agreed. He took me into a corner that wasn't as lit as the front of the store and had me bend over a bench. He then pulled his zipper down and proceeded to place his penis into my rectum. Because the size of my rectum was small and not lubricated, I felt some moisture in my butt. It felt as if he had licked his finger and placed some saliva in my cheeks of my butt. His penis was forcing its way into my butt as I cried and gowned. He drove his penis back and forth a few times with great force.

My head began to hurt, and I felt as if I were about to throw up. Suddenly, I felt like urinating but couldn't. After trying a few times, he heard footsteps and my uncle's voice. He had sufficient time to pull his zipper up, but I didn't. As usual, the person that threw the punch never gets caught, only the one that retaliates. As my uncle entered the shop, he observed me trying to pull my pants up and became annoyed with me. He quickly drew his yard stick that he measures his cloth with and struck me a few times with it, while calling me "nasty."

I ran out of the store, sore and in pain and totally embarrassed. I ran across the street into the field where green bananas were growing. I pulled my pants down and proceeded to wipe my rectum with a banana leaf. The leaf had blood on it, and my butt was extremely sore. I sat in the bushes for a while and cried and wished how I would enjoy killing that man. I so wanted to walk back to the shop and slice his head off and actually watch it fall off. This is where the Devil had complete control of my mind. I swore from that day, that if I would ever see that man again, I'd kill him. I've been to Grenada twice since the incident, but I haven't been lucky enough to see him. I think it might have been possible that I saw him and didn't recognize him, but I would never forget a face like that.

Life continued on as usual and no one ever asked or spoke about what happened to me. My uncle acted as if nothing took place and continued to talk to me as usual. For me, I knew that I had been raped and what took place in the corner of his shop was real. For those that knew, and chose not to talk about it, it was their choice; and that was alright with me, but in my eyes, I prayed daily for him to be punished by God in due time. One night my cousin Jaclyn and Ali decided that we would have a cook up in the bushes like the older people did. We got our pots, vegetables and other ingredients together and went down as close to the river as possible. We started a fire and began to make a big pot of soup and had some soft drinks and bread to go along with it. While the food was cooking, we overheard some noise not too far from where we were. We decided to stake out what was happening. We walked between the fig trees and coco trees. As we got closer we could see a light shining and a few people talking. We stayed low and looked on. What we saw was quite crazy. Three men, quite large in statue had a naked woman tied to a tree. We couldn't see her face or theirs, but we could tell that she was in distress. She sounded like she was apologizing, and that she was asking them not to hurt her. They continued to fondle her all over her body. They slapped and touched her in her private areas. One of the men had something in a bottle, and he opened it and released it onto her body area. She screamed "please don't do that." Suddenly, one of the men pulled a short cutlass and sliced her

63

gently on her chest, causing her to bleed. She knew not to make any unnecessary noise, fearing for her life. I don't know which one of us made a sudden noise, but we had to stay very still and low. The men were looking carefully in the bushes. One of the men untied her as she fell to the ground in tears and most likely in pain. We knew that if we didn't leave the area we'd be caught, and in all likelihood killed. We crawled swiftly on our knees back to the camp area and threw everything into the water and ran like the wind. The next day we met and promised each other that we'd never tell anybody what we saw. After this day, neither of us has ever spoken about what we saw on that full moon night. I guess living in the Islands came with the good and the bad. I recognized why some of the kids had such an advantage on me.

Christmas time was the best time to be in Grenada. The people were full of spirit and everyone was in a great mood. My aunt Merle and her friend seemed to care about each other. My uncle Jude was never at home because he was too busy chasing all the girls on the Island. I think he might have had a good time with most of them. Grandma and Grandpa were busy preparing for the festive day. My sister Maureen was busy with her friends, or spent her time beside our grandmother. One of the customs at the time while I was in Grenada was to slaughter a cow in public. I found this act to be very entertaining, but some people might see this act as being cruel and barbaric to the animal in today's time. However, in those days, I think it was meant to be a celebration and a way of providing food on the table as my grandparents sold the meat for money. The practice was to place a rope around the head of the cow while tying the other end to the tree. Another rope would be tied to one of the legs of the cow, while tying the other end of the rope to the same tree. Once this act is complete the butcher or the town executioner would approach the cow. The people would gather around and watch as the butcher prepares to lunge the knife into the neck of the cow. The butcher would approach the cow with an extremely long sharp knife. By this time, the cow was nervous and sensed being on someone's plate during the evening. The cow becomes rather uneasy and his head starts to twist from side to side while tugging on the tree. The butcher lunges the knife into the neck of the animal striking an artery. Unfortunate for the animal the artery wasn't severed properly, causing the cow to become uncontrollable. The cow will begin to kick and grown as it pulls on the tree. The cow begins to pull and kick so violently that eventually it will pull the tree out of the ground.

Now that the cow was loose, the task of the butcher was to control the cow so that it didn't hurt anyone. The cow was bleeding heavily and seemed to be losing its strength, due to the amount of blood it was losing. The butcher then ran up beside the cow, placing his hand around the short horns, and plunged the knife once more into the neck of the animal. This time the cow groaned out and fell to the ground within distance from where it unleashed itself. The excitement ended with applauds from the community and giving thanks to the Lord. The practice of this ceremony is to drain the blood and to sell it to whoever wants it. The joy that shines upon the village's people has always amazed me to how easy it was for them to see the killing of this animal.

The cow is skinned first by being sliced and diced apart by the butcher. Every part of the cow is used for something. My grandmother will sell various parts of the cow to the community in exchange for money to purchase other cows for the coming season. What a celebration this day is for everyone who lives within the area. I sat within inches of the butcher as he scalped the head of the cow as I watched with enthusiasm as he cuts the head off and other parts of the body.

He was very meticulous as he carved his way around the cow so that he would have as much meat as possible. The cow was used for many different types of entries in many people homes. I observed families eating the tale of the cow. There were times around the holiday season I observed family members and friends eating certain parts of the animal. I couldn't believe that they even ate the penis of the cow. A dish that's commonly made is cow heel soup. All that is used are the fatty areas of the heel of the cow and coated with salt and pepper to kill the obnoxious taste. I enjoyed the steaks and the soft meaty area of the cow. The Christmas was a wonderful time, and everyone was in a jolly good mood. Money and some clothing were given to us as gifts. We ate all that we could, and drank as much as we would like. At the end of the festive day, everyone had ingested a ton of food and probably wouldn't be able to sleep that night. But who really cared, it was Christmas.

One day after school, my grandmother called on me to have a word with me. The news that I was waiting on had finally come. My parents had sent word to my grandparents whom they would be sending for us within a month. I was ecstatic; I jumped and jumped like I had won the lottery. Thinking about it, to me, it was the lottery; my ticket to finally be with my mother was finally here. As I jumped up and down I saw the look on my grandmother's face. She had a happy look on her face; however, she also had the look of sadness. I realized for a moment that I was fixated on my joy and not thinking of how my grandmother had felt. I sat beside her and asked her to forgive me for being selfish. She understood and said that she would also be happy to be with her family after being away from them as long as we had been. She told me that she has gotten used to have us around, and once we'd be gone, she'd surely miss us. At that moment, I realized how much she loved us.

I'm going to miss my sweet grandmother. She taught me so much about humanity and how to be as a person. Respect for myself is mandatory, and once I have it, I will earn respect from others. In the weeks leading up to leaving, I tried my best to spend as much time with my cousins as possible. My cousin Jaclyn wasn't very happy to see me leave. Many times I thought to myself that if we weren't cousins, the possibility might have been there for us to be in a relationship.

Jaclyn kissed me on my lips one evening before turning in for the night. She looked at me and said that I was special and to never let anyone tell me otherwise. She said that she would miss me, and that she'd always hold me close to her heart. We hugged each other for a long time and in return, I kissed her softly back on her lips. The following evening I decided that I'd pay my other cousin Crampton a visit. We never really spent a lot of time with each other, only because of his strange behavior. On this particular night, I decided that I'd sneak up on him, scaring him out of his boots. He was sitting under the house near a fire with his mother. His back was turned to me, so I knew that once I touched him, he'd jump out of his pants. His mother saw me as I placed my hand on his shoulder. Crampton jumped like a bunny leaping out of the bushes. He picked up a piece of a stick that was beside him and struck me with it, piercing a hole over my left eye brow. Blood was everywhere as I struggled to stand on my feet. I made it halfway out of his yard as I fell to the ground. I knew that I had been injured, but I had no idea of the extent of the injury. My grandparents and aunt were called and attended the scene. My grandmother had my uncle drive me to the hospital. I woke up the next day in the hospital with bandages surrounding my head. My head felt like it had been hit by a truck, and my chest was very sore. To this day, no one would tell me why my chest was hurting, so I assumed that maybe I went unconscious. After spending the night and a part of the next day in the hospital, I was released to go home. My grandmother was not very happy and as a result of his cunningness, she had a few words with Crampton and his mother. I knew that Crampton did that act deliberately, and there were no reason for that.

I had approximately three weeks before I left Grenada. So I decided that I'd make it my last mission to revenge Crampton. He had to have known that I wasn't about to let this go without paying him back. I staked out Crampton every day for the last three weeks while in Grenada, but I didn't have an opportunity to punish him. The morning that I was preparing to leave Grenada, I went over to Crampton's home and knocked on his door. I knocked several times to no avail. Finally, I yelled out to Crampton that he might have gotten away with this for now but rest assured, I will not forget him. The bus had arrived and we were ready to leave. Some of my cousins had arrived to see us off while the others chose not to say goodbye. The drive to the airport seemed forever as we drove through the country area. I reflected on the first time I met my grandparents and the remainder of the family. I smiled as I thought of the fight that I had with my aunt Merle. It's amazing how one's heart can change.

Chapter 3

I'd become very close to my grandmother, and I enjoyed being around my aunt. The time in Grenada was well spent, remembering the moments of my adolescence. Grenada is truly a place of peace, joy and tranquility all bundled up into one. I came to Grenada with a disdained taste for it, and now I leave with fond memories and a hole in my heart. We arrived at the airport and the moment that I knew I would dread was upon me. As I looked into my aunt Merle face, I could see the love she had for me and how she's going to miss us. My grandmother had a glimpse of a smile on her face along with sparkles in her eyes. Usually once the eyes sparkled it meant a detection of tears to come. My grandmother's voice was crackly and soft. She told me that she wanted me to grow to be a fine young man, and that she's going to miss us very much. I hugged her and told her that I'd never forget her and that she's the best grandparent whom any child can ever ask for. I thanked her for her kindness and for all the one on one conversation shared. I also told her that I'd do my best to remember everything that she has taught me. I told her I was sorry I caused her the grief that I did. She responded by saying, "if I didn't then I wasn't a kid at heart." As I kissed her for the last time, my heart felt like it was about to split in half.

Life was about to take another turn as we embarked on a new adventure. I knew not what's ahead for me, but what I did know, was that I'd face it head on. The air hostess was warm and friendly to us. She made us comfortable and fed us anything that we asked for, within reason of course. As I sat and pondered about what's to come, I continued to have flashbacks of my grandmother. I was already missing her, and I hadn't been away from her for more than an hour. The air hostess approached us to let us know that we'd be landing within the next fifteen minutes, so we should buckle up.

As I looked out the window, all I could see is snow. I had never seen snow before, except at the movies. The hostess waited until the plane was empty and then escorted us out to meet our parents. As we approached the entrance to the public, we stopped for a brief second. I took a deep breath while my sister was inpatient and full of excitement. We were off to the welcoming party. I thanked the air hostess as my grandmother wished of me, and proceeded along. There they stood, three smiling faces. Well technically two smiling faces and one face with a slight smile on it. My sister was off like a bullet. She ran directly to my father, I thought, and then to our mother. As I walked slowly towards them, it almost felt surreal. I felt as if I was traveling in slow motion. There I was standing among three people who were staring at me, as if they had never seen me before.

The tears flowed from my mother's eyes with joy. She was overwhelmed with joy to see me. I must say that my eyes had filled with water to see her also. As we embraced for a few seconds it almost felt like minutes. If it wasn't for me, gasping for air, I think she might have still been there hugging me. That journey went well and now it's time to make it two for two. As I stood there with a smile on my face, I had the task of deciding which one of the two men was my father.

Now you have to remember I didn't see exactly which one of the men my sister actually went to. All I knew is that she ran towards a man. I decided that I'd walk towards the gentleman with the smile on his face. What a mistake that was. That gentle man was my cousin on my father's side. The look on my father's face wasn't suited for television. I said "Sorry," as I approached him and shook his hand. The look wasn't as accepting as it was from my mother. I knew right then, that this was the beginning of hell for me. The drive home was long, because of all the snow that had fallen and that was continuing to fall. This was the first time I actually saw and felt the snow. As we drove home with my cousin in the front seat and my mother in the back with us, I could feel the joy that penetrated my body from my mother's happiness as she was so elated to finally see us again.

My mother continued to look at us, as if she was on a tour of another country. She was really happy. I couldn't say the same for my dad. We arrived at our new home that was settled near to a park and a school. We lived on a street by the name of North Cliff Blvd. My father parked his car in the garage, and we entered into the house from the garage. Before entering the house, I could remember answering to my grandmother. I said, "yes Grandma," but no one answered back. My mother said to me that my grandmother was on my mind, and that's why I thought I heard her voice. I believe it was my grandmother trying to warn me of what's to come. We placed our luggage in our perspective rooms and returned to the kitchen to be lectured by our father. I hadn't been here a day, and he was already laying down his strict rules. The first issue he spoke about was our safety. He wanted us to know that we're no longer in Grenada, and Canada is far larger and much more dangerous. He expected us to follow the laws of the road and of the schools. He then spoke about schoolwork. Under no circumstances would he accept us not being able to memorize our timetables.

Every night we would be tested on our tables from two to twelve. He stated that the person who didn't know his or her timetable would be punished by way of a spanking. I knew right then that this was his way of trying to punish me for what had happened at the airport. Within two days, he had me just where he wanted me. I had some difficulty remembering my timetables. He went to his room and returned with a thick brown leather belt that seemed as if it had my name on it.

I think I received approximately five lashes about my body. My mother stood within striking distance, as if she were prepared to stop him at any moment. I took my beating and went to bed bruised and achy that night.

The next morning we rose and prepared ourselves for school. I wasn't in the mood to eat so I just drank a glass of orange juice and went to school. My mother did her usual good byes at the door with little hugs and kisses. On this morning, she whispered in my ear to try my best and not to get myself into trouble. She was trying to guard me from my father.

School was tough and very unfriendly. The kids were mean and all had terrible attitudes. One kid in particular, had an issue with me from the first day of school. He would spit wet papers onto the back of my head using a straw. He taunted me at every moment he had and provoked me at recess. One morning while class was being taught, he spat one of those wet papers onto the back of my neck. I got up and pushed him and told him to stop it. This reaction sparked off a chain of reactions. The teacher had him come to the front of the class and apologized for disturbing the class, and he also had to say sorry to me.

He said his apologies with a great deal of resentment. As he walked by my desk, he said to me "after school you're dead." Now not being accustomed to that type of language, I actually thought he was going to kill me. So as soon as school was over, I made my way to the rear of the building, where I tried to leave through the side entrance. A gang of about six to eight kids had spotted me leaving from the back. I dashed across the school playground and made my way down the street. I felt like I was running through the woods from a bear. The kids were relentless. Everywhere I ran, they were on me like white on rice. I could see my home from the top of the hill as I ran down the hill, and as I got closer to salvation, I could see my father sitting on the balcony.

Screaming and yelling for help as I fell to the ground, I begged for him to help me. I got up as quickly as I fell and ran across the street to my front yard. The pack of wolves, per say, had stopped chasing me and proceeded to walk back to the school. I asked my dad why didn't he help me, but he just sat there while he smoked and ignored me. I went into the house and proceeded to tell my mother what had happened. During my story, I was interrupted by my father wishing to see me in the basement. Something told me that this wasn't going to be good. I met with him in the basement near the cold room. He lectured me about having to pay taxes for our education and additional expenses for clothing. He said that he could have understood if I had stood my ground and fought like a man rather than run like a bunny in the tall grass. He reached into his rear pant pocket and pulled out his favorite belt. He called it the Everard special. Without any sign, he proceeded to swing like a wild man at me. The belt was striking me in the head, the legs and arms. I felt that mercy was not one of his softer sides. He seemed to be completely out when it came to me. After screaming loud enough for my mother to hear me and hopefully the neighbors, he stopped. I curled up into a corner like a ball and just cried and cried and cried. My mother came down the stairs and sat beside me and told me that one day everything would be all right. I had no idea of what she was-talking about at the time. I think my mother was beginning to realize that my father had it in for me, but was having a hard time understanding why.

That night I had very little sleep due to the pain I was in and how I had to change to survive in this country. I never experienced anything like this while I lived in Grenada. The school I went to didn't have kids that acted like that, so this was quite new to me. I rose a bit late that morning because I had to wear the appropriate clothes so that the kids and teachers wouldn't ask any questions. All morning the red head little bully was taunting me, and implying that he's going to kick my ass at recess. I said very little to him as some of the other kids looked at me.

Something told me that the other kids were afraid of him, so they did whatever he asked. The bell had rung for recess and the kids made their way out to play with their friends. I didn't have any friends yet except for the three kids that would say hello to me, whenever they saw me. I decided that I would play basketball at one of the unoccupied nets. I shot the ball at the net over and over trying to have it enter the circle. Suddenly, the red head appeared and stood directly in front of me. I moved to the side and tossed the ball at the net again but missed. The red head that I speak off name was Heat. I heard the other kids calling him to play football, but he was more interested in provoking me. He walked over to the ball and kicked it away. I looked at him and ran after the ball and returned to try again. He kicked the ball away even further this time. I asked him this time not to do that anymore. He said "And what?" This time when I returned, I stepped away from him, looked at him before I shot the ball and released.

Without any hesitation Heath had approached the ball and gave the ball the hardest kick that I couldn't believe how far I would have had to walk to retrieve the ball. My heart began to pump as I looked at him with that grin on his face. For a brief moment, I remembered the beating I took and all the kids that were chasing me. At this point, I lunged at him pulling him down to the ground by his hair and punching him directly into his face. All the kids were yelling, "A fight, a fight, a nigger and a white!" At this time, one of the teachers approached and attempted to pull me off Heath.

Because of the rage that I felt, I think I had blacked out and struck the teacher in his face also. Finally, they were able to remove me from Heath. Justice was served by me! The teacher took the both of us to the principal's office and had us sit in the waiting area until we were called. Heath was called in to give his side of the story. After fifteen minutes or so, he summoned for me to see him. I told the principal exactly what had taken place without leaving any details out. I figured if I wanted the respect of the principal, even if I was wrong or right, I had to tell the truth.

While waiting in the hallway, my mother had been called to the school. Due to my altercation with the boy, it was the school's policy to request that the parents attend the school. The principal explained what had happened to my mother. He also felt that I wasn't to be blamed for the fight. He also told my mom that I was a good kid, just quiet at times. He observed that regardless of wherever a fight might have been, he recognized that I was always present. His decision was to suspend me for a day, which included the said day. He felt that because of my honesty and the restraint I had towards Heath, he felt he was justified in his decision. Heath had a cut above his right cheek, and his lip was bleeding and swollen. He had an opportunity to speak with the boy and felt that he was not entirely honest with the event that took place. He requested that his parents attend the school, but they weren't able to reach them. He suspended the boy for three days excluding that day.

I returned to school the following day to be greeted by the kids like a hero. My suspicion all along was correct. The reason they supported Heath, was due to his bullying. That was the first time I felt at ease since Heath was away. The following week Heath had returned from his vacation (suspension). As usual, he sat directly behind me, but on this day he didn't spit wet papers at me. I think he had learned his lesson. The bell had rung for recess, and all the kids were out having a good time. I spent my time shooting baskets by myself.

The other kids were about to start a game of soccer. Heath approached me and stood directly in my face without saying a word. All the kids were prepared for another fight. Then he did the unthinkable, he shook my hand. I was asked to join them in a game of soccer and even played on the same team with Heath. Life at school was beginning to be enjoyable. I had accumulated a fair amount of friends, and that made me very happy. The school year was about to come to an end, and I had become friends with two guys who lived near me.

One of the boys lived approximately two blocks away from me, and the other boy lived a few houses away from me. Their names were Johnny and Frank. Frank was the one that lived on my street and Johnny lived a few blocks away from us. Frank was the first person to introduce himself to me. He had such a sincere demeanor. He asked if I would like to meet his family and have supper with them. This was the first for me, so I had to ask my mother if that would be alright. I told Frank that I would meet him at his home before supper was ready. I wanted to clean myself up, seeing that this was the first time being in another person's home. His family greeted me with warmth. They were wonderful and completely down to earth. I remember eating a hamburger for the first time at his home. That was the nicest burger I ever tasted, although I had never tasted a burger before. The burger flowed with juices and the cheese melted in your mouth like chocolate. Within a few weeks, I had met numerous people that had lived on or near by our street. Every morning myself and Frank walked to school together. We would walk towards Johnnies' home, and then we would all walk to school together. We were known as "The Three Amigos." We did everything together. We went to the park together, even washed our bikes at the same home together. I can recall getting into little situations, and somehow one of us would appear to back the other one. There was a girl on the street that I totally liked. She had the same last name like my mother's maiden name. Her name was Susan Ross. When we had any games that could involve the girls I always tried to have her on my team. She was as beautiful as she was kind. Her parents had many children, and one of them was severely disabled. It reminded me of when I was in Trinidad. Some of her siblings never spent any time with the boy, but I did observe Susan sitting with him on many occasions. He never really came outside. He usually sat on the front balcony for a brief moment and would make his way to the back of the house. I figured he probably was embarrassed as he was teased by the public.

We were about to begin our new grade. Grade seven was at a separate school, just across from D.B. Hood. The schools sat on the same property but only went up to grade eight. This is where I observed a girl whom I would have a long lasting relationship with. She was in grade eight while I was in grade seven. Her name was Robin Clyke, and she had a smile as bright as the Sun. She never took her eyes off me. For some reason, no matter where I was, there she would be. Eventually, as the school year went on, we became friends. She invited me to her home to eat with her and her brother and her family.

My father worked many hours and spent very little time at home. He always seemed to be either at work or on a business trip. As time went on, I started to see a pattern in my father's behavior towards my mother. He wasn't an affectionate person towards her. Many times I would see her crying, but I never knew the reason for her tears. This started to concern me, so I tried to be at home a little more. My father was a serious man. He smiled very little with my mother and especially with me. Saturday evenings would be the only time that I would see him with a smile on his face. I think the reason for his happiness was because he was going out with his cousin and friends. He buttered my mother up with playful pinches here and there and with little kisses on her cheek. I was confused by this behavior because during the week he acted like a dead fish, and once the weekend appeared, he was like the little drummer boy. I guess my mother enjoyed whatever affection she would receive from him and blocked out her beliefs. He would walk by and pinch my sister while handing her his change from his pocket. I knew better to ask how about me, so I just looked on and kept my questions to myself. My father enjoyed dressing well and driving nice cars. He had a very expensive taste when it came to material things. His practice was such that he would never give my mother a time of his return, from wherever he was going, so as a result she would never stay up.

Sometimes I could hear him turning the key in the door, because he always struggled due to his impairment. The following day he would sleep the majority of the day. Once up, he would sit and watch television without saying too much to anyone of us for most of the day. That happy go lucky guy had disappeared again, only to return in a few more days as the weekend closed in.

The type of activities that I participated in while in Grenada had been significantly different. To begin, I never had an opportunity to learn how to ride a bike. Learning to ride a bicycle was very important to me. Everyone whom I came into contact with had owned a bicycle. One evening after school I asked my father if it would be possible to purchase me a bicycle. At first he said no, so I didn't ask him again for some time. Approximately, two weeks later I confronted him again with the same question. This time he looked at me and then looked at my mother. I was guessing that after seeing how my mother looked at him, he felt some type of obligation. That same evening he took me to a bicycle store near Eglinton Ave. and Oakwood Ave. The store was filled with all types of bikes. The owner of the store had known my father, so we had good assistance in purchasing the proper bike for me. At the time, for whatever the reason, my eyes became fixated on an orange twelve-speed racing bike. This bike was manufactured in France and had a good reputable name. The owner of the store felt that I had picked out a fine bike, not only to mention fine dollars. I had him tune it up and added a few accessories on the bike for me. We paid for the bike and waited around while they tuned and added the accessories that I asked for. We placed the bike into the back seat with one rim off so that it wouldn't be scratched in the trunk. My father drove approximately half way home and stopped and had me take the bike out of the car. At the time when we stopped, I thought he was going to assist me in learning how to ride. This was not going to be the case. He told me that I wanted a bike, so now learn to ride and get home. I spent countless moments trying to balance and peddle at the same time. It just wasn't happening and I was becoming frustrated. I sat on the sidewalk for a brief moment to calm down and began to think. I looked left and then I looked right. My little spider senses were starting to tingle. Something inside of me had me stand up, and it finally came to me. I walked the bike to the top of the hill and push myself off and tried and finding my balance. So I did just that. The first try was scary and wobbly. I realized that I didn't fall, so I knew that I only had some difficulty steering and peddling at the same time. I tried it again, only this time I focused on peddling and changing the gears while I was on the flat surface. With every try, I saw an improvement and that gave me more and more confidence. I decided that if I could put it all together, I would be able to make my way home without any problems. So I walked up the hill again, after walking up the hill so many times I was beginning to run out of energy. As I sat on the bike all proud and beaming from ear to ear, I observed some of the residence looking at me. They smiled and gave me that nod of the head.

Their encouragement gave me that spark that I needed. I had a sip of water from my water bottled that I purchased with the bike, and made the sign of the cross as I prepared for the challenge. As I flew down the hill, I felt an exhilarating feeling that came over me. I knew that I had considered the task of riding, so I thought hopefully my father would be surprised to see me. The sun was beginning to go down so I wanted to get home in the light so that everyone could see my new bike. I ran into the house, called my mom and dad to the front door and showed them that I could ride. My mother had a nice smile on her face, and my father nodded his head and walked away. All my friends were surprised to see me with a new bicycle. Everyone wanted to have a ride on my bike. I told them to be careful, and they're only allowed one ride. I didn't want my bike to be damaged or jinxed. The following morning when I woke up, I ate quickly and I was off riding everywhere. I wanted to be the best on my bike and I wanted to build my stamina so that my endurance would be endless. Within a few weeks, none of the kids on the street could handle their bike like me, or ride as fast as I could. I realized that just a few weeks ago I couldn't even ride and now I was probably the best rider on the street.

As I lay in my room, I began to think. If I had it in me to learn how to ride then there is no reason why I couldn't learn how to play all the other sports. I called my friend Frank that night and asked if he would be willing to teach me how to play all the other sports. The first things on my list was to learn how to skate. It looked easy but I had a feeling that it really wasn't. He took me to an arena in the area and allowed me to wear his extra pair of skates. I didn't want to purchase my own, unless I liked it. I fell every three feet on my big butt. As quickly as I could rise, just as quickly I would fall. Frustration was beginning to kick in. He made me practice walking first, and then he had me hold on to the railing and try little steps. This seemed to be working, and I felt as if I might enjoy this sport. Gradually, I was skating longer distances without falling and or holding on to the railing. I could feel my confidence building each time I went around the rink. Before I knew it, I was skating without falling or holding onto the railing. I wasn't an expert yet, but I had the hang of what to do.

We called it the evening and decided that we would return the following day and the following day until I was good at it. A few weeks of training had me sore in the butt area and on my shins. I wasn't about to quit now seeing that I was just a few more practices before I could skate with the good guys. One evening I decided that I'd go to the rink by myself and test my ability. I watched for a while as I looked at some of the good skaters do their stuff. I wanted to be able to do the same thing, so I decided that this was going to be the evening that I crowned myself.

I was moving around the rink pretty well. The other skaters were skating really low to the ground when they went around the corners, so I needed to do that also. I was trying to emulate every move they made until I tried stopping. The problem was that I had forgotten to learn how to stop while in training with Frank. The guys would take off with a burst of speed and then suddenly stopped. So, not realizing I didn't know how to stop, I took off like a jet doing all the fancy moves and crashed into the boards busting my chin open. I was never so embarrassed, not to mention that I was in a lot of pain. My chin was cut open pretty well and blood was flowing from my chin to the ice. They had to call for first aids to assist me to the locker room. They cleaned me up and bandaged my cut with gauze. I saw the doctor the following day and was given a clean bill of health. The wound would heal and I would be able to continue to skate.

As the weeks passed, my skating ability continued to improve to the point where I was capable of challenging some of the other skaters to a skill assessment. I decided that I wanted to learn how to swim. All my friends on the street would gather together and walk to the swimming arena. At this pool only the good swimmers swam in the deep end. The deep end had three diving boards. The diving boards were situated at three different heights. To dive of the highest board, usually meant you had no fear, and you were a pretty good at swimming. I looked on with great interest and eagerness to learn. I approached Frank again and asked him to teach me. Swimming wasn't going to be the easiest task to attempt. I knew that Frank would have to be very patient with me. For days, I couldn't do anything until, one day Frank shoved me into the deep end. He wanted me to get rid of my fear and to try some of the techniques he thought me. I panicked at first until I went under a couple of times. It didn't look like Frank was about to jump in and save me, so I had to settle down and breathe. I started to kick my legs and use my arms like a windmill turning.

I found myself moving and gradually I realized that I was beginning to understand the format. Frank had me swim a couple of lengths to build my lung capacity. After that he asked me to come out of the pool. This is when he explained to me the art of treading water. It took me a long time to actually get it right, but after a few days I learned. I decided that I would practice as often as possible until I was good enough to participate in the events with the guys. Frank and I went to the pool one afternoon about an hour before it closed. He wanted the pool to be fairly empty so that we could concentrate on diving. First he showed off his skills, and I was very impressed. It was almost like if he was trying to show me how to dive in slow motion. He would stand and explain how to arch his back and point his hands and toes. He made sure I kept my eyes open at all times to anticipate where I was going. I performed small dives that carried a name of belly flop. Over and over I dived until I began to get sick of being in the water.

That evening wasn't as successful as I would have liked it to be. We returned almost every evening until I began to get the hang of it. Finally, out of nowhere, I performed an almost perfect dive. The practices were beginning to pay off. I started to dive off the platform almost gliding like a swan in the air. Frank believed I had gotten the idea and I was now ready for the next level. He placed a chair just at the edge of the pool and suggested I dived over it without knocking it into the pool. I watched him perform it a couple of times. My first two or three times at diving over the chair, I wasn't as gracious as Frank was. Over and over I continued to knock the chair into the pool. I stopped and looked at the chair for a second or two, and decided that I was not going to knock it over any more. I was off and over I went like a bird taking off the ground for the first time. I felt so proud of myself when I realized that I hadn't knocked the chair over. I performed that dive over and over until I knew that I wasn't going to knock it over anymore. I thought I was ready, but the word belief was up in the air.

Frank performed a few dives and he made them seem so easy. We decided that we would skip one of the diving boards and challenge myself to the big times. My first dive was almost like a cannon drop. Water was splashing everywhere. My next dive wasn't as bad, but I still had to make a few adjustments. I stood still as if I was about to perform in the Olympics. I bounced a couple of times and dove into the air like an eagle souring for food. I arched my back slightly with my toes pointed and my hands straight out and entered the water like a bullet piercing through an object.

The dive was as close to perfect that would cause any judge to give him a score that was as close to perfect. Frank clapped and gave me a huge high five. I was now ready to sore with the big boys. We decided that before we left, we'd have one more dive for the road. Frank dove first, and it was a beauty. He did a flip in the middle of the air before he entered the water. I decided that to beat him I'd try something new. I did a running dive, springing high into the air as twirled once in the air before entering the water.

The plan didn't go as well as I would have wanted it. Before entering into the water, I lost sight of how low I really was and smashed my mouth against the bottom of the pool. This would cause me a great deal of pain, and as a result of smashing my mouth, I cracked my front tooth. My face was all bloody and I had to be hurried home to be taken to the medical emergency. My mother wasn't very happy with me, and my friend felt bad. The surgeon examined me and all would be OK. He placed a material on my tooth to stop the pain and fixed my tooth to make it look natural and told me to try my best not to chew on it for a few days. My friend Frank was happy to learn that I'd be alright and back in good form again. I figured I had learned all the sports that I felt would be a problem to me when amongst people from this Country. Playing baseball, basketball, soccer, and football were all sports that you can pick up on your own. My father continued to be fairly strict with me. He even went to the length by telling my friends that if they were to ever see me smoking, that he would like them to mention it to him. Most of my friends thought that, that was an odd thing to say to them. They looked at me as if they wanted to ask me if I was being abused. After a while, of nothing being said, I changed the subject to practicing for the street hockey tournament that was coming up.

For the past little while, even before I was introduced to them and the game, they were challenging other neighborhoods to decide on who's the best block in the community. We decided between us who will play what position, and decided that we'd have a good practice the following day after school. After school that day, we all rushed home so that we could eat and prepare to practice. Everyone met in front of my house to practice. The day was perfect to play outside. The sky was blue, the wind was perfect for playing and my spirit was high.
At approximately fifteen minutes into the game, my mother asked if I could take the laundry to the laundry mart to have

the clothes clean. Without thinking I said "No, I'm playing right now."

My mother then said to me "Everard I'm not asking you again, I'm telling you."

I found myself responding by saying "I'm not washing any f---king clothes today." What possessed me to say that, I have no idea. What I didn't know, was that I was about to dig myself out of a whole. I dropped my hockey stick and ran into the house. I tried apologizing to my mother, but she had already decided to call my dad. I could hear her talking to him on the phone while I stood in the kitchen. After her death defying phone call, I asked why couldn't she just forgive me and have me take the clothes. She felt that as a child, I had disrespected her in front of my friends and I had to be thought a lesson. My father was home within ten minutes. He came through the front door, like a man looking for a gun fight. He asked me to take my shirt off. He said that he was having a difficult day with his work men and that they're costing him additional dollars. I asked what that had to do with me. I said to him that wouldn't it be nice to move away from our Stone Age custom. I explained that in his eyes everything seemed to do with someone being rude or mannish. He pulled his shinny black belt out of his waist, like Clint Eastwood pulling his gun out of his holster. I decided that I already knew that he was going to brutalize me, so why take my shirt off. So by not removing my shirt, it sent him into an animalistic rage. He started to swing the belt like it was a sword in his hand. Every blow that landed on my skin was a damaging blow. We started off in the kitchen, but I thought it would be to my advantage, so I ran into the basement. This was the worst thing that I could ever have done. He cornered me at the far end of the basement and began to go to town on me, like a boxer finishing off his opponent. The belt was striking my face and every part of my body. Blood was beginning to show through my clothing and my muscles were becoming numb. I fell to the ground in mercy of him and hid under the bed for protection.

I felt like an animal that knew he was going to die, but was hoping for a miracle. He started to jump on top of the bed, causing me to split my lip open from the force of the blow to my mouth. Realizing that I felt safer under the bed, he grabbed a hold of one of his crutches and began to poke it into my ribs and legs. Knowing that I couldn't withstand the assault for much longer, I came out with my hands up in the air and barely standing. Being in the rage that he was in, he swung the crutch, hitting me in my ribs. This blow caused me to fall to the ground. My mother began to scream, by asking him to stop. She was in a hysterical state. Some of my friends who were standing outside, attempted to speak with my father to rescue me through an open window. They asked him to stop beating me, because he might kill me. He yelled at them, causing them to flee from the property. Before deciding to end his slaughtering, he kicked me in my ribs as he made his way upstairs. My body lay almost lifeless in my mother's arm on the basement floor. In my head, I could hear little bells ringing and my heart felt like it was about to pierce through my chest. The tears flowed from my mother's eyes as she wiped the sweat off my face. My nose was bleeding. My legs were filled with cuts and bruises. My back looked like I had been through a mauling. As I lay on the ground I felt as if my rib had been broken, but I was too afraid to ask or look.

My mother looked at me that evening and said to me

that, she'd never ever again involve my father in any disciplining again. She did hold true to her word, but she wasn't strong enough to protect me. An entire week would pass before I was capable of attending school. All of my friends would call the house to ask about my well-being. My mother told them that I was fine, but I wasn't feeling very well. We both knew that they didn't believe her, but it was the best story we could come up with. I returned to school after being on mercy resting to the welcome of my entire class. They were so happy to see me that most of the class got up and hugged me. I knew now that the teacher and the students knew. I knew that if I admitted to anything, that my home would be investigated, so I continued to tell them that I fell down the stairs and I had caught a cold. A whole two weeks would pass before I would be able to participate in any gym activities. The teachers were convinced that I had been injured. They knew how competitive I was, so missing gym meant something serious was wrong.

I got by that moment with a great deal of pressure. Every teacher in the school that knew me stopped and spoke to me. Things were back to normal, and I was back hanging out with my friends. Life was wonderful away from the house. My biggest fear was being in the house at night. I felt that this could be the moment when I did something that could cause me grief. I began to sleep with my pilot gun on my chest. Hours would pass with me staring at the door handle. Thinking that at any moment he'd barge into the room because of something that I had done during the day.

Every morning, before I got up, I noticed that my gun would be at the corner of my bed. My mother would enter my room while I was sleeping and would place the gun in a spot that would seem less confrontational. I knew that she knew that I was afraid of him, so I did whatever I could to protect myself. When walking around him, I walked with my eyes to the ground and walked as quickly as possible. I did my best to watch television during the moments that he wasn't at home. We enjoyed watching the shows when my dad was away from the house.

Winter was upon us and I hated it with a passion. Every kid had his chores, and my chore was to shovel the walk way and property. I had no problem doing that because it gave me an opportunity to be outside. What I did have a problem with, was washing the car in the cold weather. He was obsessed with keeping his car clean regardless of the weather. In the early hours almost every Saturday morning, he would have me out in the garage washing the car sometimes even before I had breakfast. The look on my mother's face said it all. She wouldn't have the opportunity to prepare breakfast because he would make sure to see that I didn't have a chance to eat so I had to work in the cold on an empty stomach. I had a bucket filled with boiling water and would wash the car in small spurts. Drying the car was almost impossible, because the water would turn to ice quickly. I had to wash and dry almost simultaneously with the washcloth in one hand and the drying cloth in the other. The task of washing the car played on my nerves, so to avoid going mad, I thought of my cute little friend at school.

Once I was done cleaning the car, my appetite for food was usually gone. My hands felt like leather. I had very little feeling in my hand, but my mother would have me sit with a semi cool rag to bring the feelings back to my hands. The toughest part of it all was no "thank you." He'd walk into the garage and inspect the car, and then usually at night he would take it out for a drive. The process would play itself over and over until he realized that it didn't bother me anymore.

My father had a serious addiction to cigarettes. He smoked approximately a pack and a half a day. He initiated me as his cigarette lighting person. Whenever he was in the mood for a cigarette, he would have me light one up for him. I would open the pack of Rothmans, place a cigarette in my mouth and puffed on it until I saw smoke. The smell of the cigarette was disgusting. I had the strangest job of lighting cigarettes for many years.

I can remember the look on our guest's face when I would return with a lit cigarette in my mouth for my dad. They had that look of "what the hell is going on in this house?" None of the guests would inquire or say anything, but they were intrigued. I must say that, the only thing that I did was to have it lit and burning. Never ever did I share in smoking or attempted a few drags. Sometimes if my father was having a bad day, he would have me run to the store and purchase a pack of cigarettes. The catch was, depending on the urgency, he would have me go either without a jacket or shoes. Many times I traveled to the store in the midst of the winter without a jacket on, or my shoes being barely tied up. I can recall the attendant asking me why I was out here without a jacket on numerous of occasions. My skin would feel as if it was burning to the point that once I was back in the house, I would itch for an hour or more as my skin became bumpy with a rash like bumps.

My mother would argue with my dad's madness at lengths and at times even threaten to leave if he continued to treat me like that. Summer was around the corner, so my father and my cousin had decided to give the house a makeover. If my memory serves me right, I think it was in the month of May when my cousin and a few friends of my dad came over to give him a hand. Everyone had a job that they were working on. My cousin Lennox was working inside with my dad painting and varnishing the floors. Cousin Lennox was in charge of painting, and my father was varnishing the floors. My job was to get everyone whatever they required to do their job. The day was beautiful, sunny and my friends would stop by from time to time to say "Hello." For some reason, I was asked to get something from outside for one of the workers. After handing over one of the tools that they were requiring, I made my way into the house from the front entrance. Having no idea at the time that along my way, I had accidentally stepped in some paint that had spilled on the grass. Because it wasn't visible to me, I stepped in it and carried it into the house with me accidentally. I walked from the front door to midway through the hallway before my cousin would ask for me to stop. He said "Everard, please don't walk any further."

I asked, "Why not?"

He looked at me with a disturbing look on his face as if he had seen death. He said, "Everard, you've stepped in paint, and you've walked through the house with it." He then said "I hope your dad isn't going to go crazy over this, because we can fix it." My eyes slowly moved towards my feet as my heart started to feel as if it was about to explode in my chest. I can feel my bladder losing control and little drops of urine was trickling down my leg. Perspiration was beginning to consume my body. I felt as if I was going to have a heart attack. Cousin Lennox approached me and assured me that everything was going to be ok. "It was an accident that anyone of us could have done," he said.

While my cousin was speaking to me my father entered the front entrance. His eyes automatically fell to the floor. The rage in his eyes was uncontrollable and seemed like a man that was about to commit murder. He looked at me and didn't even ask any questions as he began to walk towards me like a man who was about to fulfill his intention. I couldn't tell you about the speed that he had moved with. He was like a hungry lion attacking his pray.

Unfortunately, for me, my mother had left for the grocery store. My Cousin Lennox tried to stop him from his assault on me, but he was already out of control. He swung his belt like lighting hitting the roof top of a building. I had no way of covering myself from the onslaught to me. I could hear my cousin yelling at him to stop and at the same time trying to hold him back. My dad seemed as if he was in a world of his own. With every blow, he spoke to me, while the sweat dripped of his face. I lost some hearing in my ear from the belt striking me on my ear lope. Finally there was additional help from other relatives and friends. By that time, I had no control of my limbs, and I was convulsing like a chicken that had just lost his head. My eyes had been swollen and my ear was bruised and swollen. Both of my hands and forearms were cut and extremely swollen. I had blood pouring out of my mouth because I had bit down on my tongue so many times. I tried to stand, but because of how bruised and swollen both of my legs were, I required assistance to be carried to the bath tub. My cousin and other members had me sit in the bathtub with mild water in it. I think I had laid in the tub for over an hour, until my mother returned. My mother returned from the grocery with my sister singing and happy from the little conversation I overheard. After ten or so minutes, she inquired about my whereabouts.

Cousin Felix and cousin Lennox explained to her what had happened. I could hear her running to the washroom. Her eyes had lit up with anger as she tried to comfort me. I didn't want to be touched because of the pain that I was in. I asked her not to say anything to dad, fearing that he'd retaliate against me. She left the washroom and continued to ask him if his intention was to kill me. He asked her, "Why don't you take a look at the floors?" My mother asked if the floors were more important, or if he felt better by hurt me.

She threatened him that one day she's going to leave and he'd be sorry. His response to her was "I guess your king is more important to you, than I am." I missed another week at school, but fortunately my friends weren't around to witness it. After so many beatings for absolutely nothing, my feelings for my father were changing by the minute. I knew he had a problem with me.

One evening when he returned from work, he emptied his pocket of lose change onto the centre table in the living room. He probably had about ten dollars in loose change. Maureen and one of my other sisters had picked up some of the money and placed it into their pockets. Thinking that it will be Ok to do the same, I took about two dollars worth in change. That was a bad move to make. He asked about the remainder of his change. I responded that I took it. He said something about working and not having a change to buy something to drink. He grabbed me by my throat and suggested I put it all back. I reached into my pocket and placed the money on the table quickly so that I didn't blackout. He removed his hand from my throat, but left me with a serious slap to remind me not to do that again. At that point, I knew for sure that I was not loved. I didn't know why and I didn't care to know anymore. My thought was making sure that I stayed out of his way and not to do anything to upset him.

Frank had a motorcycle and a scooter. I wanted to learn how to ride in the worse way. Being able to ride to me seemed as it was the coolest thing ever. I believed that I wanted to ride for a few reasons. I believed that it would give me an opportunity to be free, and to release all my feelings and thoughts while riding. Riding not only made you cool, it portrayed an image of being tough and cool at the same time. Girls always loved a man on a bike, so this would give me an opportunity to meet some nice girls along the way. Finally at some point you get to the point in your life when you're not afraid anymore. So by riding you knew that at any time your life could be taken from you, or you could take your own when tired. Frank taught me to ride, and within three days I was riding as if I'd been riding for years. I had a gift for vehicles and I knew it. My biggest dream was to become the best racing car driver ever. I loved speed and anything that had risk; I felt that I had to be involved.

I think I developed a carefree attitude by being tortured and dismissed all the time. I approached my mother and spoke to her about my desire to someday ride a motorcycle. She didn't know that I had already been riding and riding on a regular basis. I asked if she could speak to dad about assisting me with some money to buy my first bike. I explained that I had been saving my money from the part-time jobs that I had. She wasn't very keen on the idea, but she agreed to speak to him for me. My sixteenth birthday was in two weeks, so I wanted to have my test done, so I could have my bike for my birthday.

Surprisingly, his response was favorable to me. My mother made him feel guilty to a point with regard to the way he had been treating me. I didn't care how he felt, I just wanted the bike. I made an appointment to be tested on my birthday and was fortunate enough to pass. That afternoon I flew home and told my mother of my success in passing the motorcycle test. I asked if she could call my dad at the office and remind him that he promised to take me on my birthday to purchase a motorbike. She called as I suggested. He had forgotten and didn't even know it was my birthday. Again I didn't care because I didn't expect anything good or bad from him anymore. Maybe I shouldn't say that, because I often thought of the worse only. I am grateful to my mother for her true love and assistance in persuading him to buy me such a gift. He came home extra early that day, so that we'd have sufficient time to get everything done. He had a friend in the motor vehicle business, so he recommended us to a store that he knew of. I couldn't wait to get there. The car drive there was very quiet. I didn't say a word more than thank you and that was all I said the entire time. Once there I made my way into the show room and within seconds I saw the bike that I would like to have. It was a burgundy Honda 750 cc. It came with a nice screen and a little area on the dash for a water bottle.

I couldn't wait to sit on her. She knew who her master was, and wanted her to serve me well. I spoke to her in the show room while they worked on a fair price for the bike. I told her that I'd be good to her and in return, I expected the same from her. She agreed and we had an instant connection with her. The deal was done and they had just enough time to prepare the bike to be ridden home that evening. This was going to be the first time that I actually rode on the main roads for any lengthy distance. The ride at first was scary but fun. I felt as if I could do anything and not be injured. I rode all the way from Mississauga while my father stayed behind me for the first twenty or so minutes. Once he believed that I was alright, he left me on my own. I didn't go right home that evening. I had to pay a visit to all my friends to show them my new toy. All my friends were surprised and happy for me. I asked that they didn't ever mention the words "be careful" to me when I was riding. Franks' parents bought him a motorcycle shortly after I got my bike. Now we were like the riding Ban Di Dos. We rode everywhere together. He took me places that I'd never been to or have ever seen. The countryside was beautiful and smelled wonderful. This was what I needed all along during the times that I got myself into trouble; I would never have been beaten up because I would never have been in the house.

I took my friend Susan for a ride on the back of my bike and I felt that she never wanted to come off. She held onto me so tight that although at times, I had some problems breathing, but I didn't want her to let go. One day out of the blue my father had mentioned that he was thinking of buying himself a bike also. So he invited the same people we bought from, to have lunch with him. My mother thought that he was going out of his mind, or was just jealous of how happy I'd been.

The owner of the store did arrive as he said, and they sat and spoke about any and everything. The couple indicated that they wouldn't be staying as long as promised due to a situation that had risen. My father decided that he'd get them something quick to eat, so he asked what they would like to eat. They requested a hamburger if it wasn't too much of a problem. I asked if it would be alright if I took his car to the store to get the burgers. He agreed and gave me some money to buy some burgers and drinks. Frank accompanied me to the Harvey's hamburger restaurant. We bought sufficient burgers and drinks, so just in case they wanted seconds. We were so caught up talking about where we're going to go next, when we did go riding again. I placed some of the burgers on the roof of the car while getting into the car and drove off. Suddenly, I felt as if something was wrong and searched between us and observed that most of the burgers weren't in the car with us.

I panicked for a short second and then spun the car around. We went back to the same spot where we took off from. The burgers weren't at the Harvey's restaurant as we initially thought. We followed our trail home and saw the burgers on the road that was damaged by the cars. Panic came over my mind. Frank could see that I was in a fearful state. We arrived home without the burgers but with the drinks. I explained to my dad what had happened and the guest said that it was ok.

The look from my father's eye told me that if the people weren't there at that moment, he might have killed me. He gave me some more money to go back and to the restaurant to buy the burgers. This time Frank and I were very careful with the burgers. Frank was wondering if I was going to be alright. He sensed the fear in me and asked if I was concerned for my safety tonight. I told him not to worry, that it's over. The burgers were delivered nice and hot, and my father had a smile on his face when I arrived with the burgers.

As I walked away, I remembered that I had owed him some change, so I returned it to him. He had a look that represented "you're so lucky" on his face. I wasn't about to forget after what had happened that last episode. Frank spoke to me for a short while and then left to spend some time with his family. I was left with that unpleasant thought of whether I was still in trouble or not. I decided that I'd pay no attention to it and just carry on as usual. The people were preparing to leave, so I made my way over and said my good byes to them. To this day, I still don't know the real reason for them being at our home; however, I thought it would be in my best interest if I didn't ask any questions.

I made my way into the basement to tend to a project that I was working on. While I was sitting in the open area of the basement my father confronted me. I had a suspicious feeling that he wasn't completely over with me. The smile that he appeared to have on his face was only to make himself appear to be an understanding person for the guest. I gave him a once over quickly and observed that he wasn't wearing a belt. I found that to be uncharacteristic of him. He stood approximately two arm lengths away from me. He spoke with anger and said that he felt that I embarrassed him. Without any notice, he reached into the rear of his back and pulled out his favorite belt. I asked for some mercy and expressed my sorrow but that wasn't sufficient. He had me cornered and he knew it. He swung the belt quickly and violently as I tried my best to cover my face and head. Every time he swung the belt, I could hear the belt cutting the air as it landed on my body. My mother ran down the stairs to my aid to prevent him from going any further. She had no idea that he planned on disciplining me. I used the word discipline with great care, because his way of disciplining is what one would call mental and physical abuse. I had nowhere to run because I was cornered between the furnace and the hot water tank on me. I felt like a cat being thrown into fast moving water and hoped only to be rescued. My father and my mother went at it for at least an hour. She had enough of his contempt for me and couldn't understand the reason for it. I knew that one day I'd grow to a young man and he wouldn't be able to abuse me like that anymore. Everytime he touched me or even spoke to me, I felt like a woman that had just been raped by a family member. I did my best to avoid being in his view or having any verbal conversation. There were many times I felt myself growling like a cat whenever I thought about the things he's done to me. I developed an image in my mind as being a lion and devouring anyone that tried to harm me. I'm sure that he'd heard me growling or screaming at times like a big cat. Many times I wanted to pounce onto him and bite him all over his face and body. I fantasized eating his face off and watching him bleed to death. I knew that I was too small and besides, my mother always preached that I should never strike a parent. She used to say that I should follow the commandment of God.

One Sunday my father decided that he wanted to give his car a complete clean up. That meant compound waxing, then regular waxing. This job would take the most part of the day. I think he knew that I had planned to go on a long bike ride with my friends. My friends and I had planned this riding adventure ride for a while. We went out to the front of the street and started to clean the car. He washed the car with regular soap first then he'd wash it all over with turtle wax soap. My friends had no idea that I wouldn't be able to make the trip. He had me vacuuming the inside of the car and the trunk of the car. I didn't think the vacuum had picked up any dirt from inside the car and probably only a few pieces of junk in the trunk. My friends were beginning to wonder whether I'd be coming with them or not. They wanted to ask my father if he would allow me to come with them. I asked them not to ask him because it could only make it worse for me. My mother did ask on my behalf to allow me to go off with my friends. His answer was a definitive no. He said that he had a lot of work to do on the car and he required my help. The day was bright and sunny and my heart was breaking in two. I couldn't allow him to see me crying so I sucked it up. The guys had no choice but to go ahead because they couldn't see that I had no chance in leaving. We finally completed cleaning the car late in the evening hour. After spending so many hours on the car, I had absolutely no desire or energy to spend any time with my friends. I went in and had something to eat and went directly to bed. Sure I was upset but I had no control over my life.

The next morning I rose to a wonderful breakfast by my mother. She did that because she knew that I had had very little to eat on Sunday, so she wanted to wipe away that terrible day from my mind. The remainder of the summer went along quite smoothly, and we were on the verge of preparing for back to school and winter. All the kids on our street enjoyed playing soccer in the snow with a tennis ball at the rear of my house. There was a laneway at the rear, so we all enjoyed playing at the back because there was very little traffic. We decided to have a friendly game of soccer with just a few of us. Approximately six houses from where I lived, another kid that we rarely played with decided to join us. He was a bit older than us and only came out when some of the older guys were out playing hockey. On this day, he decided to hang out with us. I didn't know him very well or ever had any interaction with him before. We started the game of, with three people on each team. No one played in net; we only protected the net when necessary. Frank, Johnny and I were on the same team. We were kicking Enyo's team pretty badly. I had a feeling, based on his attitude, that he wasn't having fun because he was losing. For some reason, he wasn't impressed with the way I was playing. He felt that since I was black, I shouldn't be able to play soccer hockey as well as some of the white kids. He began to torment me by calling me names. He said that hockey wasn't a game for "coons." Frank and Johnny told me that I should ignore him. They asked Enyo to stop with his remarks and to just play the game. We played light checking, but not from behind. I attempted to kick at the ball but slipped and fell on my butt. Enyo purposely fell on me and started to shove snow in my face and down my clothes. He placed one of his hands close to his mouth and then spat in it. He took that same hand and slapped me with it in my face.

After slapping me with his hand, he then looked at me while sitting on top of me and said "How do you like that nigger? Now do you see who runs things on my street?" This infuriated me tremendously. My mind went black as I threw him off me. I started to growl and scratch as I punched and tried my best to bite his face off. He was trying desperately to get up, but I continued to punch and bite him on his arm and chest area. Although he was wearing a winter jacket I knew he was feeling every bite I laid upon him. I stopped as a result of the guys pulling me off him; moreover, he looked at me with fear in his eyes and asked if I was crazy. He said to me that I sounded like a cat or something. He stood at a good distance from me, after I allowed him to stand. He looked directly at me and said to me that I was f--ing nuts. After that episode, he never called me a name or attempted to touch me again. After a period of time, he actually started to be nice to me. He even invited me to his home. While at his home, he apologized to me for his behavior. I said nothing but shook his hand and smiled as I made my way out his door. I felt for the first time that I defended myself from being abused.

One evening after dinner I sat and had a serious discussion with my mother. I informed her of my intention to put an end to her misery. She was confused and couldn't understand what I was really talking about. I told her that I had seen all I could have seen, and that it came a time when a man had to do what he had to do: "Well, maybe a boy who had to do what he thought was the right thing to do."

I explained that I had two of my friends awaiting my call so that we could ambush Alice and put an end to her blaspheme. The person that I speak of is my father's mistress who formed a romantic relationship with. The plan was as sealed as a volt within the hands of a security laser. We would wait for Alice to exit her car that was always parked in the rear of the lane way. As she exited the car we would strike her on the head with our bats. After she fell to the floor, we would beat her all over her body, especially in her face and her groin area, causing her a great amount of discomfort. By beating her in these areas it would cause her to dislike her appearance and prevent my father from having any type of intimacy. My friends and I would be dressed in balaclavas and protected with gloves and dark boots. There would be no talking as we delivered a beating that was well overdue to her. Once we felt that she had learned her lesson, we would drag her back into her car and leave her there so that she would be found the following morning.

My mother would have no part of this. She reminded me of the Bible again. She said that punishment is left for God and at times we decided to take the burden on, then God would have no part of it. She reminded me of Joseph and his brothers, of how they tried to harm him and at the end, he was the one they turned to. The plan was perfect, but my mother saw too many holes with the idea. She felt that she wouldn't be comfortable with the idea of me beating someone to within seconds of her life. She was also uncomfortable with my ingenious idea, because if one of my friends were to yell my name out by mistake, my life would be over. Her main reason for not fulfilling my quest was due to her belief. As a Christian, she believed in leaving the burden to Jesus. She wasn't about to have blood on her hands, and to see me live my life in torment. She told me that, "God washes His hand from anyone that believes that they can do anything better than him," so she would prefer if we left her alone and continued to pray and let her be. After listening to her and watching the nervousness on her face, I agreed to her wishes. I believe that somewhere along the route, a mother always knows best.

That evening after speaking with my mother, I called the guys and told them that the river will not run wild anymore, so we can just meet and hang out. We met at the back of my garage in the lane way and sat and talked about what my mother said and agreed that what she said to me was right. Seeing that we had nothing to do, Frank came up with a fantastic idea. We were all short of money, and neither of us had a job, so we decided to make a few bucks in a clever way.

Saturday nights the parking lot behind my house was usually packed because of the Italian venue. On this particular evening, the hall was being used to cater a wedding. There were probably a hundred and fifty cars or more in the lot. The plan was to look for some of the expensive cars, and to let the air out of one of the tires, and then sit at the front of the hall on our bikes and wait for the guest to come out.

We knew that some of the drivers would change their own tires, but we also knew that the older ones wouldn't. After an hour or so, the guest was beginning to leave the hall to make their way home. We would ride through the lot as if we had no idea to what was occurring. Finally, one of the owners of the car summoned us as we rode pass them. The plan had worked and we were about to make a fortune that evening. We charged twenty dollars for each tire we changed and thirty if we had to take the spare across the street to be filled with air.

The look on our faces was priceless as we worked diligently through the evening. At the end of the night we had made close to six hundred dollars between us. "Yeah baby for an ingenious idea." I guess that's where the saying came from. "When one door closes another door opens even wider." If we had gone ahead with our vindictive plan, God wasn't going to bless us with an opportunity like this. Personally, I don't think God had anything to do with what we were doing. We only said that to take away our sins and guilt for what we were doing. I guess if our parents had known what we were up to, they probably would have skinned us alive. I didn't think God had played a part in our scheme, but someone had the knowledge to bless my mother to prevent us from going down a really bad road.

The following day when we got together after laughing our heads off, Johnny asked if anyone was regretful for not stripping Alice apart. At the time when asked that question I said no, because I was probably in another place in my mind because of the small jackpot we had earned.

Looking back through the years, I can honestly say that I wished I had a brief moment with her, so that I could do her my way. Time has gone, and my family has passed, and all I have is my memories, be it bad or good. So I've got to let it go and move on, but I do wish that one day God will see to it that she felt far worse pain than whatever we felt as a collective family. God bless her!

My parents had decided that they were going to look for a new home, and we'd probably be moving within the next four to five months. I told my friends about the move that my parents were planning on doing. None of them were happy with it, but we all decided that we were still going to remain friends. One night we all gathered at Susan's' home to play some games and had some eats. I always liked her from the minute I saw her. They decided to play spin the bottle. I had no idea what the game was or how it was played. We all sat around on the floor and dimmed the lights down low. Music was playing loud, but not loud enough to prevent us from hearing each other. The bottle spun and once it stopped on the person, the person that spun it got to tell that person what they would like to see done. It landed on everyone except for me for quite some time. Finally, the bottle was spun and it landed on me. Their request was simple enough; they wanted me to walk on over and kiss Susan on her lips. My heart stopped for a second or maybe more as I began to sweat thinking about what or may not happen. I got up after breathing deeply, and I walked on over, slowly to Susan, bent over and kissed her gently on her lips. After I kissed her and I was about to unlock my lips from her lips, she continued to kiss me. Everyone was in awe as we locked our lips for almost a minute. It felt great and I couldn't wait to kiss her again. The entire time that I sat there I was praying for someone to dare me to kiss her again. At the end of the night, as we all walked out to make our way home, she stopped and gave me a hug and one more passionate kiss. In return, I continued to kiss her until she decided that she had enough of my sweet lips.

We eventually moved from our old address on Bloom Avenue and made our way over to a street called "Corby Av." We moved approximately fifteen minutes from where we originally lived. The area seemed to be very quiet and had few kids living on the street. For me to have any excitement, I would have to ride my bike or motorcycle back to my old address. News came rather quickly that Frank and his family had sold their home and was planning on moving to the west end of the city. They eventually moved to Kipling and Eglinton Avenue in a very quiet neighborhood. The traveling distance by car was approximately half an hour by the 40I highway. With Frank gone and some of my other friends being involved with new people, it took away the pleasure I had in traveling to my old neighborhood.

I spent a lot of my time at home keeping myself busy by building little things that interested me. I started riding by myself for pure the interest of learning the city. I rode north towards the cottages and sometimes towards the border of

Buffalo. I eventually made friends along the way with other motorcycle riders. It was fun to ride as a group when traveling. I learned a lot of interesting things from some of the people that I came in contact with. One of the most interesting things was that, every Friday and Sunday afternoon, they held a motorcycle and car race north of the airport towards the cottages. They called it "dead man's valley."

I became very intrigued about this event and couldn't wait to see how it worked. I made it my duty to be at the next event. The first time I went, I watched as many cars and bikes appeared to race. Some cars looked and sound like they had two engines under their hood. Others just looked pretty. Some of the biker's seemed experienced and hungry to take your money at any cost. While the others were there on for the fun of it and hopefully to win.

Rules were applied and under no circumstance were they to be broken. I thought that I might participate for the first time with my dad's car for my first event. Some of the guys had been racing bikes and all the equipment to go with it, and my bike was a cross between a sport and cruise, so I felt more comfortable racing a car. Two hundred dollars entry would get me six hundred dollars with a hundred going to the bookie. There were usually ten to fifteen guys at any given event, and everyone thought that they were capable of outperforming the other one. I knew in my heart that I had a car that I could handle, and it also had a powerful engine. In my opinion, it all boiled down to who had the most guts and better driving skill.

My first race was up against a Monte Carlo that sounded as if it was a tractor-trailer. Intimidation had no effect on me at all. I knew that I couldn't lose because I would have to answer to my mother, to why I had no money. The race was about to begin and I could feel the blood pumping through my veins. We were off. The first man to get to the bridge and back wins. The bridge was about two miles away, and the road at times became one lane in certain areas, but we had to be prepared for the police. We were neck and neck for the first half a mile or so, until the lane was about to become one. This is where your mind and guts had to become one. The entire time I had the shoulder lane, so he obviously felt that I would have to slow down as the road came to a merge. This was not going to be the case on this evening. I stepped on the pedal, and the pedal was about to touch the metal as I prepared my mind for anything.

As we approached the two to three hundred markers I felt that he was about to back off. As predicted, he did, just as I thought as I flew past him. He gave me that loud honk, but that meant nothing to me. We got to the bridge with me being in front by at least two car lengths. We spun the car around quickly and began our journey back with no holds barred. Everything I learned in driving was about to be used. I had to get to him first so that he wouldn't try the same thing on me. He had no chance of catching me because I had the car up to speed, what most people would call unsafe. I could remember touching speeds of hundred and thirty miles an hour and feeling that if necessary, I still had a little left before the pedal would touch the metal. I had to win and to win it meant taking chances. I was the first one back by at least five or six car lengths. That didn't matter to me, what mattered was that I won and I was the man to beat from here on.

That evening I went home with an extra five hundred

in my pocket and with the respect of the other drivers. They respected me because I came in as the underdog that no one knew about. I did what I had to do without any attitude, and left to return the following week. That night when I arrived, I called my mother to my room where I gave her two hundred dollars without too many questions being asked. She asked questions and I told the truth. Her concern was, what's going to happen if my father found out what I was doing, and what would happen if I smashed his car. I told her not to worry that if for whatever the reason I was going to lose a race, I'd abandon the race to avoid causing an accident. The next time l went out, I out drove and out raced almost everyone until I had an incident where one of the drivers felt that he was going to win regardless of whatever happened.

I had to abandon the race as promised and give it to him because of his stupidity; so on that night he did beat me because of his reckless and god fearing ways. That night it cost me six hundred dollars because of my hesitation towards his stupidity. He had me in the curb lane and at the edge of the lane that was filled with gravel and sand. Because we were nearing the merger I knew that I had to get to it first. This time the driver must have found out about my style of driving, and that I wasn't going to stop and just go for it and call his bluff. What he did was so unfair. He waited until we were almost at the fork, and began to merge his car as close as possible to mine, so that I would ride the gravel. By driving on the gravel it took away the safe handling of the car, creating the potential of me losing control of my car at that high speed. To avoid any catastrophe, I slowed to a slow speed without touching my brakes so that I could re-enter safely back onto the surface. For this reason, I lost my first and only race competing in a car. I drove back to the finish line at an average speed extremely upset at myself, but I knew what I had to do from that day on. This gave me the time to think about my rematch with him. I assured him that evening that the next time we met, he'd never see my bumper and he'd need a bottle of Windex to wipe the mosquitoes off his windshield. I realized that he wanted to win at any cost even if it meant hurting me. So I took my father's car to a garage where he normally gets his car serviced. The owner of the store was a friend of my dad, and new me well and liked my enthusiasm. I asked him to do whatever he could to make the car faster without making it louder. He asked "Why?" and I said, "don't ask."

I paid him the money, which thankfully wasn't a lot. He did it as a favor and as an experiment. That Friday night I was back and prepared to win my money back and also to teach the little nut a lesson. I never said much at the camps, I only drove.

This time when we flipped the coin, it fell in favor of me. We sat in our cars and waited for the towel to be dropped. We were off and my tire spun very little but had a lot of pull from the engine. The car felt like a rocket, and it was handling like a car on the track. I slowed down for a brief second so that I could make eye contact with him for a second.
We were about nine hundred yards away from the merger, so I wanted to show him that I didn't need to be like him to cause him to drive on the shoulder. As I approached the merger, I glanced at him and waved good bye as I floored on the pedal pushing it all the way to the metal. The race was over, in my opinion, before we even had started. I arrived at the finish line many seconds ahead of him to the noise of

many happy drivers. I guess the bet was on me to take him. I took my winnings, which were what I had lost the previous week and an extra four hundred for this week. He approached me as I was about to enter my car and said to me "you're good; you're real good and you've got skill, where did you learn to drive like that." He asked. I said, "I thought myself, but most of it lay in God's hands, with a little of guts."

The school year was about to begin as I was about to enter grade ten. My mother and my father were having difficulty getting along. I felt as if I should be around for support for my mother. I knew that my mother was afraid of my dad, but kept her feelings to herself.

I was fortunate enough to have a few friends that I knew to be in my classroom with me. At the rear of the class sat a heavyset boy. At times he would steer at me, as if I had done him something. Every time the class made fun of me, he would laugh and laugh loudly so that everyone could hear him. This really annoyed me, so I walked over to his desk when the teacher had left the room. I pointed my finger in his face and warned him to be careful. As I walked away, I poked him on his chest with my finger and knocked his books off the desk. When the teacher returned, I asked permission to visit the washroom. While in the washroom I heard the door open and shut violently. I turned around, and to my amazement there he stood, Fuzzy, the boy from my class. I knew something was about to happen when he looked at me and said, "Take your time," as I tried to finish urinating. For some reason, that was the longest I ever took at a stall to urinate. I felt as if I should stay there for the entire time. I stepped away from the stall and asked him if he had a problem. He looked at me and said, "No one embarrasses him like I did." Suddenly, without notice he kicked me and knocked me to the ground. He started to pound on me without any care at all. Fuzzy picked up the garbage pan in the wash room and smashed it over my back. He dumped all of the garbage onto me and walked away.

As he approached the door, he stopped and turned and said to me, "I hope you learned a valuable lesson you f—king punk."

As I lay on the floor with garbage all over me, I could only look at him and say to myself, "Next time buddy, next time." I felt rather embarrassed about what had happened and didn't' want anyone to know what had happened. I went home that evening and asked my mother if she could have my father enroll me into a Kung Fu school. She asked why I wanted to enter the school so badly. I told her what had happened at school, and I didn't want that to ever happen to me ever again. My mother convinced my father to find me a good martial art school. He wanted to know why he should enter me into a school. He suggested that one day I would try to use it on him. She told him that we didn't raise our children to raise their hands upon us. He said to my mother that the day I thought of it, which would be the last day I would ever raise my hand again.

He took me to an instructor whom he knew about at Oakwood and St. Clair Av. area. He taught me from scratch everything that I should know at the level that I was starting at. Month after Month I attended, not missing any classes. Before you knew it, I had moved up in rank and was continuing to move on up.

The school that I attended was one of the best schools at that time in basketball. I played volleyball also while participating in basketball at least twice a week. One week before our semi-finals in basketball, I attended our regular practice with my volleyball team. During the practice, I dove for the ball and I injured my wrist and a couple of my fingers, causing my fingers to swell. The first aid person around helped me and suggested that I see my family doctor the following day; the doctor confirmed that the sprain in my wrist and my two fingers caused the swelling.

The basketball game was to be held on that Friday afternoon in our gymnasium at about 2:30pm. Due to the fact that we had won more games than most of the teams, we had home court advantage which gave us a better start. This was a game that I really wanted to play, but it was not meant to be. I sat on the bench and cheered my team, as we played with all the energy and emotion. At half time, I decided to venture out into the hall way to use the washroom. As I exited the door from the gym I couldn't believe what I was seeing. I stood about ten to fifteen feet away and watched as one of the students from our school was yelling and pointing his finger into his girlfriend's face. At one point when she tried to push him away from her, he grabbed her by her chest collar and slapped her in her face. At this point, I had to interject. I walked towards them and asked Mugsy to step away from her, or he'd have to deal directly with me. Mugsy looked at me and asked me to mind my own business. I asked Starlit to step away before things got out of hand. Realizing that I wasn't about to back down, he threatened me by telling me that I'd got something coming. I told him that because of his boyish ways, I was going to take Starlit away from him.

Two weeks later after school ended, I offered Starlit a ride home. She seemed to be intrigued with my offer and happily said "yes." Once at her home, she offered me an invitation to come in and sit for a while. Well, you can just imagine what I was thinking at that moment. I humbly accepted and made my way in. After a minute or so of talking, we gradually approached each other. I guess there would be no need to disclose what happened from there. What I can tell you is that she was amazing and out of this world. Suddenly there was a knock at the door while she was expressing her emotions. The voice sounded a lot like her ex-boyfriend. I said "ex" because he didn't know that his girlfriend had just left him. He began to bang on the door while calling my name out as if he knew that I was in there. Starlit approached the door and without opening it, asked him to leave. The fury was in him and I knew that he wasn't going to let this go.

Weeks would go by until one weekend a performer was playing at the waterfront. My friend and I decided that we would attend this function to see this amazing band. Once at the event, we were spotted by Mugsy and his friends. Right away I knew that we had a problem on our hands. Mugsy and his friends were approaching us quickly, and we didn't have our other friends to back us up. The only thing we could have done was to run and to run fast. It was a big crowd so it made it more difficult to try to leave. Unfortunately for us we ran the wrong way and were trapped between a fence and his gang. Now we had no choice but to stand and fight. Our backs were to the wall like a cat being trapped by a dog.

Fortunately, for me, whenever I traveled away from my neighborhood, and I felt that the possibility for any potential violence was high, I would make sure to carry my nun-chucks with me. I usually placed it in the back of my waist, which was covered by my shirt. We were at a disadvantage because we were wearing sandals while the other guys were in their runners. I began to swing violently at them striking a person on their shoulder or leg. Eventually, we were cornered and a beat down was delivered. We took a few harsh blows but managed to force our way out and ran to my vehicle.

After we left the waterfront with our lips bleeding and a few bruises, we made it known that if we run into anyone of his friends or Mugsy himself, we would make sure to remind him of this day. One day after school while watching the track and field athletes training, we happened to see one of Mugsy associates. We walked over to him and introduced ourselves and told him that we were about to send a message to Mugsy. I can remember the young man trying to put up a fight but we over powered him and really gave him the type of beating that would send him to the hospital or remind him to never mess with us again. Fortunately, for him, when we were finished with the beating, he only had a few cuts, a busted rib and a broken finger.

We knew that the school was going to talk about it the next day and that Mugsy was going to try and retaliate. Before Mugsy could have an opportunity to plan his next move, we added two more players to our team and approached Mugsy the following day after coming from a track and field tournament. The majority of our school had attended this event at another school in the down town area. We knew that we all had to travel across the subway and our stopping point for most of us would be the same. We saw Mugsy with another fellow that was known by the police for being in the prostitution business. After the train stopped, we made our way up to the ramp quickly so that we could have the upper hand on them so that they wouldn't have a chance to plan an escape route. Mugsy came up the stairs first and shortly after his friend followed, we were all in an area that was vacant and no one was passing through until the next train arrived. Mugsy had the look on his face, as if he had seen death. I looked at him and reminded him that I never forgot, and that I would only give up if I was dead. Without granting him an opportunity to talk, we began to beat on him and his friend. The beating was severe and swift. During the beating, I can hear Mugsy begging for mercy, but on this day I was all out of mercy. I reminded him of what he had done to Starlit in the hallway of the school. After begging like a little child that's being assaulted by an insane adult, he agreed that he would never bother us again, and that he would leave Starlit alone from that day on. Mugsy was a mess and his friend knew that if he was to open his dirty mouth ever, we were going to give him the same treatment. Mugsy's friend took a beating that would send a message to his friends, and hopefully he'd think twice about retaliating. We walked away from the subway with both men moaning and their clothes all torn up. I would think they must have laid there for some time before leaving. After that incident, we didn't see either one of them for at least two weeks and once recovered, we never had any trouble again. Justice was served and we were now known as the bad boys, where ever we went.

After the school year had come to an end, we still continued to keep our gang together but as time went on, I found myself moving more and more towards understanding the Word of God and the purpose for me being on the earth. I realized that not everything is solved by violence and that if I prayed about it sincerely, many great things could happen. Starlit and I eventually parted and moved on to new things in our lives.

One night after we had all turned in for bed, I overheard my mother and father arguing. The argument sounded like it was very intense and possibly could lead to violence. I heard my mother screaming and asking my father to let her go. I ran up the stairs to see what was happening and observed my mother on the floor. She had some of her hair in her hand, and her lip was swollen.

She picked herself up of the ground with great difficulty, and made her way into the living room to lie down. My father had soaked her side of the bed with cold water so that she couldn't sleep. He also pulled her by her hair of the bed, pulling out a handful of hair from her head.

The following morning she didn't look very good and complained of a headache. As I stood in the kitchen with her for a while, and then I confronted my father and warn him to never try that again. I knew that although I was enrolled in martial arts, that presently I was no match for him. He was still too big and much stronger than I was. My mother begged of me not to get involved. As a son, how can I not say something when you see someone abusing your mother? Within a few weeks, they had another fight. It seemed as if my father and mother were getting into confrontations on a regular basis.

One of my functions in the house was to pick my mother up from work every evening. I enjoyed the drive to Sunny Brook Hospital to pick my mother up. It gave me an opportunity to be away from my father. My mom and I would have all sorts of discussions about our future. She definitely wasn't happy but she still loved him. For the life of me, I couldn't understand why she would still feel like that way for him. Sometimes I would park the car in the garage and at other times I would park the car on the street.

On this evening I decided that I'd leave the car on the street. We made our way up to the stairs and opened the front door. What we saw with our eyes was unbelievable to the eye. My father and Alice, the so-called "secretary," were involved in an affair. My mother and I observed Alice with a white towel wrapped around her as she made her way to the washroom. My father was in his boxers with no shirt on. He had a surprised look on his face and had difficulty looking at my mother.
Alice eventually came out of the washroom and stood at the front door. He said nothing to either of us as she made her way out the door. I was not sure if he felt guilty, or if he was upset at himself for being caught. He didn't have the energy to pick his wife up, but he had sufficient energy to have a relation with this degenerate of a person.

My mother sat on the sofa and dropped her head to her knees and just cried and cried. There was nothing that I could say that would make the matter better. She slept on the sofa that night while my father slept in the bed that he had just finished having a relationship with Alice. The following morning my mother was so tired that she had difficulty getting up. My father made himself his breakfast quickly and left. As he walked out the back door he gave me a look that meant be careful.

My mom eventually got up and called her sister Monica and spoke about what had happened. They shared everything together. Aunt Monica was an outlet for my mother, and I was sure the same for my aunt. Slowly but surely, the entire family was turning against my father. On many occasions, my uncles wanted to pay my father a visit, but my mother didn't want any violence, so she always pleaded with them not to get involved.

Again, within a week or so, they had another fight. It seemed as if my mother could do nothing right. He came home late from work and for whatever the reason, he just wasn't in a good mood. I was not sure what my mother had said to annoy him, but it couldn't be that bad to justify him slapping her about. I made my way up to the stairs from my bedroom in a flash. I wanted to make sure this time that he didn't get carried away. She had a bloody mouth, and it seemed as if she had a bruise above her cheekbone. I asked him to stop hitting our mother and to try speaking instead. He turned around and grabbed me by my neck and threw me across the living room like a rag doll. I stood up and looked at him and asked him if he felt good with what he was doing to us. He walked over to me and slapped me a few more times and attempted to throw me down the stairs. I caught my balance and returned back up the stairs. I looked at him this time and said to him, "Dad please remember this, 'a cub stays small for a short time, and then they eventually grow up.'"

He asked me to explain what I was trying to say. At first I said nothing to him, but I changed my mind suddenly and said to him, "Exactly what I said is what I meant" My mother walked on over to me and stood beside me and tried to smile.

He felt angered as she did that and said to her, "You can only protect him for so long." The next day when my father had left the home, she called her sister again and explained to her while crying as she told her what had happened. I overheard her telling her sister that she's afraid that one day he might kill her out of anger. From what I gathered, both my aunt and my mother were crying on the phone together. My mother wanted to do something, but she didn't know what to do.

Saturday night was upon us and my father and my cousin were up to their usual. He was dressed to the hill and my cousin always had a way with mother. They got along well although my mother wasn't condoning his ways. He walked out the door without saying a word and didn't return until late that morning. My dad would take these unexpected business trips that seemed a bit ridiculous. He would tell my mother that he was going on a convention for contractors to advertise his business in a larger way. We weren't stupid and thought twice about his lame excuse. My mother worked just as hard and contributed to the home probably even more than him. The time that he spent away from the house was like a vacation on a whole to us. Every time he returned from his trip, we observed that he always complained of a headache. I believe that it was his way of trying not to be involved in any conversation in the home. My mother knew that eventually she would have to leave, because that was no life to live, as a person. The kitchen had some patches in the ceiling that needed repairing, he asked me to assist him with the repairs. My mother was busy preparing our evening meal, so the kitchen was busy. I was not sure how the events unfolded, but he became annoyed at me for something I had done wrong.

He immediately came down from the ladder and started to yell at me. I guess being frustrated, I turned my back and started to walk away. That was definitely the wrong thing to do at the time. He grabbed me by my shoulder and spun me around and slapped me in my face. I fell against the wall and received another slap for being rude. My mother couldn't help but to ask why was he doing this. He turned around and slapped her also. This slap sliced her lip open, causing a huge gash in her mouth. She seemed so defenseless that I wanted to stick the knife into his stomach to put a stop to all the torment. He decided that he'd work on the kitchen another evening and went out for some time. We had no idea when he left the house where he went. I had to find out exactly where he went to unwind, so I asked my cousin Lennox but he was evasive in his answer.

One afternoon my mother received a phone call from my father indicating that he would like me to come and pick him up. This was odd seeing that he had his own vehicle, and I had no idea of his whereabouts. I took the phone and Alice explained to me exactly where they were situated. All this time I couldn't imagine that they were so close to us. I arrived at the home, which was one of his worker's homes. He had rented the top of the apartment for Alice to live. This was extremely convenient for him; seeing that we only lived about ten minutes from his worker's home. Alice explained that he had a massive headache and that he had forgotten how to get home. She asked that I drive extremely slow so that the car didn't go over too many bumps. Once in the house he acted as if his head was about to explode. He moaned and groaned for many hours until the pain passed.

My mother took him to the doctor to be checked out, and they explained to them that my father suffered from a certain type of headache that's much worse than a migraine. They did agree that it was possible for his memory to temporary leave him. I couldn't believe how concerned my mother still was over him. She was truly a child of God. Regardless of all the ill treatment she suffered from my father's hands she was still willing to help him. I thought to myself how things have a way of turning against you. As she took care of him, I wondered if he'd ever realize how much my mother loved him. One thing for sure the house was a bit peaceful for a while, and besides, now that he knew that I knew where he spent his time, he might be a bit nicer to me. I didn't have the heart to tell my mother the truth, so I told her he was at Joe's home, the brick layer worker. It seemed to work because she didn't question this, so everything was good, in my opinion.

On my way home, I would make it my duty to drive by the address to see if his car was parked outside. The majority of the time if he wasn't at home, he was at the address. Spring was around the corner so the weather was becoming warmer and the days were much longer. My father told my mother that he and my Cousin Lennox were planning on taking a short trip to Chicago to purchase some clothes. He bought the majority of his clothes either in Chicago or Detroit, so they had planned a trip to the States. The truth was that they were planning a party at cousin Lennox's home. Apparently, it was well advertised by mouth, and a lot of their friends were to attend. The house was well stacked with alcohol and food, and they hired a disc jockey to spin the music. I didn't know that my father was a jealous man.

The party was a success and the entire guest that was invited attended. Lots of eat and drinks, and with the music blasting, everyone was in great spirits. This was what I was told. One of the guests had an interest in Alice (my father's mistress) and was observed to be flirting with her. This was a "no-no" in Lionel's world, especially when you were someone not known to him. The word had spread quickly to my dad, so he approached the gentleman and made him aware that whatever the intention was, that he should try it with someone else. Words were exchanged and my father walked away thinking that all was under control. There's a saying that says "two male rats could never live in the same hole." It's obvious that this man felt whatever vibes Alice was sending, meant that she was interested in him. My father approached Alice and inquired if she felt like being with the gentleman. She had no interest in my dad, and she did not want him talking to her. Armed with what he had just heard, he approached the man again and suggested that he left the party. Words were exchanged, which lead to threats. My father didn't take kindly to his attitude and threw the first punch. From what was told to me, the fight was one to see. My dad was all over him like an alley cat. The gentleman landed a few punches, but not nearly as much as my dad did. The fight ended up in the driveway as a result of my father throwing him out of the front door. While the guy was on the floor all bruised and battered, my dad kicked him with such a force that he broke his foot as a result. Thankfully, for my father the fight had taken place nearing the end of the party. My cousin Lennox assisted in helping him to his feet and placed him in the car. He transported him to the hospital, where a doctor saw him almost immediately.

As a result of the seriousness of the break, he required surgery to repair his foot. They placed four pins into his foot and ankle area to keep his foot together. He spent a few days in the hospital to check for any reaction as a result of the pins in his foot. He was discharged and returned home to be questioned by my mother. He told us a lie that seemed possible of occurring, so at the time we had no choice but to believe him.

For a few days he hung around the home trying to keep himself occupied. These were the days I kept myself out of the house. I knew if I stayed anywhere that's within eye distance of him, the likely hood of me being in trouble for something was grave. After a week, once he was capable of placing a little bit of weight on his leg, he was up and about.

After a couple of months, the cast was off, and he was able to do most of the things by himself. As he continued to go out more and more with his mistress, I decided one evening on the way back from picking my mother up from work, to show her where my dad stays when he's not at home. First I had to decide if my mother would be able to handle whatever I told her. I started off by saying, "Wouldn't it be nice to finally see where dad and his mistress hung out?" She indicated that she asked cousin Lennox the same question, but he avoided the question. I wanted to know, whether it bothered her if I showed her the location on the way home. She said at this point nothing really bothers her anymore when it comes to my dad. I decided that I'd show her because she deserved to know. I looked at her face after I showed her, and although she said nothing bothers her, it was expected for her to be a bit hurt. We both knew exactly where he went when he said that he's going out or on business. My mother decided that it would just be a matter of time before she left.

A few months after, my father decided that he was going on a business trip again. This time we were prepared for his lie and deceit. We found out that he was on a cruise somewhere in the Caribbean. He left the car keys for the Lincoln in my care, so that if necessary I could use it. My mother would apply for extra work at various hospitals, including the Toronto General Hospital at College Street and University Avenue. We had some interesting conversations as always along the way to her work. We arrived a little bit early as she liked to do, so we sat in the car and spoke for a little while. The time was advancing on her, so she decided to leave. Once she was out of the car, she said her usual goodbyes. Hoping that she would refrain from speaking the words that I'd asked her not to say, she still told me to "be careful." I believe that once someone tells me to be careful, it puts a hex on me.

I looked at her and said, "How many times have I asked you not to say that word"? She gave me that big smile, waved at me and walked away.

My dad rarely drove his car, but only took it out on nice days, or if he was going somewhere special. I loved driving the car whenever I got the opportunity to do so. Approximately, fifteen minutes away from the hospital I decided to take an alternate route. This area had beautiful homes and gorgeous cars in their driveways. My attention was on the road, but from time to time I would look at some of the homes and cars.

Suddenly, a car swerved into my path causing me to step on my gas to avoid hitting him. At the time there was a fairly old car in front of me. The other driver wasn't paying attention to the road, so as a result of his stupidity, I had to implement my defensive driving to avoid a major accident. The distance between the older car and me was quite short. I tried my best to stop without colliding into the rear of the car, but I was unsuccessful in doing so. The front right bumper came into contact with the left rear bumper area. The damage to both of the cars weren't as serious as I thought it would be. Unfortunately, the car that I struck was an old Antique ford wagon. The car had a broken taillight and damage to the paint. First I apologized and then asked the gentleman to give me an opportunity to fix his vehicle without the police being involved.

He agreed that he would have a few estimates done and will contact me with the appraisal amount. He did contact me and I agreed for him to have it fixed as soon as possible. I had the headache of trying to have my father's car repaired before he returned from his trip. I took the car directly to the dealer where he had the car serviced on a regular basis. I pleaded with the tradesmen to have the car fixed before the weekend. They told me that they'd try their best to assist me. The gentleman with the antique car informed me that his car will be ready on Saturday, and he will be coming by on the Sunday. I suggested that he called me first, and I'd meet with him at the corner of my street.

My dad's car was ready and looked exactly the way it did before the accident. My father returned from his trip late in the evening on Saturday. He came home and unpacked and went straight to bed. The following morning after having his breakfast, he went to the garage to check on his precious car. I couldn't tell you how afraid I was as he inspected his car. Both my mother and I had pins in our body because of being so nervous. He gave the car a good go over and returned. Nothing was said, so we took his silence to mean everything was alright. Now the gentleman called and said that he's just around the corner from our home. I instructed him that I'd be right out, so I'd meet him at the top of the street. For whatever the reason, he decided against meeting with me at the top of the street.

Just as I was preparing to leave, he was making his way up to the stairs. He rang the doorbell and created a panic in our household. I answered the door and kept him away from the door and window. I gave him the money quickly and thanked him and hurried him on his way. Once he was gone, I took a deep breath and returned into the house. My father enquired to why the gentleman was coming here on a Sunday. I told him that it was the store manager from my part time job and explained that I had closed the work by mistake and couldn't re-open it, so I took the remainder of the money home with me. Nothing else was said, so I was grateful that everything worked out.

Chapter 4

I enjoyed dancing very much, so I decided to join a dance group that my friends started at school. Every evening we would get together for a half an hour and practice. We heard about a contest that would be taking place in the city and would end up drawing a lot of people. The organizer had printed in the paper that it would be a two day contest, that only the top three performing groups would receive a prize.

After my father and my uncles were involved in an argument that almost came to violence, I decided to visit my friends who were at a roller rink. This rink was almost like a club, and everyone came out to party and have some fun. I left my home that evening without my blades and went to the club. The doormen at the club knew me rather well so I had no problems entering the venue and made my way in and had a seat in the corner of the club near the bar. After sitting for a while as I tried to blow off some of my steam, I observed a young lady that I just had to speak with. Yeah, she was fine and seemed to know how to use her assets to promote herself. I walked on over and started up a conversation about skating. She noticed that I wasn't wearing my skates and wondered why. I explained that I just wanted to hear the music and to relax. I offered to buy her a drink and to possibly have a moment at a table with her to get to know her better.

On my way back from the bar, I noticed another chump trying his best to get her attention. She ignored him and this bothered him. I approached her with my drink as she accepted it. This individual turned to me and asked me to get lost. At first I thought he was talking to a dog or a cat, by the way he spoke. I told him that I wasn't going anywhere and that the young lady and I were involved in a conversation. He then took a hold of her hand and through the glass of wine onto me. This really angered me, so I placed my glass of beer onto the table and immediately tackled him to the ground. I began punching him on his face and body. At one point, I could remember kicking him in his ribs a few times. After being pulled away from him, I broke lose and returned and jumped on him before he could rise. I attempted to bite him on his chest. For some reason, as I tried to bite him and too leave him with an empty spot on his chest, I believed that I must have bitten down on his cigarettes. This was to be his lucky day. The bouncers escorted me to the door. The lady whom I was attempting to have the conversation with, also came outside while the bouncers were escorting me out and thanked me for helping her. She was sweeter in the light, and I had a short moment to see her sensitive side. She gave me a hug and a kiss on my lip that tasted like sugar and asked for my number. I gave it to her, and I never asked for hers but told her that she should never bask on this day when two men fought over her. All of this was just a man trying his best to avoid a woman from being abused mentally or possibly physically because of her reluctance to communicate. She smiled and I walked towards the car.

We practiced diligently for weeks for the upcoming event. There were five of us, and we were all talented at something. I explained to my mother that I had joined a dance group at school, and we were intending on performing at a nightclub the following weekend. I knew that she would have an issue with me being in a nightclub. I explained that it would be well supervised and all I wanted to do is dance so that we could win the purse money and our trophies. Reluctantly, she agreed, but she made me aware that if my father got word of it, he'd probably go mad. So I told her I'd wait until he goes to bed, and then I'd sneak out. It was agreed on and on the Friday night, I did just what I had said I would do. We were the fifth or sixth group up from twelve. Most of the groups were good, but they all danced similarly. I explained to the guys that we had to come on strong right from the start. The name of the group was called "Lock Lightning." I could hear the crowd with every move we made as they chanted. My heart was filled with joy and for the first time I felt like a star. This was the first time I felt happy and fearless in a long time. The group that I managed was up next, and I really wanted them to do well.

I managed an all women's group that had five beautiful dancers performing. They also had a wonderful reception as they started. They were gracious but at the same time had a bit of thug and edge to them. At the end of the night the top seven groups were called out. In the first four names that were called, neither of our names was mentioned. The fifth name was "Lock Lightning" and the seventh name was "Lady Divas," the group I managed.

We went away elated that we made the top seven. We had a few hours the next day to practice and come up with something new. We decided that we would dress our robot dancer up in lights. Alan was going to be our ticket to victory, and I would be the one to kill them with the Sanford dance.

The girls were on their own and wanted to try it. They were happy that I got them this far, but they too felt that they had a weapon. I told my mom that I'd be back as soon as the show was finished. We were the fifth group up, and on that night with all the rushing, I forgot my dance shoes. I had no choice to dance in my multi colored toe sock. The audience took a liking to it, and we were on our way to being number one. Alan came out in the dark with lights all over him performing the robot. They had never seen anything like that before. Everyone in the audience had their jaws wide open. Alan moved like a robot, and I ended the show with a sample of the Sanford dance, which drew a big ovation from the crowd.

The girls were directly behind us, and they looked smashing that night. They teased the crowd that night with some dirty funk dancing. The fellows in the crowd wished that they could be between them. They bounced of each other while touching their body parts. The energy was whacking and their timing was on with every move they performed. They ended the show by laying kiss cross over each other. The moment that we were all waiting for was near. The DJ played some bounce rock skate music as he announced the winners. In third place was a group from Windsor. "Lock Lighting came in second place, and first place went to the Divas. I don't think any of the guys felt disappointed because we came in second place. We had money in our pocket and the girls whom we worked with did well. From that day on, where ever we went, people recognized us. I knew that I couldn't hang around for very long fearing the outcome, if I was to get caught. Most of the guys along with the girls knew that we weren't allowed to be in the club after our performance, so they all went out afterwards for something to eat.

I made my way home, and once I got to the top of the

hill, I revved the engine of the car slightly and then placed the gear into neutral and shut of the engine. I had to be precise with the parking because I wouldn't be able to start the car again. Thankfully there weren't any cars parked near my house. I closed the car door real softly and tip toed up the stairs. I opened the front door as quiet as I could; however, with the squeaks from the door, I weren't sure if it had wakened my father. Once in the house, I took my shoes off my feet and placed them into my hands as I tiptoed across the living room floor. I had no idea what had happened, but the only thing I knew was that I was having problem breathing.

I had an electric cord around my neck and at the time the only thing I knew, was that I thought I was going to die. My father had wakened up and was extremely upset that I was out at that hour in the morning. My mother woke to the sound of me struggling as I tried to remove the cord from around my neck. He eventually removed the cord from my neck as a result of my mother screaming. After releasing the cord from my neck, he swung the cord two or three more times, striking me on my leg and back area as I made my way down the stairs.

The following morning I spent my time sleeping and resting my neck and back. My mother felt at fault for allowing me to go. It wasn't her fault, I said because my dad was crazy and didn't like me. I told her that I was thinking of returning to my martial arts. She served me my breakfast in bed and sat with me for a little just to cheer me up.

After my father went out in the afternoon, I eventually made my way out of my cave, meaning my security room. I knew that I got beaten up pretty good that night, but my joy was still on our accomplishment. I felt so proud of myself and especially of my friends. My mother was starting to have a lot of headaches, so she saw her family doctor. The doctor felt that she was suffering with symptoms like migraines. He suggested that she spent some time resting. My Aunt Winifred had heard about her condition and offered to have her stay with her until she felt better. She traveled to New York City and spent at least two months with my aunt. Luckily, for us, my aunt Monica also offered to have us stay with her. I think my mother felt much better knowing that we were staying with one of her family. While our mother was in New York, I decided that I would return to my martial arts. I thought by doing my martial arts it would allow me time to meditate. Classes were on Thursday nights, so I took full advantage of it, seeing that my mother wasn't around. I knew that I was better than some of the students who were a rank or two higher than me. I had an opportunity to choose whomever I wished to spar against. I chose a brown belt and was successful in beating him up. After the instructor told the class that it's not good enough to be strong at our Katter. He explained that knowing Katter isn't sufficient enough. The instructor looked at me and said, "Well done."

He asked if I would like to try someone else. I looked at him and said, "I'd like to try you." He looked at me, as if I was crazy and suggested that I try someone else, but I said, "No such thing today." We began to spar and for the most part, I thought I was doing well. I decided to try a spinning heel kick, and hopefully I would knock him to the floor. He timed me perfectly as I leaped into the air, as I turned my body around to spin; he connected with a kick right to my ribs. I fell to the ground in excruciating pain. I knew then that I had a long way to go before I can teach a class. He picked me up with the assistance of a fellow student and assisted in wrapping my ribs with a tensor bandage. He then insisted that I go home and have it looked at by a doctor the following day.

I continued to go to the classes, but I had to be easy on myself for some time. Although I wasn't sparring, I was developing my skills in other areas. After four years of studying with him, I left and trained with another instructor. I stayed with that instructor for about a year and a half. Eventually, I started to learn from people that I knew privately.

The holidays were coming and Christmas was just around the corner. My mother had returned from her stay with her sister, looking much better than she did before she left. Christmas was always big at our home. We enjoyed the foods and looked forward to having some of our relatives visit. I looked forward to the many gifts I received every year. I always bought my mother something that she needed.

I enjoyed looking at her face when she opened her gift. As for my father, it was usually a tie and shirt, or cufflinks. After having such a wild year, I was looking forward to a peaceful jolly Christmas. Christmas Eve we spent part of the day shopping and preparing for Christmas and at night, we would spend the Christmas in church. Thanking God for having mercy on us and asking him to pave the road for a better life and that His children would seek refuge in Him.

We had a wonderful breakfast and a belly bursting dinner. A couple of my friends had dinner with us because they either celebrated their holiday at another time or their families were not around. That was fun to have someone else at the dinner table with us. It took away any unpleasant tension from the room. After dinner my friends left to be with their family for the holidays. I went down stairs to my room and spent some time on the phone with my friends talking. At around 8:00 pm, I heard some screaming upstairs. I couldn't believe that on Christmas Eve night my father would lose his cool with my mother. I hung up the phone and ran up the stairs. I was right; my mother was lying on the floor with my father holding her by her hair. This angered me very much. I decided that this was going to be the night that I became a full-grown lion. I asked him to take his hands off my mother and to never touch her again. He walked over to me and asked if I were trying to disrespect him. I replied by saying, "That isn't true, I'm only disrespecting what you do."

He looked at me and said, "So you think you're a man now?" He had been working on the kitchen ceiling, so he had some of his tools lying on the kitchen counter. He looked at me and said, "I'll show you what a man is." So he picked up a chisel to use upon me, so I reached for his extra long screw driver and proceeded to walk towards him, as he was approached me to lunge the screwdriver into him. My mother was fearful that someone was going to be injured, so she started to yell at the top of her lungs, "Murder!!!! Murder!!!!" She stood directly between us as she was yelling "Murder!!!" at the top of her lungs. As a result of her screaming, my father placed the chisel on the kitchen counter to avoid her from having a breakdown. I told my mother she didn't have to worry, that I wasn't going to be the one that would be murdered here tonight. He stood away from us and smiled while stating to me again that I felt like a big man now.

136

I knew that the Devil was in our presence and was trying to ruin the special night, as Jesus was the one we should be fighting over. I said to my father that I wasn't rude to him, but I didn't appreciate the things that he had done. Before he left the house, I turned to him and said. "I told you that even a cub will grow up. I'm no longer a cub, I'm a lion now."

As he stood there with fire in his eyes, I asked of him a favor that he refrained from touching my mother in a physical manner again. After he left, my mother fell on the couch and said to me that she knew for sure now, that she had to leave. She cried for some time while I sat there and said nothing. After a while, she started to smile and looked at me with her funny self and said, "So you're as bad as a crab for your mother, aren't you?" We both started to laugh and made the best of the night. Christmas morning we were all up early, except my dad. I guess he was probably replaying his actions in his head. We waited for him to rise and then we all opened up our gifts. My mother had a smile from ear to ear although just last night she was being abused. Once the gifts had been opened and hugs and kisses all around were given, we sat down for a breakfast that was fitted only for a King. My mother went all out with this breakfast. We had everything that we could possibly want to eat. The table had a bit of life at it, and most of all she was happy. Thank God for that. He looked at the relationship that we shared with each other, and for a moment I almost felt that he wished he had the same with me. He said to me that she's your queen, and I replied by saying that she surely was my Queen, and no one was going to take her away from me.

My father did assault my mother once more a few

weeks later. This time he shook her around viciously rather than slapping her. I was not condoning either abuse, but for the most part she wasn't injured. A couple of months had passed, and the house felt as if we were in a garden of some sort. I began to ponder that it might be as a result of me standing up to him. Ever since I stood up and became the Lion in the house, the mood in the house has settled down considerably.

We were able to laugh and play with one another without fearing for our safety. My mother had her step back in her, and she actually seemed happy for a change. Her brothers had still refused to come to our home, fearing that if they saw my dad that they might be tempted to initiate a fight. Her sisters came by quite often and hung out with her and even went out together.

A fair amount of weeks had passed without any controversy, but for some reason on this day, everything came to a head. I think whatever the reason, my mother had run out of patience. She ran over to the phone without any hesitation and called her brother, Thomas. She told him that she didn't think she could continue with the relationship with my father any longer. After speaking to her brother, she told my father what she felt for the benefit of our children and her mental health, and it would be best if they considered parting their ways.

My father was like a caged tiger, just pacing back and forth in the living room. He was in an agitated mood, and unwilling to listen to any solution at the time. The phone rang and my mother picked up the phone. On the other end of the phone was her sister aunt Cita. At the same time, my mother's brothers were outside of the house preparing to enter the premises. My father was suspicious of whom she was talking to, so he took the phone from her hand and enquired to whom he was talking with. Once he realized who it was and that my uncles were indeed on his property, he rushed out to the garage and found himself a steel bar to defend himself with. He rushed back to the front door with the steel bar in his hand and encouraged my Uncle Thomas and Uncle Winston to come and get him. This was a show-down from the old west. My uncle Thomas was carrying long scissors, while my uncle Winston had himself a butcher knife as his weapon of choice. Things were out of control with all the yelling and threats and I believe that one of the neighbors saw what was happening and called for the police to attend.

The neighbor across the street told my mother not to worry, that the police had been called. Fearing for her brothers' safety, she encouraged them to leave before the police arrived. They were bent on teaching my father a lesson and didn't want to leave. With the sound of the siren from a distance, she tried to hurry them of the property. Once my father felt hat he had sufficient time to run into his car, he started the engine and attempted to run my uncle Winston over.

Realizing what was about to happen, I placed myself between my uncle and the car, forcing my father to apply his breaks, while the car came into contact with me, knocking me to the ground. This angered my uncle, but based on the limited time he had, he had no choice but to drive away. I believe if I hadn't done that, my uncle could have been hurt severely or possibly killed. Seconds after they left, two police cruisers appeared on the scene.

They asked my mother to step away from my dad while they spoke to her. She avoided any answers that could possibly place her brothers in trouble. She said that all it was a misunderstanding between two brothers and a brother-in-law. She said that she believed the neighbors over reacted and everything was alright. Without a solid confession, there was nothing that they could do to my father. Again my mother saved him from being punished, because of the underlying love that she still felt for him.

That Sunday was the opportunity that my mother was waiting for to finally make her mind up. She knew that regardless of what she did, my father wasn't about to change. He was a selfish emotionless person towards her, and asking him to change his ways was not going to happen. To change you must want to, and you must have feelings and love toward that person.

She decided that she was going to move within a week, hopefully on the Monday morning after he left for work. In the meantime I tried my best to change his way of thinking. Every morning on the way to work I'd try and help him to realize that my mother was going to leave him if he didn't say sorry and work on changing. I didn't want to betray my mother but for some reason I felt it was best if I tried to help keep the family together.

Sunday evening we had a fantastic dinner and then sat and watched television together for the first time in many years. Was he sensing something? I don't know, but it was nice to see the living room filled with everyone in it without any fears. After he watched a couple of his shows he went out for some time. We all knew where he was going, but too much damage had been done for anyone to be upset. I asked my mother if she still had plans on leaving on Monday, and she advised me that she had already ordered the truck. She had asked for the truck to arrive after 9:30am and not a minute before.

Monday morning was here and I rose with a sad feeling in my stomach. Although he had been terrible towards me, I still looked at him as my father. I guess the same thoughts must have been running through my mother's head. She married him and thought that he was going to grow old with her and love her until she was no more. On the way to my job, I asked if he had ever thought of some of the things that he had done to mom in the past years. The only thing he kept on saying was that if it wasn't for him, none of us would be where we were, and that included my mother. I guess his head was hard and if his heart was still this hard, then I guess my mother was doing the right thing. I didn't think that God would give my mother more than she could handle. She was a God fearing and loving person, so He was with her in every step she took. I knew that once my father arrived home and realized that the house had been emptied out, he'd be in a shock. I pictured him standing in the house, stunned, with a weird smile on his face. The first thing he'd probably do was to call Alice and explain to her what had happened. Once he was over the initial shock, he would contact me to find out what happened. Everything that I said happened exactly as I pictured it. The only thing that was a bit different was his appearance at my work. He showed up at my job and wanted to know if I had known that my mom was moving out. I had to pretend like that was a shock to me also, so I acted as if I was surprised. He asked if I would be allowed to leave work, seeing that there's been a crisis in the home. I asked my manager for some time off, due to a situation that had happened. He took me directly to the house and indeed my mother did move out.

The only thing that she left was his bed for him to lie on. There was a little bit of food in the refrigerator and a few linens to clean up with. All of my belongings had been removed from my bedroom, so he knew that she was expecting me to stay with her. I told him that I'd spend the remainder of the week with him, and I'd join my mother on Saturday night. I slept on the carpet in my room for the time that I was there.

It bothered me that Alice had broken up our family, and even though she knew that my mother had moved out as a result of her, she still had the gall to come into the house and give my dad some company. I knew that Alice had to pay for what she had done, but this wasn't the time to focus on her. Saturday arrived and I woke up, prepared a little something to eat and sat outside and just thought while I ate. Once my father woke up, I said my goodbyes' to him and left. He wanted to know where my mother was staying, so I told him that she was at my uncle Fitzroy's house.

We stayed at his home for about a month until we found an apartment on Bathurst Street. The apartment wasn't the greatest, but it was clean and it was a fresh beginning for us. We knew that it would be a bit difficult until we get used to it. My mother said that we all had to chip in and try and do our best to be happy. Life was about to take on a new path but with the strength of God, we knew that we were going to be OK. My father had tried to contact my mother while we lived at our uncle, but it wasn't very successful. He didn't get the support from her family that he was hoping for, so after a period of time he decided to leave. That was the beginning of an all out war against each other. He carried a strong hate towards them that never left his system. The feeling was mutual among the majority of the family towards him. He did have one or two that spoke to him, whenever they saw each other. However, the anger and dislike towards the majority of the family, was embedded in his soul.

I now had to work full time at the Bi-Way Store so that I could support the home and myself. I had my car and motorcycle insurance to pay, and also to assist with paying the rent. Once I had a routine going, everything began to fall into place, and life wasn't as bad as I thought it would be. I left school half way into my grade twelve and pursued a managerial position at the Bi-Way store. I worked my way up from being the stock boy, to assistant manager all within a year and a half. The manager and senior manager both felt that I had portrayed good work habits to be promoted so quickly. At the time the Bi-Way stores paid fairly well, so I didn't have too many money problems. From time to time I'd take my car up to dead man's valley for a race or two if money became a problem. My mother still felt that what I was doing was unsafe and it could cost me my license or my life. I always reassured her to have faith in me. I told her that I had her spirit with me and that God was always looking over me.

I won a lot of races in my time and during it all, I never cheated nor did I have to resort to any unfair methods. Whenever I made an entrance after being away from the scene, I was always welcomed. There were those who always felt they had it in them to beat me, and those that heard about me and felt they would be the one to beat me. I continued to say, "To be the man, you've got to beat the man." As time went on, I was faced with more and more challenges. I decided to purchase a Trans Am, brown in color with a nice big bird on the hood.

This was the car of all cars. I felt as if the car was built with me in mind. The car loved me and I loved her. Knowing that they were so many drivers out to dethrone me, I decided that who's better to work on my car than my dads' mechanic. I loved the car but not as much as he enjoyed working on her. He had me feel her out on the highway a few times until he got it right. The big bird was now ready to enter the big bad world of unprofessional world of racing.

The outcome was the same every time I raced. Some races were an entire blowout, while some races had some serious competitors. I had made some good money breaking the law, and I loved every moment of it. I always wanted to be a Smokey and bandit type of character. I believed in my heart that there's a little bit of bad in all of us. I may be wrong, but we all enjoyed when the bad guy gets away from the law sometimes.

My mother had no problems paying her rent and paying her bills off. Eventually, I purchased a new motorcycle but never raced with her. This was the first bike that I considered racing with, but soon realized that my skill in riding was good, but not superior enough to beat the guys who raced on a bike for a living. I perfected my riding skill over the years, but I still stayed away from the track. I knew my strengths and racing required a different mindset, and I hadn't developed a mind for that. I decided that I would take some of my vacation time in the summer. What I wasn't thinking was, although I'd been on vacation, most of my friends didn't have the same schedule as me. I spent most of my time driving or riding around by myself. I decided that I'd ask my mother to ask my father if he needed any extra help. It seemed as if he wasn't too enthusiastic in having me work for him. He agreed and he had me start the following day on a job that was in the east end of the city. I arrived nice and early and prepared to work for my money. My cousin Lennox worked on all of the jobs with my dad. I believed that they had a partnership going or at least an understanding. Most of the men knew me, so I felt comfortable being around them.

My father placed me in a room where the walls required some sanding and suggested that I do it right. There was a lot of work to do on the walls in this room, so I got to it. The wall had been plastered and was all ready to be smoothed so I spent at least an hour and a half standing before I decided to take a short break away from the dust. I stood at the entrance where a door was required to be hung. We stood at least two stories up from the ground and spoke about my teenage years. The house didn't have any front stairs at the time so they placed a ply wood as stairs to walk on to get into the house. Cousin Lennox and I were talking casually when out of nowhere I felt a blow to my ribs. My father had walked up from behind me and struck me with a two by four piece of wood, out of anger on my back because he felt that I had spent too much time in the room, and the walls still weren't smooth enough. The blow knocked me right over the ledge, causing me to fall on my back. I lay on the ground in excruciating pain for a moment. My cousin Lennox came down and assisted me to my feet to make sure that I'd be alright. I had a bruised rib and cuts from the fall.

My head felt like I had been in a field filled with marines on an exercise. Once on my feet I felt like walking up the platform and striking my father in his head with the shovel that was on the ground. He stood at the ledge steering at me, as if he wanted me to confront him. I looked directly at him and told him that as long as I lived, he would never see me work for him again, never ever. I dropped his stupid tool belt on the lawn and walked over to my car with my cousin's assistance. I went directly home and explained to my mother what had happened. That evening when my father called her, I could hear her telling him exactly what she thought of him and the reasons why she left him.

One afternoon we decided that we were going to have a family night and just watch television together. My mother cooked a nice meal for us, and we all sat around and watched some of our favorite shows. The phone rang and it was our dad on the phone. We could tell that something was wrong by the look on mother's face. She stood silent for a while just answering by saying only, "A-ha." After she got off the phone, we inquired about the look on her face. She told us that our father had just told her the doctors said he had prostate cancer. She felt sad for him, and we understood that she still cared about him but she couldn't live with him. The first thing that came to my mind was God was punishing him for all the things he did to the both of us. I told her not to worry because she didn't have any control over his health. I reminded her that she could have died from all the blows that she took, "So please remember that." He had his operation within a week and stayed in the hospital for a while. They had some complication after the operation, which to this day, I still don't know what it was.

Eventually, he was released from the hospital, and based on what the doctors felt, he should be alright. They felt that they caught everything just in time, but they wished to see him frequently for the next little while. He was back to his regular self, and from time to time he would pass and see my mother. I couldn't understand why she maintained a relationship with him, even when she knew that he was still involved with Alice. With the help of her family and great friends, we were able to get her to entertain the idea of meeting someone new. Many people asked for her hand, but she refused them all. One man whom she spent some time with, had her thinking all over again, and this had us all happy for her. He came by the house many times and some of my mother's family even met him. Some liked him, while the others didn't, but we all suggested that she went slowly. They saw each other on and off for a few years. I started to have doubts about him when he was never available when my mother needed him the most.

After a period of time, without us saying anything to her, she stopped talking to him. The mother whom we knew was back on her feet again. We missed that spicy mouth woman who was never afraid to say how she felt; the lady who laughed from her stomach and not because she wanted to make you feel good. We were all happy once again to see her eyes glitter and to see her back dressing fine as ever. Doreen always had something to say when she felt that it was time for her to give her advice. Her words were sharp but truthful. She had every phrase that you can think of. Fu Manchu had nothing on her at all. To this day, I think everyone of us has used some of her paraphrases in our day-to-day language. My brother and his family would come to Toronto in the summer time to spend a few weeks on their vacation with our father.

From what I found out later, is that whenever they were here, he would take them to a cottage up north. I couldn't understand why he never asked if I would like to join them. My entire childhood was spent without any interaction with him, and now that I was in my adult years, it still continued to be the same way.

As a child I enjoyed fishing, but so many times I wished he would have taken me fishing or just for a drive up north. Whenever I wanted to go fishing he would tell me to ask my uncle to take me, so I did ask my uncle to take me fishing and while we were fishing, he said to me that "It would be nice if one day, your dad joined us to go fishing."
Robert and his family decided to spend a few weeks of their vacation visiting my father. They had never spent any time at my house when visiting. They would visit my home, but they never slept in my home while on vacation in the many years that they had been visiting our father. One day I decided that I'd ride my motorcycle over to my father's home to visit and spend some time with them.

We sat around and talked about our time as kids and all the trouble that I used to get myself into. My brother Robert was sitting in the living room with his wife and child. My father and I were in the kitchen talking. My father had said something about my mother which I wasn't too appreciative of. I felt that my mother had tolerated his foolishness for many years, and she didn't need his filthy mouth speaking bad about her. I chose to speak up for her by reminding him that if it weren't for my mother and his ex wife, he probably wouldn't be where he is now. This angered him, and felt that I shouldn't be talking back to him in his house and especially speaking negative about Alice. As I sat in the kitchen with my back turned to my father, he retrieved a knife from the counter and walked up behind me. Suddenly, I felt a sharp object around my throat that felt cold and jagged at the edges. He had one hand on the back of my neck, while the other hand was around my throat with the knife. He started to speak with a loud voice, as if he was in an agitated mood. I guessed by my attitude, he felt that I was out of order and by retaliating when he spoke about my mother, offended him. He asked if I felt like dying in his kitchen, or would I like to leave with a scar to remember him by. I decided that I'd reserve whatever answers I had for another time, so I said absolutely nothing. I felt the blood trickling down my neck, and as it dropped to the floor, I began to boil with rage. Robert and Alice persuaded him to put the knife down, because they feared what might happen. He kept asking me if I "felt like a son of a bitch now." I continued to say absolutely nothing. As long as he had the knife to my throat, I said nothing. The experience of having a knife to your throat was like being in the ocean with a life preserver that wasn't completely filled with air.

My only choice was to wait it out and to act as if I was not afraid. Alice finally got my dad to release the knife from around my throat. He said to me that if I ever talked to him in a disrespectful manner again in his house, he'd cut my blasted neck off. I got up from the chair and made my way to the side door entrance. As I started my motorcycle, my brother Robert came outside to see me off. He told me to take it easy and not to try to get daddy upset next time. He was trying to convince me that our father didn't mean what he said, and he was only upset because I spoke up about our mother.

I started to wonder in my mind if he was for real or

just a big kiss-ass. For a brief moment as I listened and looked at Robert as he talked his gobble-gobble nonsense, I wanted to punch him in his face. I'd always believed that I was the only one with a voice in the family, and it'd been branded by blood, I still am. Every one of my siblings were "yes" children and had no voice of their own.

Working for the Bi-Way stores can be taxing on anyone who worked for the company. So once the weekend came along, I looked forward to unwinding. The place to hang out at was called "Heavens," a social spot nightclub. You never knew whom you might see at Heavens on any given weekend. People from everywhere would gather in hope to meet someone. The DJ played music that would have you forgetting your problems and would place your body and soul in a place of euphoria. The ladies were as fine as the lines of the body of a Rolls Royce. The guys lined the bar in hope to purchase a drink for that fine lady, and hopefully be that one passenger whom she'd offer a ride.
On this Friday night, I received a call from a friend indicating that all of the guys were planning on going to Heavens. He indicated that on this night all the ladies were free until 11pm. We knew that if Heavens was having a ladies night special, then all the fellows in the city who knew anything about Heavens night club, this would be the night for all the so call players. I had my hair cut and pampered myself with a hot towel shave by the barber. My ride was clean, and I had money in my pocket, and it being Friday night, I felt that everything was going to turn out just right.

I had a pretty good reputation among the bouncers at the nightclubs, so regardless of the time or price, Everard would be alright. To show my gratitude at the end of the night, I'd always make sure to place some money in their hands before leaving, as a token of thanks. The club was jamming and the music was pumping. Ladies were everywhere and the air smelled like animals on the prowl. We were standing around in a group looking around for that right girl. I noticed this beautiful girl that stood approximately 5ft 6in tall with wavy long brown hair. She had legs that were long and well shaped. Her eyes sparkled from afar as if she had tears in them. She stood in a way that would prohibit any man from approaching her. A bet was placed between me and the guys where I'd have only 15 minutes to try and have her dance with me on the dance floor. Once on the floor I'd have to get her to dance with me to a slow song before we get off the dance floor. If I were successful at this challenge, they'd have to pay me eighty dollars and a drink for my friend and me. I approached her like a cat preparing to groom their mate. She looked at me with those big brown eyes and said, "Excuse me."

I looked at her and said, "I've noticed that you've been standing by yourself for some time, and I was wondering if you would like to have my hand to dance on the dance floor."

She snuffed at me, as if I wasn't worthy to be seen with. I took a short step back and looked at her and said "it's obvious that there isn't a line up to dance with you, so I recommend that you take advantage of this opportunity, because it may never come your way again." She broke into a smile and took my hand as we walked toward the dance floor. The first part of the bet was had come to an end, and the slow songs were about to start. I had to find a way to get her to dance with me without looking desperate. I decided that I'd thank her for her company and casually walk away.

As I started to walk away, she stopped me and asked if I had a problem slow dancing with her. I said "not at all," I just didn't want to wear my luck out. It worked, like a charm. She was like candy in my hand. Every time we turned on the floor, I showed the guys the signal for eighty dollars. Once we were finished dancing, I introduced her to my friends and had them purchase a drink for the both of us. We enjoyed each other's company the entire night. She spoke to me about any and everything that night. She told me that she was traveling to Barbados on Sunday with a close girlfriend to visit her family.

We decided to leave the club a bit early to beat the crowd. We took our time walking towards her car. The night was warm and the sky lit up brightly as the full moon shined. Once at her car, I knew that I'd want to kiss her, but I'd have to do it in a cool way. I placed her inside of her car and had her buckled up as the engine warmed up. I leaned over and gave her a subtle kiss on her cheek. She pulled me closer to her and asked if that's the best I could do. The magic had worked and she was now ready to be my girlfriend. Before I walked away, she told me that she wished that she didn't have to leave, but she wishes to continue to see me when she returned. "The feeling is mutual," I said, and I did look forward to spending time with her when she returned.

I had arranged to pick her up from the airport when she returned. I picked her up just after midnight from the airport. Because of the hour, she asked if it would be possible to spend the night at my place. I knew that my mother wasn't going to be happy, but I did it anyway. I slept on the couch that night, and I offered her my bedroom. The following morning I rose to see her sitting on the couch staring at me as I slept.

My mother had gone to work so I didn't get the third degree that morning. She had absolutely no clothes on but the comforter she covered her body with at night. She crawled into my little bed and started to seduce me. Before I could think clearly, we were already making love to each other. That morning was like paradise, and every man should be this privilege to wake up in the morning like this. She didn't want to stop that morning at all. I felt as if we were going at it for at least an hour and a half already. She said to me that she'd had sex before, but this was love making. I tried to get dressed after we ate and showered, but she still wanted more. I promised her that in due time she'd get as much of me as she wanted when God joined us together. By the way, we had to do it one more time, just for the fun of it. We spent almost every day together and at times that didn't feel like it was sufficient. Wherever I went, I found it odd, that although I didn't tell her where I was going, she would find herself at the same location.

We dated for some time before we started talking about being together on a permanent basis. I realized quickly that being with her wasn't going to be an easy time. Anytime we had to go anywhere, I wasn't allowed to meet her at her home. She told me that her parents wouldn't be very hospitable towards me, because I was not Jewish and being black placed me in a prohibited fly zone. Her parents would not approve of me being with their daughter under any circumstance. She would walk approximately two blocks away from her home, so that her parents wouldn't see her with me. She explained that she didn't have a very loving relationship with her parents. Her father owned his own company, and she was employed by him. Her half brother from the mother side was also an employee at the company, and their relationship was like water to oil. One day she showed up at my job in Whitby to pay me a visit for lunch. The visit was unexpected but most welcoming. We had an enjoyable moment until she informed me that she had quit working for her father. She explained that he was too much of a bully, and that she couldn't handle being yelled at any more. She wanted to seek employment elsewhere so that she wouldn't need her parents for anything I encouraged her to return to her job and apologize to her father. She wasn't happy with my suggestion, but because she respected me, she took my advice.

My mother had found herself a very nice condominium that was located near the subway. My sister and my mother had moved into their new place, so I had sole possession of the apartment. Esther decided to move in with me at the apartment after my mother moved out. Living on my own for the first time certainly was an adventure. We had a good thing going and enjoyed being on our own tremendously. Her parents were terribly annoyed at her for moving out and even more so for moving in with me. I couldn't understand why she had so much money on her, whenever we went anywhere.

Every Friday she had approximately $1,000.00 on her, which caused me some concern. I really didn't know how much she was being paid while she worked for her father, but I didn't think it would be that much for a week after taxes. We had many enjoyable moments while we were dating, and after living at the apartment for some time, we decided to move into another apartment that would be brighter and roomier.

Esther had decided to leave her father's business and got a job in the computer field working for Jerry Phillips. At the time Jerry Phillips had owned his own company and wasn't in politics as yet. We stayed at the apartment for at least two years. The building was clean and quiet but had an evil spirit lurking somewhere within the wall of the building. One morning on my way to work, I observed a letter that was printed and stuck to the bulletin board. The letter read, "Can all niggers, please seek room and board somewhere else." It went on to say that, "As a result of black people being in the building, many of the white residents are moving out." The tenants in the building had a meeting to address this type of racism. We left the meeting feeling as if nothing was resolved and felt that it might be time to move. Esther took it upon her shoulder to look for a home that would be enjoyable for the both of us. After a Month or so she came home one evening with a ton of energy. She had found a home that was for sale not too far from where we lived. The house was beautiful and I never bothered looking at any other homes. It was the only home I had looked at, and felt that this would be the home that I raise my family in. Within two months we were out of the apartment and in our new home. I proposed to Esther and set a wedding date for September long weekend.

Esther had dinner with her parents one evening and informed them of her intentions. She asked if they would be willing to come and if her father would be willing to give her away on that day. The conversation didn't go very well at all. They told her that if she got married to me they'd be terribly hurt, and they would definitely stay away from her on that day. They even told her that they'd see to it that no family members or friends attend such a farce. Esther returned home with hate and anger built up against them. Whatever anger she had towards them before, it was twice as much now.

Our wedding date was nearing, and her family still hadn't changed their minds. I had to find someone that would fill the role of her father. He needed to be approximately the same age and height. I wanted the guest to believe that her father had given her away. We had gorgeous weather on the day of our wedding. The sky was blue and the temperature was perfect, seeing that we were running all over.

I remember showing up to the church asking myself "What are you doing?" I knew that I loved her, and that we got along really well, but I wondered if I would be able to handle the abuse and if it was going to be possible to mend such a gap. For now I just had to get through this nervous moment. As I stood at the front preparing for her to walk down the aisle, an urge took over me to run. My friends held onto me while the pastor had a quick word with me. The music began, and my life was about to take a huge change. "For better or for worse," right. She looked beautiful and I just couldn't believe how emotional I felt. I realized right then, how lucky I was, or I told myself that. I couldn't wait to hear her say our last name. We took a ton of pictures at Edward's Gardens. While we were being positioned to have one of our pictures taken, we had a quick glance of her father's sister at the garden. We believed she came to the garden for many reasons. She probably came because she felt as if she had an obligation to Esther. The other reason was probably to confirm that we did get married so that she could relay the information back to her brother. Nevertheless, by the time we were finished taking our pictures, she was nowhere to be found.

The reception was well done, and the guest enjoyed themselves. We stayed until midnight and then we had the limo take us to the hotel at the airport. We planned our honeymoon night exhausted but extremely happy to be with each other. The time we spent in Las Vegas and Los Angeles was out of this world. We gambled, ate well and took in the shows as well as have some quiet moments to ourselves. We were lucky to meet a lot of movie stars and to have them sign our books for us along with a few pictures. While in Vegas, we had an opportunity to sit in the front row, alongside Ann Murray. That night we were entertained by the Temptations and were given a bottle of champagne as a gift. At the end of the show on the way out, we had the pleasure of meeting Dan Ho from the hit show "Hawaii Five O." The hotel was filled with entertainers, and we were ready to party and have a good time. We had a fantastic time on our honeymoon and were ready to meet the world head on.

We knew that we would face many challenges as a biracial couple, but we weren't about to let it affect us. After being back at home for a while, Esther felt that for her to get anywhere in life, she would have to complete her grade twelve. So I worked to carry the home on my wages so that she would be successful in completing her studies. We both knew that we wanted children, so we decided to work at it and hopefully, with God's grace, we'd have a beautiful child.

Esther came home one evening and out of nowhere she said to me that she was seeking the help of an assassin to murder her parents. She wanted them dead at any cost, and she would stop at nothing to have it done. I couldn't believe what I was hearing and thought that she was just trying to pull a prank on me. I looked at her and asked if she was serious? She told me that she hated her parents so much that she couldn't wait to see them dead. Esther was serious as a heart attack and I knew if I didn't do something soon, we could be facing a serious charge.

That night I had to be harsh and tough on her. I told her that if she was intending on pursuing her wishes, I'd have no choice to leave her. I didn't want to be a part of it, because the law would see me as being the person that encouraged you to seek their death because of their money. She cried for about an hour and continued to shed her tears about their death. She so wanted them dead that I had to think long and clear about our marriage. After a few hours had gone by, she came into the bedroom and agreed not to follow through with her feelings. Esther didn't have a job but for some reason she always seemed to have a wallet full of hundred dollar bills. She explained to me when asked about the money that she stole it from her father's safe. I started to wonder if I ever knew this woman that I married. She explained to me that one evening she stood at a distance while her father was opening the safe and recorded the numbers. She made herself a copy of the combination and worked at it until she got the right numbers. She explained that her father would never miss the money because he never counts the money. The money that he placed in the safe was money received from the customers as a result of purchasing goods without paying the taxes. I asked her to stop doing it because if she was ever caught, the consequences would be severe.

I explained to her that her family doesn't like me as it is, so if anything happened, they would blame it on me. I wanted her to stop immediately, but she said to me that she'd stop after a few more times. After three or more times, she did stop stealing from her parents. Esther was in the early stages of her pregnancy, and she informed her family. For the first little while, her family continued to stay away from us, but as she grew closer to her delivery date, they started to come around. I remember her mother visiting at our home and still not being able to look at me and breaking down crying.

She was still uncomfortable with the idea of her daughter being married to a black man and her daughter carrying a child for me. As time grew closer to the delivery date, they were much better with the idea of me being a son-in-law. I couldn't believe that the mother was sitting in my living room discussing with her daughter names for the child. To me that was a remarkable turnaround. I knew that the only reason for the change was due to the birth of our child. We decided to call the child Austin if he was a boy and Sweetness if it was a girl.

The basketball finals were on and my team was in the play offs. The game was in the fourth quarter with about six or seven minutes to go when Esther came down the stairs holding her stomach. She said to me that her water had just broken. I couldn't believe that of all the nights for the baby to come was on the night when I would get to see my team take the championship. I assisted her up the stairs and helped her into the shower so that she could clean herself up. The pain was intense as we prepared for the hospital. I had no chance of seeing the game end, however I was about to see a newborn come into the world. I thought to myself that, this was going to be a better seat in the house. Esther continued to moan and groan for many hours. We were into the ninth hour and still no baby. The doctor came back into the room to check her and indicated that she's dilating at a faster rate. He felt that within the next hour or so, she should be ready to deliver. At about thirteen and a half hours into her delivery she was taken into the delivery room. I tried my best to keep her calm, and I continued to wipe the sweat of her forehead.

Before the doctor started the procedure, Esther insisted that he knew that there was a possibility that the child could be born with twelve fingers. She wanted him to know that because I had twelve fingers when I was born so the doctor and staff wouldn't be alarmed when he was delivered with twelve fingers. The baby wanted out and he was making no bones about it. Esther could feel that he was pushing against her walls, and it was a matter of minutes before he arrived. The doctor urged her to continue to push, while I paid attention to what was happening to her.

It totally was an amazing moment to see your child being delivered into this world by his mother. Indeed, it was a boy, and he did have twelve fingers as Esther suggested. I must say that I had the best seat in the house and that no basketball final could have ended as great as this. They wiped him off and slapped him gently to cry and then handed him to me. At that moment, I felt like the world had stopped, and I was the only man in it. I was never so happy. Austin was as quiet as a lamb in my arms.

Unfortunately, when I handed him over to his mother, he wasn't as quiet. I believe that at that moment was when Austin and I connected. The news was out that Esther had delivered a bouncing eight and a half pound baby boy. Esther rested for the afternoon and later that evening. Every relative

160

and friend came to the hospital to visit. I couldn't believe the look on Esther's parents face. They were over whelmed with joy. Her father couldn't stop talking about his grandson. Everyone in the hospital could have seen the joy on their faces. My mother finally had her grandson, and she didn't want to put him down at all. I knew that Austin would be loved like no other. My mother was already making plans for him in the hospital. She couldn't stop talking about all the things she wanted to do with him. On the other side stood Esther's parents, and they were making their own plans for Austin as well.

After two days, Esther and Austin were released from the hospital and were about to take on a whole new life. Esther was to stay at home mom for at least three years. She wasn't comfortable with anyone taking care of him as yet. His grandparents spent a lot of time with him at their home. He learned how to swim at an early age as a result of her parent shaving a pool in their back yard. Austin was the only grandson in the family and seemed to be a problem with Esther's brother. Her brother had two girls and always wanted to have a boy.

Now that Austin was the only grandson in her family, her brother felt very envious because he felt that Austin would be treated like a king. Shortly after Austin was born, I had an opportunity to attend the police college in Aylmer. Every police agency from all over Ontario would attend this college for training and education to become a police officer. Leaving my family behind for twelve weeks was very difficult on me. Since I was a little child I had three dreams in my life, and one of my dreams was to become a police officer. The first two weeks were extremely difficult, but as time went along I conditioned my mind to it.

Once every so often I would come home for the weekend. Myself and two other fellow officers would pack up and spend it with our family. Being at the college could literally drive you crazy if you didn't take a break. I was in my eighth week at the college when I received a phone call from my wife. Esther informed me that my mother had been in an accident and that her foot and ankle had been broken severely. This news came at a bad time for me, because I was about to enter into our exams and physical training marking.

I needed to be focused for me to do well, or everything I dreamt of would be for nothing. I knew that I would have to call my mother, but for the first time I was fearful of my ability to concentrate. One afternoon after my classes, I called the hospital in Toronto and asked to speak with her. It was wonderful hearing her voice because I hadn't seen her or heard from her since I left. From her voice, I could tell that she was in agony, but didn't want to alarm me. I found out that her foot was broken badly and would require surgery. Having her laid up and not being able to work, brought another set of problems that I wasn't prepared for. I told her that I'd check in with her after her surgery the next day. The doctor explained that they're waiting for her blood pressure to lower before they could operate.

As a result of unfortunate fall at her friend's home, we wouldn't have realized that her blood pressure was out of control. The operation was a success, and they placed four pins in her ankle and foot area to keep the bones together. Going into exams, all I had on my mind was my mother. Focusing on the work that was before me, became much more difficult. I started thinking about her financial situation and how it would affect her life. I understood that the Landlord Tenant Act exceptionally well, and enjoyed studying the Liquor Control Act and the Highway Traffic Act. I had some difficulty with the criminal code and finding the cases in the code. Performing in the self-defense class and driving the police vehicles came effortless. Graduation was two days away, and on that day, all our family and friends would be welcome to see us graduate. On that day as we marched as a class, and I had an opportunity to meet Sir Lincoln Alexander, the Governor General of Ontario. He stood directly in front of me and spoke to me for at least a minute. He said that "he was very impressed with the way I marched, and how I wore my uniform." That meant so much to me, to be the only officer out of hundreds to have an opportunity to speak with him.

As I glanced in the bleachers, I could see how proud and happy my mother was. My wife seemed very intrigued in the marching as all the forces of Ontario marched with their respective class. It definitely was something spectacular to see, if you've never been exposed to such an event. At the end of the ceremony, we all gathered with our families and took pictures along with a tour of the facility. Once we were finished, I went back to my bedroom and changed to prepare for the long drive back home.

Esther had suggested that we all meet at her parents' home to eat and enjoy the moment. My mother drove with my wife, and Maureen drove her own car. It took me some time to gather all of my belongings. I had to drive my friend home because we took turns driving to Aylmer. On the way home the conversation surrounded our graduation. My friend wanted to know what Mr. Alexander said to me. We were so happy to be out of the college and to move on from there.

We left at a decent hour, so I found it strange that the traffic was so bottled up. We realized the reason for the pile up. Someone was involved in a serious motor vehicle accident. People were lined along the side of the road looking at whatever was going on. As I drove by the accident, I had a quick glance at the vehicles involved. I turned to my friend and said, "That vehicle on the side of the road looked like my sister's car." We didn't pay much attention to it and continued on our way. Along the way, I had small thoughts of envisioning the possibility that the vehicle may have been my sister's. I dropped my friend off at his home and made my way back to Esther's parent's home. I found it to be a bit odd that I had arrived before my sister. I thought maybe she went to visit our dad before attending the gathering. We sat for at least an hour and a half before my mother started to worry. I began to think back to the accident along the roadside that we passed. I began to wonder if the car on the side of the road was indeed my sister's car.

My system was feeling very unsteady, and I felt as though we were about to have some bad news. The door bell rang and the energy that I felt from the room, in anticipation that Maureen was at the door was remarkable. Everyone had their eyes fixated at the door to see her walk through. I opened the door to be greeted by absolutely no one. I looked north and south to see if it could have been someone who may have rung the door by mistake. As I looked at their faces, I could see the emptiness on their faces. At this point, I think we all knew that something had happened to Maureen.

I believe that the spirit of Maureen was sent to the door to alarm us of her situation. Shortly after the door incident, the phone rang. The person on the other end wished to speak with a relative of Maureen. My mother's face had the look of terror all over it. I answered the call and spoke to an officer who had been at the scene of the accident. He informed me of the severity of Maureen and the urgency of attending the hospital. He didn't release much info about her state, but he did say that she was in a critical state. Maureen had been air lifted to the hospital, due to her complications and the urgency was to get her into the emergency as soon as possible. I had just arrived from London, and now I found myself returning to London for what could be a horrifying experience. The drive was long and depressing as we tried to do our best to think positive.

My mother sat in the back seat and hummed from time to time and prayed with passion. My thought was on how I was going to deal with my mother if the news wasn't pleasant. She already suffered with her blood pressure and being in some discomfort as a result of her foot. This could send her right over the edge. We arrived at the hospital a minute or two before Maureen arrived. She was covered with a blanket; her head was wrapped tightly with bandages with blood stains that covered it, and an IV was running through her veins as she lay motionless.

There were all kinds of wires that were attached from the monitors to the majority of her body. The sight of her on the gurney was nerve wrecking. Having to see Maureen in that position had a distinct effect on my mother. She screamed and cried, until she collapsed momentarily in my uncle's arm. I admit that it was very difficult even for me to take, but I knew that I would have to show my strength for my mother. My father was contacted, but as of this day, I have no idea who contacted him. He arrived after Maureen had been brought into the emergency room. Someone filled him in on what had happened by one of the attending officers on scene. Maureen was in the operating room for quite some time.

We were all on pins and needles in anticipation of good news. After being inside for over an hour and a half, a doctor came out to speak to us. I would like you to picture the events that played out as he opened the door. The door swung open and there he was with spots of blood on his white hospital going. As I stood and watched as the doctor walked toward us, it felt almost as if everything was in slow motion. His face had the look of a man with upsetting news. His cheeks were flushed and his eyes had a sad look to them. He spoke with a very soft voice, almost as if we were in a library. He encouraged us to follow him to a room where he would like to sit and talk to us. Everyone followed as if we were soldiers walking into a field without knowledge of what to expect. He sat directly in front of my mother as he spoke, while my father stood a few feet away. He explained to us the severity of the accident and the situation that she was in as he spoke. He informed us that Maureen had to undergo an operation to save her. She had internal bleeding and her back was broken. We wanted to know how serious of a break to her back she had. Before going further he explained that Maureen had passed away on the operating table and needed to be revived, as a result of her being without oxygen for more than four minutes, due to the seriousness of the nature. He explained that Maureen was shocked more than usual to get her heart running again. Because time was against us, she lost a small percentage of her cognition. Everyone in the room had a somber look on their face as the doctor continued to speak. My mother did not give up on her question with regard to her walking. He looked at us with great sorrow in his eyes and told us that at present it didn't look as if Maureen would ever walk again. The news of Maureen never being able to walk again had both my mother and father upset. My mother held onto his arm and cried while asking if there's anything else that he might be able to do. He told her that all the results weren't back yet, but from the test and lack of leg movement his summary was based on that. He explained that Maureen would undergo a few more operations, and she would need a lot of care. After hearing everything that the doctor had to say, we asked when it would be possible to see her. Maureen wasn't in the position to see any visitors as yet, and they're still working on her as we spoke. As the doctor rose to his feet, and asked if there were any more questions that he could address, my father turned to me and said: "Why couldn't it have been you, Everard, laying on the gurney, rather than Maureen?" I couldn't believe that my own father would say something like that to me. Everyone, including the doctor looked at him with awe, and turned their eyes onto me. I hung my head and walked out the room. My heart had been broken even more. I felt as if I was responsible for her fate, and that I probably should have been the one laying there. I struggled to wonder if what my father had said to me was indeed correct.

I should have known that Maureen was an inexperienced driver, and I should have insisted on her traveling along with my wife. Maureen spent a fair amount of time in the hospital undergoing physiotherapy and learning skills all over. She had lost a certain amount of her short-term memory, so it made it very difficult and extremely challenging. Maureen had become very resentful and for the most part, refused any type of treatment. My mother decided that she would try to assist by having Maureen spend a weekend with her to hopefully give her a break from the environment that she was in.

The idea of having Maureen spend some time at my mother's home to hopefully bring a bit of light to her situation was a total failure. Maureen was not cooperating in any fashion, and this made it very stressful on my mother. At the end of the weekend it was obvious that Maureen was going to be a difficult person to work with. My father didn't make matters any better for us at all. For whatever the reason, Maureen had become defiant towards the nurses, which made their job even harder.

We believed that our father had total control over Maureen and, being close to him, she had agreed to whatever he said to her. She believed that whatever her father said to her was the gospel truth, and everyone else was trying to interfere in her business. Her hands were folded in front of her, and her answers were very evasive. She continued to use phrases that led us to believe that her father had threatened her to keep her mouth shut. Maureen had placed our father in charge of her financial situation, which meant any claims or counter actions with the lawsuit was to be handled by our dad.

My mother was removed as the primary person of Maureen's insurance policy and caregiver for no unknown reasons. My mother had been removed as the executor of the insurance policy. My father now had all the power to her money. Maureen was discharged from Sunnybrook Hospital after six months. She was transferred to Lyndhurst Hospital for approximately a year and a half. After getting her to a point where she was capable of sitting upright in a chair and being able to feed herself, she was transferred to Gage Hospital. Maureen had spent her entire time at the Gage only spending holidays and a few weeks here and there at our father's home.

We believed that our father used some of the money that he received as a settlement to build a custom built home with all the amenities for the possibility of Maureen residing with him. Maureen had a nurse who would provide her with the care needed at least three times a week.

After a while, as it became strenuous on the wallet and harder to assist her with the proper care that was required, he decided to have her stay at the Gage hospital on a permanent basis. I believe Maureen became very resentful for a period of time because of being moved out of her home. Her improvement had been very limited over the past years. We believed as a collective group that Maureen may have done better if she had the assistance and support of her family. Because of my father's influence and underlining fear towards Maureen, she'd been unable to make any real progress.

Maureen's ability to read or write had been diagnosed as being somewhere between a level 5 to 7. She spoke with a bit of confusion at times. Her ability to write, read or retain any information was very limited. To have Maureen understand how important a situation was had been virtually impossible. Her rationalization was as good as having a discussion with a hungry lion. Maureen saw and heard things that hadn't been seen or heard by anyone but herself. She still relied on the nurses to assist her with the changing of her clothes.

My mother began to suffer with headaches on a frequent basis. Her blood pressure was high and required constant monitoring by her physician. Ever since the accident, the hustled and bustled of trying to take care of Maureen brought her a lot of stress. Seeing her daughter in the condition that she was in, was very difficult on her mentally and physically. She began to look a bit worn down and the laughter that she once had, wasn't as prominent as before. Many times I would sit beside her and try my best to get her to smile. She always gave me a smile, but behind the smile, I saw the grief in her heart.

After my mother separated from my father, I made it my daily duty to continue to pick her up from work, whenever she worked the afternoon shift. I would leave wherever I was at 1:30pm. I continued to do this, although I lived in the other end of the city. On this night, I decided that I wanted to relax for one night and told her that I wouldn't be there that night to meet her. She had no problem with that, because she knew that I was always there for her.

On this night, she made her way through the city by bus and subway. After being dropped off by the bus about a block and a half away from her building, she took her time walking because of how warm the night was. As she got closer to her building, she saw a tall slender blond haired man approaching her. She became concerned and held on to her purse a bit tighter. The gentleman made eye contact with her as he got within a few feet of her. He acted as if he was about to pass her, but spun around and grabbed her by her shoulder and threw her to the ground. He tried his best to get her purse off her but was unsuccessful. Realizing that time wasn't on his side, he tried to get her to lie on the grassy area of the sidewalk. The mother whom we knew wasn't about to have some street punk take advantage of her. She did what she was best known for: scream. She began to scream and scratch at his body and face. Realizing that at any moment someone could see or hear her, he decided to give up on his attack. After the attack, she made her way home and called the police. Nothing came out of her complaint, but she knew that the assailant would be wary of being caught if he ever tried this again. After this catastrophic situation, I made it my duty to see to it that she arrived home safely whenever she worked the afternoon shift.

One evening after my mother had returned from visiting her niece at the hospital, she went through her regular ritual by preparing her usual cup of tea or in its place, a warm cup of milk. After making herself comfortable she called her brother Thomas and had a conversation with him. From what I understood, my mother was feeling unsettled and had complained to her brother about the way she was feeling. She got off the phone and drank the cup of milk that she had prepared. After she drank the milk she sat on the chair for a short while and began to feel extremely hot. Out of nowhere her head felt like it was on fire, so she called her brother Thomas out of fear. Feeling as if she was going to collapse, she made herself to the door while crawling on her knees. As she crawled towards the door, the phone had been left off the hook, and my uncle could hear her screams for help. Realizing that she was in desperate need of help, he called for an ambulance to attend her building. The neighbors in her building had heard her screams and came to her assistance.

They realized that my mother was in distress; so they placed her on the ground and tried their best to make her as comfortable as possible as they too called for an ambulance to attend.

The ambulance did attend and prepared her for transportation to the hospital. My uncle had arrived just in time to see her being taken to the Western General Hospital. That evening everyone in my mother's family attended the hospital to hear what the doctor's prognosis. He indicated that my mother had experienced a severe attack. She was diagnosed with a brain aneurism, and that she would likely require an operation to save her. They needed to bring a team of doctors in order to decide exactly what steps should be taken to remove it. In the meantime, they'd medicated her to keep her comfortable and will have to wait for her pressure to settle before making any attempt on removing the aneurism.

Every one of us was nervous and extremely concerned about her. For the next week, I visited my mother twice every day, sometimes three times a day. I had no desire to eat or for anything else in my life. My ex-wife knew how depressed that I had become, and I survived only on the spirit of Jesus. There were times I asked God to remove her pain and strike me with it so that I could carry her burden. Mother's day was within a week, and her birthday was on the 28th of May.

The doctor promised that they were doing everything that was possible to prevent her from having another attack. They received another attack that could be even worse. Knowing that the possibility was eminent, they're doing their best to have her ready for an operation on Monday. They'd decided that Monday would be the day to perform the operation. If my Mother were to have another attack between those days, then that would bring everything to a halt.

I remember visiting my mother on the Wednesday at the hospital right after work, and seeing a change in her. I felt as if we were behind the danger and the operation would be a go. She spoke to me about how she was feeling much better and how scary it was for a moment. She teased me about leaving me behind to see the pearly gates of heaven. We laughed a little although in the back of my mind, I still had a fear circling. She spoke to me about being able to be a fantastic grandmother to Austin. As I was leaving, I asked her to be in the same mood that she's in when I returned the next day. I decided that I would visit her on my lunch hour rather than seeing her first thing in the morning. I felt that seeing she looked so well yesterday that the probability of her being ill again was slim. I walked into her room and saw a woman completely different from the one I saw the day before. Her face had the look of a person that had already given up. Her eyes were red and so sad looking. I attempted to give her a hug, and I had to quickly release her. She said that she had another attack late last night and that this one wasn't very good. Looking at her lying in her bed so motionless, broke my heart into many pieces. She began to speak to me, as if she knew that she wasn't going to be around for long.

As we spoke about not giving up and being strong and believing in God, she looked at me and said, "God never gives you more than you can bear." After saying that, she said to me, she believed her time had come. Regardless of what she said to me, as the tears ran down the side of her cheeks, all I knew was that she was going to be around long enough to have the operation. She asked me to come a bit closer so that she could talk to me. She asked me to be the best man that I could be without selling my morals short. She wanted to know that I'd do my best to forget whatever happened in my life with regards to my dad. She told me that it's impossible to love a child as much as she had, but she loved me more than words can explain. My mother explained to me, I was the one that kept her smiling each and every day and that if it wasn't for me, she didn't think she would have been able to make it all those years. I had to stop her as she spoke to me and make her aware that she hadn't left this world, and I intended to see her tomorrow and the day after that and so on.

I knew that she had come to the fork in the road when she asked me to ask the nurse for her belongings. Inside her bag were her bankbook and other important belongings. She asked me to take her bankbook to her bank and withdraw all her funds and to use it to assist my sister with. She wanted me to promise to be in my sister's life and to never abandon her. She asked me to beware of my father and to do my best to never disrespect him or to lay my hands on him. I promised her everything that she asked for. Before I left the hospital to continue my job, I reached over and gave her a kiss and a hug that was as gentle as possible not to cause her any extra discomfort. I looked at her in her eyes and told her, that no matter what happened to her, I'd never ever forget her as long as I lived.

That evening after work, I decided to go directly home, due to how mentally and physically tired I was feeling and after seeing my mother in the condition that she was in, had drained me of all my hope and spirit.

For the first time, I felt as if she wasn't going to make

it. My heart felt as if it was on fire and my brain felt as if I had a six-hour exam for a job that meant everything to me. My mother meant everything to me, and this time, there was no one to correct my papers. I knew that if God truly wanted her to be a part of the world that we lived in, he would have her stay. I got home to see a beautiful little boy with big brown eyes all happy to see me and on this particular day, I knew that this was what I needed to bring a sense of balance back to my life.

Esther had prepared a meal for me to eat, but my appetite had left me after seeing my mother. I lay on bed with just my pajama pant on and stared at the ceiling wondering to myself, what I'd do without my mother. Esther closed the door and had decided to distract me by making love to me. As much as I enjoyed our moment together, at the back of my mind, I felt a burning sensation. I sat at the edge of the bed and prayed that the phone wouldn't ring until after we had finished making love.

As we were enjoying a quiet moment with each other, the phone rang. The look that came over both of our faces had that feeling of anxiety. It was almost like being in a movie when neither person knew if they should pick the receiver up to speak to the officer. We had no reason to be afraid, so why were we behaving like that, we had no idea. Esther answered the phone and handed the phone to me in a hesitated motion. I answered with my heart beating like a gazelle being chased by a Cheater in the Safari.

The doctor said to me, "Mr. Knights your mother has had another attack, and at the moment she isn't waking up." He instructed me to attend the hospital as soon as possible and to alert her brothers and sisters. I felt as if I had been given a drug that prevented me from moving, but still capable of feeling all the pain being inflicted upon me. I had my ex-wife contact all of my mother's siblings and inform them of what had happened. I arrived at the hospital and met with the doctor in charge, and he explained to me what had happened.

After all the general formalities were over, the only thing I wanted to know was whether she was going to live or not. He explained to me that the likely hood of her regaining any consciousness was extremely low. He told me that my mother's brain had died and there was nothing that they could have done or at that present moment do. He said that we could leave her on the life support machine for a few days and see what might happen. He explained to me and my mother's family that if we were to leave her on the machine for any extended length of time, the possibility was that she could live without the machine once it was removed. However, her brain would still be dead but her heart will be the only thing living. I had a difficult decision of deciding on the fate of my mother. I visited my mother in the room where they were monitoring her around the clock by a registered nurse. Her eyes were covered with bandages to prevent them from protruding through her head. Her ears were filled with cotton and bandages to stop the flow of blood from soiling her clothes. She had no movement in her hands as I tried my best to get some kind of response. Her mouth had a tube that ran with some type of fluid to keep her from probably feeling any unnecessary pain. I sat with my mother for at least an hour praying that she might hear me and show some sign of overcoming her situation. My eyes were filled with water that probably could have filled a small bucket. I had never begged anyone so much in my life to do whatever they could to bring her back to me. The anger that was inside of me was more than a lion in a fight for his life. I started to point the blame toward my father and confirming that everything that had happened to her was as a result of his abusive ways towards her. The nurse became concerned for me because of my behavior towards my mother. I shook my mother a few times out of anger, feeling that she would leave me too soon. Her hands were warm and soft, just the way I remembered it. I placed my hand inside of her hand hoping that just maybe she might feel my pulse and my pain as I spoke to her.

The nurse gently placed her hands on my shoulder and suggested that I left for a while to give some of my mother's brothers and sisters an opportunity to be with her. As I stood in the hallway I couldn't understand how quickly words travel. Within that short period of time at the hospital, so many of my mother's colleagues and friends had gotten word and appeared. I always felt that she was a supernatural woman, but I didn't know how much. It seemed as if the entire world loved her.

Her smile and laughter were infectious and regardless of the day that you were having, she always found a way to brighten it. Some of my mother's siblings were divided when it came to removing her from the life supporter. I felt some hostility in the air if I were to remove her from the machine. I had no idea of what to do. All I thought of was if my father was a good man and a husband, he would have been here as we spoke, to comfort her. My father was on a camping trip somewhere up north with his wife. I couldn't believe that although he knew that she had been admitted to the hospital for testing and observation, he still had the heart to go fishing and camping.

After he returned from his trip, he visited with Maureen only to be told that his true love was probably going to pass away. Hearing this news, I received a phone call from him that night wanting to know if what my sister had told him was true. I had been asked to try and stay out of any argument or resentments with my father. So I told him that it was true, and that I'd been charged with the decision of either removing her from the life support or granting her a chance of having a miracle by staying on the machine. He suggested that if I valued his opinion, then I'd release her from her pain. She was already gone and mentally she's not with us anymore, so in his opinion, being the person that we all knew her to be, she probably wouldn't want to live like that anyway. I told him that night that I did have a lot to think of, and I must involve the remainder of my mother's family before I made my decision.

For the next few days it was extremely difficult for me to work. I felt as if I was having a mental breakdown.

Life wasn't the same for me anymore. The sun never shined the way it used to. I had nowhere to go for my morning breakfast while I was at work. I began to think to myself that my mother was going to die, and my sister acted as if she's almost dead. I felt as if I had no reason at all to continue to live. Many times at night I would get up and stare at my ex-wife for a while. After a while, I'd walk into Austin's room and lie beside him and think and cry. My entire world had come to an end.

After a week without sleep and very little to eat, I decided to call the family together to have a final meeting. I spoke to the doctor first before making my decision to make sure that there was absolutely no chance of saving her before

I make my decision. I needed to know that I was making the right decision, and I wouldn't be looked at like a murderer. I already felt as if I was taking my mother's life, and I hoped and prayed that the remainder of the family would be supportive.

We met on a Tuesday night at my home, and I allowed everyone to make their plea with an open mind. I decided that I'd forgo whatever decision I had made and go along with the majority. We had to agree that once we had a majority, I would not be accountable for requesting that the doctor remove her from the life support. We went around the room asking only to answer by saying "yes" or "no." The majority was in support of having her removed from the life support machine. I concurred with them, but made it known that this was still something that I was still not comfortable with. The following morning I attended the hospital with my ex-wife while her parents babysat Austin. I spent a half an hour with her, and tried my best to explain my reason for doing so. I felt in my heart that somewhere in her, she had the ability to hear me, but didn't have the ability to show it. As I cried my soul out to her, I asked her to forgive me for whatever problems I had caused her. I asked her to remember all the funny moments we shared, and that she always called me her protector. I recommitted to all of her wishes and assured her that as long as I lived, I'd do my best to fulfill them. My mother always said to me if for whatever the reason that my marriage didn't work, she wished I found someone who would truly look out for me. She wanted me to be with a woman that was caring, homely, and that had strong feelings for keeping a family together. She knew that Esther and I were having problems, and that her family never liked me, so she wished that I'd meet someone that was strong enough to love me without worrying about her relatives. I explained to her that the doctor felt that by keeping her on the machine it only enhanced her chances of staying alive eventually without the assistance of the ventilator. Once we removed her from the machine she'd continue to breathe on her own, but she'd have no bodily functions. I tried to get as close as possible to her as I told her my intention. I looked at her with every ounce of strength in me and told her that I intended on removing her from the life support machine. I decided it would be the right thing to do, and we all thought collectively that she wouldn't want to be remembered like this. I asked her to forgive me once more and I walked out of the room. I stopped and asked that she pleaded with God to forgive me for taking her life. As I stood there, I felt as if I was about to walk into the sunset and never return. I told her that I wouldn't be able to sit with her after they'd removed her from the ventilator because I didn't think I would like to have that vision in my mind of seeing her leave us that way.

As I walked towards the door, I stopped and looked over my shoulder and told her thanks for being my mother. The doctor asked if I was sure that I didn't want to be there with her as she leaved us. He suggested that it should take about two to three hours before she passed, and once she had passed, he'd inform me. The drive from the hospital seemed like forever. My thoughts were strictly on her and the times that we shared together. I had never felt that empty inside as I did on that day.

My stomach felt as if it had been suctioned out. I walked into the house and went directly to my room and began to cry all over again. Suddenly, the phone rang, and it was the doctor informing me that she had indeed passed away. The task of preparing for her funeral was like me walking to the death chamber. I hadn't heard of a person welcoming their time of passing from this world. So knowing that I had to walk into a funeral home and discuss particulars about burying my mother in a casket wasn't about to happen.

I placed the unpleasant task of choosing a casket and all the other uneventful moments in my Uncle Fitzroy and Uncle Walter's hands. After walking inside of the room where the director showed us caskets like he was showing us cars, I decided to walk out. I chose a burial spot that was close to the road as possible so that in the event Maureen wanted to visit her mother she would have no difficulty in doing so. Everything was a go and the hours of visitation were arranged and the date and time of the funeral was arranged and provided to family and friends.

As the guests paid their respect to my mother, I saw the pain on their faces and the love and respect they held for my mother. I stood beside my mother many times during the course of the night, and at times I thought I had seen her breathe. I knew most of the people that saw my reaction believed that it was my mind playing tricks on me. However, being in the frame of mind that I was in, I believed that there was a sign of my mother showing her presence to me. On the last night of visitation after all the guests had left, the immediate family held a short sermon for my mother. My Uncle Fitzroy and my Aunt Winifred led us in prayer and reminisced on the glorious days we shared with my mother. They prayed that God would bless her and take her under His arms and have her watch over the remainder of us. The moment for me to speak was not at the funeral home; I reserved my words for the day of the funeral. That night I slept very little as I tried to imagine what the next day was going to be like. All I saw in my mind was a bunch of flowers and a sea of people with tears in their eyes. We arrived at the church only to be greeted by hundreds of people already seated and standing along the sides of the church walls. My heart was inside of my throat as I walked into the church to see how well the church was decorated. The time had come for us to proceed with the ceremony. I assisted in carrying my mother on that day because it was the last time I would have an opportunity to hold her.

As I walked pass the pews, it was visible to me the love that her fellow human beings felt for her. We placed the casket at the front of the church, and had it open one last time so that the people could say their last goodbyes after the sermon. Our pastor had known my mother for many years and felt that this was a sad lost to our community. He explained that he felt sad for everyone that lost a love one. However, losing my mother wasn't just a loss to him, but she was a loss to humanity. He saw her as an inspiration to others, a woman that carried the fire of Jesus Christ inside of her at all times. She glowed whenever you saw her, and regardless of your ways, she had a way of making you feel like changing. She was a mother, a wife, a leader, and most of all a true friend to every one of us. He reminded us of how fearless she was to those who confronted her. He took our memory back to how many times anyone of us thought that we could get away with talking down to her, or even raising our voices, how she would quickly put us in our place.

"Doreen our Angel," he said as he paused and wept, "Jesus has sent you from heaven to inspire us and to share your life with us, making all those that have come to know you happy. Thank you for your short visit, as Jesus felt that you'd done what you were asked to do. Jesus has asked for you to return home, so we look forward to seeing you in the near future, and we know that although you're not here in flesh, that you'll never leave us." The pastor asked for those that would like to speak about their memory with Doreen and opened up the congregation for a few minutes. Everyone who walked up to the microphone to speak said almost the same thing about our beloved mother. She was an angel sent by God to live among us for a short time to love, laugh and teach us. The moment that I feared was upon me. I was asked to speak on behalf of the kids. I looked at everyone standing, sitting and even kneeling and broke down and cried. As I composed myself, I thanked them for sharing their love and kindness with my mother. I recognized what a great life my mother lived and only wished that I could fulfill her footsteps that she left behind. I wanted them to know that my mother wasn't just a mother to me. She was a great friend and a person that I could share whatever was on my mind with. She was my protector from the day I migrated to this country. Many people didn't know how powerful she really was, until they heard her speak. Her mouth was as deadly as a man with a sword. No one could touch her children or act, as if we weren't good enough. Now that she's gone, I didn't know what I'd do without her in the short time I have left on this earth.

I walked towards the coffin and thanked her for being the queen in my life and fell on the casket wishing that she wouldn't leave. My uncle Fitzroy assisted me back to my seat and returned the microphone to the pastor for his closing hymn. Before we sang, he gave everyone the last opportunity to say their good bye to her before closing the casket. My aunty Merle couldn't control her emotion. Her sister Monica and Annacita were torn up inside to where they had difficulty standing. I knew that my aunt Monica would have a hard time understanding why God had to take their favorite sister away from them. Aunty Winifred tried her best to be the pillar for the girls but, even with all the composure she showed, she eventually fell apart. The pastor asked for us to stand and to sing our hearts out, as we sang one of her favorite songs for the last time. "Rock of Ages" brought every person to their knees as we walked slowly through the isle towards the front door. I felt as if we were held captive, and we would never see some of our love ones again. The church was so noisy, that it was extremely difficult to hear the song. As I approached the Hearse, we stopped for the honor guard to salute my mother before she was placed into the hearse.

Everyone had released their hands from the casket as it was on the trolley ready to be pushed into the hearse. I couldn't bear the thought that this was going to be the last time I see her, physically, again. I didn't realize that the entire time while I was sobbing over my mother, the police honor guard was still standing at attention. The funeral director placed her into the hearse once I had removed myself from the casket. I pulled myself together and looked around and saw the sea of people that had turned out to pay their final respect to my mother, and it had me completely numb.

There were six police cruisers and four police motorcycles to escort us to the cemetery. The people lined the sidewalk three deep and for at least two blocks. As we drove by, they threw flowers and roses at the Hearse. My heart was barely beating, and my hands were shaking as if I were suffering with Parkinson's. The drive to the cemetery was slower than I thought, or was it because my thoughts were elsewhere. My sister decided that she didn't want to leave the car to see our mother be placed to rest. I had no idea how the conversation of my father attending the cemetery became a discussion.

My uncle Winston and my uncle Thomas were on the lookout for my father. They felt that if he were to attend the burial that this would be a lack of respect to them. I assured them that Esther had mention to him not to attend the funeral because there's a possibility of being attacked. The cemetery had very little standing room where my mother was being placed to rest.

As the preacher preached, I had this overwhelming desire to throw myself into the hole with my mother. As the forklift threw the sand into the hole to cover the casket, I decided that I should keep my mother company. I didn't care to be on this earth any longer without her. My clothes were soiled with mud and debris from the ground, and I pushed my way toward being in the hole. Being exhausted, I fell on my friend's shoulder and just growled as the hole was being filled with dirt.

We departed from the gravesite, and everyone made their way back to their vehicles. As the Limousine made its way towards our home, I looked out the window and felt as if my mother was smiling at me. Knowing my mother, I was sure she was saying to herself, "Boy, you really gave your queen a going away gift, didn't you." For a brief second, I actually smiled as I thought of how she would react. I guessed the drive brought me some comfort as I had a moment to reflect by myself on our times together.

We gathered at my house and had eats and drinks and discussed how the day went. Everyone was in a somber mood, but at the same time they smiled because of the great memories. As the guest left, we were now left with family members only. Their focus turned to me and me only. They were fearful, of how I intended to move forward. I knew that I would have to find the strength from somewhere, but I also knew that I required some time and patience. My Aunt Monica and Aunt Winifred checked up on me, as if I were on parole.

My days at work were extremely difficult because I was so used to seeing her during the day. I spent most of my days at the cemetery sitting and talking with her. Very little work was completed on a daily basis. After a period of time, I was called in to speak with my sergeant. He explained to me how sensitive he was to the loss of my mother. However, he felt that I had to make an effort to move on because I would stand the chance of losing everything that I worked for. It didn't take much for me to read between the lines. I totally understood where he was coming from and made a valiant effort to try and remember her, but to give her time to rest. I made a decision that I'd visit with her only on these special days. I'd pay my respect on every birthday, Easter, and Christmas. These days are dedicated to her and the memory of all the good times we shared as a family.

After a year had passed, a stone was ordered and nicely worded and placed at the top of her grave. I thanked all of my aunts and uncles for their generosity in purchasing the head stone in remembrance of my mother and their sister. I knew that as she looked down from wherever she was, she's certainly proud and touched with the warmth from her siblings.

Chapter 5

As time moved ahead, I found myself moving along with it. I knew that I would have to live because that was what my mother would have wanted for me. I did my best to get my life back in order, and as every day passed, it got a little bit easier. There wasn't a day that passed by, I didn't think of her and I knew that by holding on to her memories, I would feel as if she were here still with me.

My family took whatever clothing and jewelry they wanted as in memory towards her. All I wanted was her bracelets that she insisted I had, so that I'd give to the woman of my dreams. Weekends were beginning to fall back into place as I began visiting with Esther's parents again.

We had stayed away for some time so that I could heal myself. I appreciated the patience that my ex-wife had with me, in giving me that opportunity to grieve. I didn't mind visiting with my in-laws, but I found it very uncomfortable whenever her brother visited. Her father enjoyed whenever Esther came over, it was almost as if he felt rejuvenated all over again. For me, seeing the mother was too much on my eyes. I always felt that whenever she looked at me, she felt like killing me. Every time we visited her parents, and her brother attended, as soon as he saw us, he would slam the door and leave. This kind of behavior really annoyed her father. They would try their best to brush it away, but it continued to happen even more as time passed. There were times when he would come to the house and try to tell his children to stay away from Austin. The kids were in love with Austin, and they enjoyed playing with him. I knew the mother understood how her son felt, but had to act as if she felt bad as a result of his behavior. Austin had sensed her displeasure of having me as a son-in-law.

One afternoon we dropped in for an unexpected visit. The grandfather was extremely happy to see Austin. Every time he saw him he would place him on his lap and tell him stories about his past as a child growing up. Esther, her father and myself would sit at the kitchen table while the grandmother prepared something for everyone to eat. My back was turned to the grandmother on this particular day. Austin sat at the far end of the table and had a plain view of everyone at the table.

As he sat playing with his toys, and coloring his cartoon book, he was observant of something that confused him and had explained to us what he had seen. After we arrived home and Esther had prepared him for bed, he explained to his mother, that while we were at her parents, the grandmother would stare at me with an evil look. He went on to explain that whenever I turned around, she would have a happy smile on her face, but as soon as I would turn my back on her, she would look at me with evil eyes again. Esther refused to believe him and said that both of her parents liked me, and it was possible that I was seeing her mother with her usual serious face. Austin was the apple of Esther's parents' eye. We started to travel to Florida to visit them around the Christmas holidays. We spent Christmas with my family, and then we would travel to Florida for the remainder of the holiday season. Their condominium was located in Hollywood Beach area. The building was primarily Jews.

There were no blacks in the building, not even a worker. Staying at the building was extremely boring and some of the folks were unsociable and unpleasant to be around. I spent some of my time working out in the gym when I wasn't playing with Austin. On one occasion while I was working out, an elderly Jewish woman was extremely insulting to me. She asked me if I had realized that there were no blacks in the building and that the equipment was only for the tenants. I felt her statement to be completely out of line and racist. I walked on over to her and pointed out to her that it wouldn't be wise to lie in the sun, because the sun tends to darken your skin. I asked her if she would be happy with, having dark skin. After educating her on what the sun could do to her, I focused on the real truth of the matter. I made her aware of why her body looked like a prune and not as healthy as mine. I referenced again to the sun and the underlining reason for lying in the sun. Before walking away, I asked if she was willing to become black, seeing that she's already half way there. I was confident as I walked away, that every time she looked at herself in a mirror she would feel really disgusted of herself.

My initial intention was to take off to an area where only black people resided and have them do to her as they wished. If she was to attempt this type of attitude in the West Indies, I was confident that she wouldn't have an opportunity to talk about it ever. At the dinner table that night, I mentioned what had happened to me in the weight room with one of the tenants. Esther's father assured me that he was going to have a word with her when he saw her next morning. I wanted to have my way with her on my own, but I guessed I would have to answer to the law for my action. However, answering to the law would be much easier than having to answer to God at the end of my life. After that experience, I spent most of my time near the pool relaxing or playing with Austin. We spent a fair amount of our time on the beach and enjoying the boardwalks.

Esther had moved out of her parents home, lived on her own, got married and gave birth to a beautiful child. With all that she had already accomplished, she still found it difficult to stand up to her father. I was not sure if it's because she knew that her brother wasn't from both parents, and that she was the only biological child from both parents, so she didn't want to ruffle any feathers and not be in control of her father's inheritance.

We were back at home where I felt at peace and loved by those around me. Esther continued to be a stay at home mother and did her best in tutoring Austin. Spring had arrived and her parents were on their way back from Florida. The weather was changing quickly, and Austin was growing just as fast. Esther's parents had taken a trip to visit with one of their family members. We decided to have a barbecue and invited a few of our friends. We arrived at the house a bit early so that we could prepare ahead of time for our guest. When we arrived, we observed Esther's brother's car in the drive way. Amos had invited one of his friends over to the house to enjoy a day by the pool. I believed he did it purposely because he knew that we were going to have some sort of entertainment at the house on that Sunday. Esther approached her brother and told him that we were here to have a barbecue with some of our friends. He said that he's also here to enjoy the weather and the pool with his friend. Esther told him that it's alright, and that he should feel free to join our conversation when all of our friends arrived. The thought of having to share the pool with black people repulsed him. Austin had changed and jumped into the pool to swim and play with his cousins. Austin was right in front of the diving board while his younger cousin was waiting to dive of the diving board as well. Abel turned to his daughter and suggested, "If he doesn't move, then jump on his back." Immediately, I said to Esther, "If your brother's child were to jump on Austin back and injured him, she can rest assured that I'll be doing my own damage control." Personally, I wanted him to do something wrong, so I could have bitten him like a lion. The taste of blood was in my mouth, and my mouth was watering for his limbs. Esther told Abel that once their father returned, she'd talk to him about his behavior. Once Abel saw that the guests were beginning to arrive, he started to pack his belongings and left with his family and friend. Once Abel left, the afternoon was a success. We had lots to eat, and we spent some of the time in the pool playing. Esther paraded around with her skimpy bathing suit, forcing her friend to change into her own skimpy bathing suit. The afternoon was well spent with some great friends and a wonderful family.

Every night we would read to Austin and I'd play one game of Nintendo with him before his bedtime. Austin would lie on our bed for a little while, before going to bed. Once in his bed he always asked for a back rub before falling asleep. For some reason, he enjoyed a back rub to help him to fall asleep. I gave him a tight squeeze and a kiss and told him that I loved him as I left the room. Esther, on the other hand, went in shortly after me and hugged him and said good night to him and left the room.

After listening to the way that she said her goodnight to her son, I had to talk to her about it. I asked why did she just hug and kiss him, and I hadn't heard you say, "I love you" to your son. She went on to explain that her parents never said that to her. I suggested her to go back to his room and tell him you love him. She agreed and walked into Austin's room and told him so.

Austin didn't even move his head, but he said to her in a quiet voice that the only reason she's saying it, was because daddy had asked her to. She was shocked that he had said so, and couldn't understand how he knew that. As she walked out of his room, he told her to close the door, because he could hear everything we said. After Esther returned, I asked her to be the one that broke the link from the chain.

Showing love to your son would fill her with joy, and the blessings would appear in various forms. From that night forward, Esther never missed an opportunity to tell Austin how much she loved him. I believe regardless of how you've been treated, you have to use those bad memories as an engine to move forward so that you can break the link in the chain.

Esther and I had a discussion one night with regard to her future. I suggested that she applied to a university so that she could prepare herself for her future endeavors. She agreed that she should look into subjects that she should take to prepare for her future. That week, she went out and registered for university classes and was accepted for the spring semester. I decided that once Esther was finished with her schooling, I would pursue a career as a Massage Therapist. In the interim, I attended night school and studied Paralegal. I enjoyed the law end of society and how it related to our functioning in our society. Esther had agreed that when she graduated from school and found a job that I would have an opportunity to fulfill my dream. She explained to her parents that she intended to go back to school and get herself a degree. Her father was always for higher education, so I knew that he would have no problem with that. I thought she might have mentioned to them that I had encouraged her to return to school but at no time did she mention my name. I felt a little disappointed that she never mentioned my name because I truly wanted them to see that I had their daughter's best interest at heart. Esther was having some difficulty handling university and caring for Austin. I did my best to remove whatever distractions she may have had. Her temperament began to change little by little. She started to make me feel as if I was distracting her by wishing to spend some time with her. At one time she said that she believed that I was jealous of her because she was improving herself. I had to remind her that I was the one that initiated the idea for her to return to school. We argued a fair amount, but it always seemed to me that she wanted to argue so that she would have a reason to complain.

Austin was now in school and attending the Montessori System. We wanted to give him the best opportunity possible in life. Originally, when we got married, Esther spoke of having at least two or three children. Now that Austin was five I felt that this might be the right time to have another child. Esther was extremely evasive with the idea. Her attitude puzzled me because this was something we

194

had discussed. I knew that something was wrong, but I couldn't put my finger on it. The Montessori school system was ideal for Austin. I believed that by him attending a private school, it would eliminate all the nonsense that happened in the public schools. He wore a uniform and he had an advantage over the public school system, which was that all the children were dressed alike, and no one needed to be jealous of the other. Each class was equipped with two teachers per classroom. I found this to be remarkable. It was almost like having a tutor to assist you when required.

One day I did have an incident that I had to address. Austin had arrived home with a black eye. He told us that there was a child in his class that continuously bothered him. He explained that during class time, the child was bothering him and calling him names and stuck him in his eye with a pencil. I found this type of behavior to be intolerable and with the world as it was, I wasn't about to sit back and do nothing. I took Austin to school the following day and asked him to point out the child to me. I asked the child to step outside the classroom so that I may have a word with him. I took the child by the back of his neck and showed him how it felt to be bullied. The child was scared out of his pants and stood still while crying. I told him to never touch Austin again, as long as he's in this school. I suggested that he informed of this incident to his parents, and to make them aware that I was willing to approach them on the matter also. I showed the child my fist and asked him to tell his father that if he was upset, to have the principal give me a call, and I'd be more than happy to address his concern.

After that day Austin never had a problem again in the school with any of the children. I believed that sometimes we couldn't wait for the justice department to decide for us; we had to deal with it ourselves. The majority of people in our society have absolutely no faith in the justice system, so I decided that I'd deal with the matter in my own way. Regardless of whatever happened after, I knew that no one would attempt to place their hands on Austin ever again, so I was prepared for anything.

Austin had developed a plethora of friends, so on his birthday, we invited almost his entire classroom to his birthday party. Imagine having at least twenty of his classmates along with their families and Esther's and my family. At any given birthday he would have at least seventy to eighty people enjoying themselves at his birthday.

One Christmas while on our way to Florida, I had an idea that I hoped Esther would be in favor of. I proposed to her that she major in Law and stayed a little longer to get her masters. I felt by studying Law, it would give her a great profession once out of school. Besides, she argued over everything with me, so this would assist her in arguing properly. At first she felt that it would have been sufficient with just graduating from a university. I explained to her that what good would it be to finish school and still don't have an idea of what you wanted to do for a living. I left her with the idea while I played checkers with Austin. I told her that she had to give me an answer before we got to her parents' home in Florida. I pressured her because I knew if I hadn't, that once she was finished with school, she would have been upset with not finding something that she might enjoy. Besides from the first time I met her, she always wondered if she had it in her to be a lawyer. The plane landed and she still hadn't given me an answer. While we were standing at the baggage area, she approached me with a kiss on my lips and told me, "Yes." She said that she really appreciated everything that I'd done for her, since we'd been together. She said that I got her back into a relationship with her parents, and now I was allowing her to pursue her career. Her parents were standing outside of the terminal with a huge smile. Once in the car she mentioned to her parents that she had something important to discuss with them. Right away her father said "then let's go out for dinner tonight, and we can discuss it there." Esther opened up the subject by saying how happy she felt. She wanted them to know that she's planning on studying a little longer, so that she could pursue a career in Law. Her parents were overwhelmed with joy. Right away he started to discuss what he's willing to do for her. As usual, I felt as if I had nothing to do with her life. Their focus was only on Esther that evening and very little was said about me.

At the end of the night, he turned to me and said you know you'll have to support her and give her time to study." I couldn't believe my ears, as Esther sat there with a smile on her face and didn't have the tits to stand up to them and defend me. Not once did she come to my defense and acknowledge that the idea of returning to school was mine. The entire time we were in Florida, I felt so rejected. I felt almost as if I was invisible in her life. It was almost as if every creative idea I had come to her with, was given while she was asleep. She made it seem as if she woke up one morning after being spoken to in her dream and decided that this was the path that she had to take.

We traveled to Orlando for three days. Austin had a great time in one of the theme parks, and at times had us all falling on the floor with his humor. I realized that I needed that time away from her parents, so that I could find a way to relax. We returned from Orlando and had one more night at their condo before we departed to Toronto. That night as we were lying in bed after we spent some time with Austin before he went to bed, we decided to have a conversation about our relationship. While we were talking about our relationship, we heard some noises coming from her parent's room. We paused for a second to listen to what it might be. I couldn't believe my ear. Her parents were getting their private moment. The old bag still had it in her. I couldn't help myself but to laugh when I heard her enjoying intimacy with her husband. As they were together, silence was broken with their passionate sounds. Esther and I tried our best not to listen, but it was too distracting not to laugh.

I'm guessing that because of her parents' behavior, Esther became aroused and wanted to intimate with me as well. I had no problems in having intimacy with my wife. She asked if I could get up and close our room door so that her parents wouldn't hear her. As I approached the door to close it, I could not avoid seeing her mom completely naked. I couldn't believe that we were standing face to face as she stood there exposed. Her mother had the look on her face, as if she was spotted by the police breaking into someone's home with bright lights on her face. We paused for a few seconds, and I smiled and made my way back to the bed. I mentioned to Esther what had just happened and she started to laugh also. What a sense of humor we both had. She asked that I didn't say anything in the morning at the breakfast table. "Of course not" I said.

Esther pulled me into her and ordered me to make her speak in her native language. We fought like two lions trying to place ownership on their territory. We all knew that there could be only one leader, and it was going to be me. She gave me a hug and said, "Do you think my mother made more noise than me and started to laugh" That morning at the breakfast table, I tried my best not to make any eye contact with her mother. Esther could see that I was about to crack at the scene, but I held it together. Her mother looked at me briefly, as if she was wondering, how much I really saw. Neither of us said anything about it, so I left it alone. In a way, I was happy with what had happened, because it gave her something to think about. If she was to ever say anything about what had happened, I would have advised her to make sure that her door is securely shut.

Esther and I were growing apart from one another, and I couldn't do anything about it. I knew that I loved her, but I didn't appreciate the way she dealt with her parents concerning me. After a while, I began to shut down and my patience for her grew thin. I took a disliking to almost anything she did. Buying gym wear to workout in became an issue for me. I could recall watching her in the washroom as she attempted to cut her own hair. She asked for my assistance and out of anger I asked her if she wanted to look like a lesbian. That comment really played on her emotion, and I believed that was the beginning of the end. We spent less and less time doing anything together. I started to stay away from her parent's home and always had an excuse for not attending.

I had a family membership at the Y.M.C.A for all of us. I spent a lot of my time at the gym playing squash and working out. On one occasion, I could recall playing squash with a few people and having them rotate in taking turns to play with me. Esther saw this and wanted to have a game with me, and I acted as if she wasn't even there. At the time I didn't care, but as I played the game I looked back to where she was sitting and saw the look on her face. I knew that I had hurt her badly, and I knew that what I had done was wrong, so I walked off the court and asked her to forgive me.

She had tears in her eyes, so I reached over and hugged her and asked her if she would like to have a chance to beat me. Those simple words made the biggest difference that day in my life. I realized that the best way to catch a bee is with honey and not with vinegar. Esther was the type of person that thrived on mushiness. There was a time in our relationship when we pampered each other with affection, however; due to my insecurities, I destroyed it and probably our relationship.

Esther had approached me on numerous occasions and asked if we could visit a relationship doctor, but being angry and macho I always declined. As our relationship sunk more and more to the bottom, Esther took it upon herself to seek therapy. While I was destroying myself and becoming angrier and angrier, she was developing her personal life. I didn't realize what was happening until it was much too late.

One day I asked Esther to follow me to the mechanic so that I could have my car repaired. Once there, the mechanic took a look at the car and was able to fix the problem while I waited. Esther and Austin decided to wait around to keep me company while my car was being repaired. On our way home, we decided to take the city route home. As I traveled along side of Esther, I observed that Austin was crying. I had no idea what had happened in that short space of time. After we arrived home, I asked her why Austin was crying. She said it was about him wanting to play without taking the time to do his reading. I believed what she said and carried on without making any fuss.

That night, we got into an argument about her spending habits. She felt that she had a right to purchase whatever she wanted, regardless if she was working or not. Without hesitation, I commented on her parents' assistance, as they had done it in the past. That comment showed vexation and a real picture of resentfulness.

The following morning, I had intentions on playing golf with my friend, however, the day was overcast and the feeling for golf wasn't in my system any more. Esther was sitting on the couch reading to Austin. Austin had a look on his face that I couldn't figure out. I looked over at Esther and for a moment I wanted to walk over her and tell her what I was feeling. I wanted to ask her if she still loved me, but I was afraid of what the answer might be. I changed my mind and left with my friend to play golf. The entire time while we were out playing, the only thing that was on my mind was being with my family. I couldn't concentrate, and the rain was falling quite heavily. At the end of the ninth hole I suggested that we stop, because there was a chance that we could be electrocuted. Thankfully, he agreed, so we headed on our way home. I walked into the house and realized that no one was at home. I remembered that Esther's niece was celebrating her birthday at her parents' home. On the other end of the spectrum, my cousin was also having her wedding shower at my uncle's home. Esther had two engagements to attend, but I had no idea which one she was planning on attending first.

The house was quiet and it gave me the opportunity to reflect on when we first met. I never believed in divorce, and I never wanted to follow the path that my father took. Just as I was beginning to relax, the doorbell rang. My Uncle Fitzroy and Uncle Walter had come to pay me a visit. Seeing them at the door sparked my interest on what reason would they have for being there. As we got over all the formalities, they began to tell me what Esther had told them. She made some strong remarks at my cousin's shower that left everyone upset. They suggested that I took a drive back to their home and try and patch things up with my wife. My thoughts were all over the place and not quite sure of what to expect. Unfortunately, when we arrived, Esther had already left, so I didn't get the opportunity to talk with her. I decided that I'd stand outside for a while before going into the house. Suddenly, the phone rang and it was for me. On the other end of the phone, it was Esther wishing to speak with me. I wanted to hear what she was going to say to me first, before I apologized to her, me still being stupid and a macho man. On that day, I felt as if the devil was in every move I made. I didn't give God a chance to intervene by releasing all my misdoings onto Him. Esther started the conversation off, by asking me to pick Austin up from his friend's place where she had left him. I asked why she couldn't pick him up, since she had brought him there. At that point was when my jaw fell to the ground so that I could catch my heart from hitting the ground. Esther said to me that the reason for not picking him up was because she had decided to end our marriage. My heart slowly stopped beating as I heard her say those words. In our entire relationship, we never ever mentioned the word breakup. I asked if she had realized what she had just said. She said she had thought about it for weeks, and she's never been as sure about anything in her life, as she was right now.

She suggested that I stayed away from her and not to attempt to come to her parent's home. I quickly informed my uncles of her behavior and asked if they were willing to accompanying me. We arrived and asked to speak with Esther. Her father went into her bedroom and asked if she was willing to speak with me. My head was on fire, and I was about to lose control. My uncle Fitzroy asked if Esther would be willing to speak with him as well. At this time, the father returned and said that Esther would be willing to talk with him meaning my Uncle Fitzroy. My Uncle Walter and I sat at the bottom of the stairs as Esther's father talked with my uncle. Uncle Fitzroy emerged from her room and said that Esther was now willing to speak with me. Esther had the look of distaste on her face as she looked at me. I couldn't believe that this was the same woman I gave my entire life to, and now she looked at me with venom in her eyes. She asked that we stood on either side of the bed for safety reasons. I wanted to know what she meant by safety reasons. I was not sure who was filling her head with all those thoughts, but I had to focus on the situation at hand, rather than arguing about her comment. More and more I felt like I was speaking with a stranger.

I couldn't bear the thought that I was about to lose everything that I had worked so hard for. The thought of having my family separated was a complete destruction to me. For the first time in my life, I begged Esther to stay and not to do what she was thinking about doing. I told her that we had a family to live for and to do whatever it took to maintain it from separating. She said that this was her family too; however, I left her with no other choice. I told her that there was always another choice, and this was not the path to take. Although I knew that I was feeling less than a man, I still continued to beg. I knew at that time that I had to and for the first time forget my macho side and fight to keep my family together. I guess my uncle could hear us talking and probably me crying. I told Esther that she meant everything to me, and that I didn't know what I was going to do without her.

After I was asked to leave her bedroom so that her and my uncle could talk, she emerged with my uncle and said that she was willing to come home tonight. She made it known that it didn't mean she had made her mind up to stay permanently, it only meant that it was a trial run for the next three weeks. At the end of the three weeks, she'd make her final decision. Her parents were furious and had the look of hate all over their faces. Her mother had tears in her eyes as Esther and my uncles were placing her clothes back into her car. Neither of her parents was pleased when she was leaving, and they couldn't bear to look at me. Her father had mentioned to my uncle Walter that he wasn't pleased with what had happened there tonight. I guessed he meant that his daughter should have never returned back home with me. Once at home my uncles assisted in placing her clothes back into her closet. After they left and we were all alone, I explained to Esther how sorry I was. She said nothing barely looking at me as I confessed my sorrow and love for her.

She suggested that the only way she would consider staying was if I decided to seek counseling. She admitted to me that, for the past couple of months she had been seeing a counselor. I agreed to seek help and asked if by doing this, she would be willing to make our relationship work. She insisted that the therapy was for me, and it was to make me a better person.

Every time I asked her to stay, I felt as if a big piece of myself worth had fallen off. I began to realize that she was enjoying seeing me beg, and she loved the power of being in control. I decided that I wasn't going to beg her anymore, but that didn't mean that I was about to give up either. I contacted my benefit department and had them suggest a counselor. I started meeting with the doctor and felt, for the first time, that I was not really at fault for what had happened between us.

Esther and I had planned a vacation getaway with a few of our friends a few months before she decided to leave. She felt that it was unnecessary to follow through with our plan. She felt right seeing that we were no longer together; she didn't want to give me any false hope, or to mislead our friends. I, in return, felt that it was the honorable thing to do, seeing that we had made a commitment and had already paid towards the trip. I realized, as time was against me, that she wasn't showing any faith in keeping our family together.

It truly amazed me how easy it was for her to destroy eighteen years of a relationship. We decided to go and hopefully by being away from any influence, she would be free to see the future clearly. I believed that whatever happened, God was with me, and if for whatever reason she decided to throw our relationship away, that God knew that my heart and soul were clear.

The first two days on the vacation were half decent. I found it remarkable that she had no reservation in making love to me. I didn't know what happened after the second day, but Esther became my worst nightmare. I felt as if I was in a nightmare and the demons were out to destroy me. Whatever I tried to do with her was dismissed without any cause. One afternoon, the other two couples were sitting in the living room, just chilling. They asked about Esther's whereabouts. I told them that she was being a little antisocial and probably didn't want to be anywhere close to me. I wanted to prove a point to them, so I told them that if she came down stairs, she'd probably lie on the floor rather than sit beside me; because I knew that she was out to hurt and embarrass me. One of my friends called out to her to have her come and join us. They couldn't believe how true I was and why would she want to embarrass me like that.

Esther and I might have gone on the trip together, but in reality, only her body was present. Her soul and energy were somewhere else rather than with me. The entire trip was stressful and agitating. I wanted the trip to come to an end so badly that at one time I almost felt like going out into the lake with a boat and not returning. Finally, the day of redemption was upon us all. I say "all" because I knew that our friends felt uncomfortable and extremely sad for me.

The drive from Huntsville usually takes about two or so hours, but for some reason I felt as if I was driving for about four hours. She sat in the car the entire trip and said absolutely nothing to me. Esther sat most of the time with her feet up on the dashboard with her other foot partially out of the window. I think she was trying her best to agitate me, because she had worn an extremely short pair of jeans that showed her private parts. Her legs were visibly open, so that the truck drivers would slow down enough to see within her legs. I had asked that she sit properly so that the vehicles wouldn't be peeping inside of the car. She said, "Don't you like hair down there?" She looked at me and said it's her body and not to touch her anymore and besides, she didn't see how this was going to work, when I continued to tell her what to do, she felt that she wanted to sit with her legs open and the truck drivers seeing her. At least some form of excitement had not gone to waste.

We arrived home in one piece without one of us strangling each other and being charged out of frustration. Austin was extremely happy to see us both. The first thing he asked his mother was if she had decided to stay together because she had promised him that she would consider it. She avoided his question and went about preparing his supper and work for the following day. This behavior upset Austin and caused him to shut down for a day or two.

One day while Austin and I were spending some father and son time together, he said to me he's sorry he didn't tell me that his mom was planning on leaving. I asked why he would say that. He said to me that his mother had ordered him to keep his mouth shut; otherwise she would have spanked him, and would stop buying any toys for him. For the life of me, I couldn't believe what I was hearing. He said to me, that the day I saw him crying in the car on our way home from the mechanic, was the day she threatened him. Austin would approach his mother daily to find out if she had decided to stay. Her answer was always the same: "If I decide to leave your father, it doesn't mean that I don't love you; it only means that I've fallen out of love with your father."

Esther began to wear some of the dresses that I had purchased for her to work, rather than wearing them when we went out. I found her action to be very disrespectful, and I refused to allow myself to become angry. Some of the dresses were meant to be worn at night with me and not to attract any unwanted attention. The dresses were partially seen through and a few inches above her knees. There were times when all she wore was her dress without any undergarment. Whenever I asked her about not wearing any underwear, her answer was always the same: She would look at me straight in my eye and say that she wore her clothing without any undergarments because she felt like being free. I realized that she was desperately trying to get me to lose my temper, so in return, I would say to her, "I hope whoever it is, he better know that I still see you naked every night."

I received a phone call one morning from a mutual friend. The person was calling to advise me that he had seen Esther on the subway, and that another gentleman was sitting with his arms around her. He also advised that they had gotten off the train, and the gentleman was carrying her attaché. I asked him if he was sure of this, and he proved it by telling me the color of the dress that she was wearing. He also inquired as to why I would allow her to wear such a dress to a professional place of business. I couldn't have placed a scale on how hurt and filled with anger from within, I felt. She arrived home later than her usual hours. After she changed and cleaned herself up, I asked if she would like something to eat. Without looking at me, she said, "Yes, but just a little."

While eating her food, I decided to have myself a beer. She asked if it would be alright to have a beer also. After she had finished eating, she began to drink her beer while sitting at the table with me. Neither of us was saying very much to each other. Suddenly, without notice she attacked me by sitting on my lap and started kissing me all over. I found this to be out of character for her, based only on the fact that she no longer wanted to make love to me or even look at me. She asked me to take her upstairs, where she stripped all of her clothing off. First she wanted to act out her fantasy. She asked me to lie back on the bed with my hands behind my head. She poured oil over my body and began sliding up and down on me as she kissed every part of my body. The understanding was that I wasn't allowed to touch her or kiss her; she wanted to be in control of her fantasy. After five minutes of stimulating me and driving me utterly insane, she turned around and started to kiss me on my neck, chest and private area.

Esther had played out her fantasy and had no energy left in her to even stand. She lay on the bed for at least an hour before having a shower and fidgeting from time to time. As we lay together on the bed, with perspiration dripping from the both of us, I had to ask her the question. I asked the reason for her doing all of this. She said that the beer got her aroused, and that she wanted to see if she felt anything for me. I couldn't believe that she had used me as a guinea pig. As we spoke more and more, I accused her of her feelings towards me due to the way she hugged and kissed me.

She suggested that, she did care about me, but she would rather have sex with me because she was already familiar with me. She went on to remind me about the difference between sex and lovemaking. She stated I'd always told her that we make love, so she wanted to show me that this time it was sex and not love making. Before I got of the bed, she turned to me and said, "Don't get used to it, because that was the last time that I would ever see or taste her again."

From that evening, I began to sleep in the basement to avoid any temptation or arguments. Although I was firm with the decision to sleep in the basement, she would find her way downstairs in bed beside me. I wasn't sure if she slept downstairs because of upstairs being warm and I didn't want to turn up the Air conditioner, or was she at war with her feelings. For the remainder of the time that we shared a bed, Esther never once tried again to make love to me.

One evening just before putting Austin to bed, Austin asked his mother if she could try and love his daddy again. He asked her to stay because he didn't want her to leave us like some of his friends' family did. He said that his friends were unhappy, and they never felt the same again. With all the begging and crying Esther still didn't listen to him. I could recall Austin holding onto her leg as she was walking and his nose would bleed and the tears would drop like rain from the sky.

One early Friday morning and bright, Esther approached me in the bedroom and told me that she had made her decision. She decided that she wanted to leave because she believed in the long run it would be better for Austin. I asked if she knew when she wanted to leave, and she said that same evening. She requested that we were not in the house while she's packing, because she didn't want to upset Austin. I agreed to her wishes and kept Austin with my Uncle Fitzroy until she was ready to say her goodbye to him. I couldn't believe that a woman, a mother would abandon her child and not attempt to resolve things. Later that evening she called and asked if it would be possible to bring Austin by to say goodbye. Austin was out of control, to the point where his nose began to bleed all over again. He started to stomp and pull on her clothing. I couldn't bear what I was seeing and tried one last time to convince her to stay. I became so frustrated, that I ended up smashing my head into the door, causing a gash over my eye. She walked into the garage, started her car up and drove off without looking back. She was gone and we were left all alone to lick our wounds. I knew that I had a long road ahead of me, and that it was going to be a tough one.

That evening Austin and I spent the night at our Uncle Fitzroy's home. We slept in a very small room together on a single bed. He held onto me the entire night as he cried himself to sleep. That night I believe my eyes must have closed for a short break only to moisten them with more tears. My entire body felt like it had left me and was in a very dark place that I was afraid to go. My heart was so broken that I felt as if I was going to die. The following morning we had breakfast with our uncle and his family and made our way over to the house after we were finished. As I walked around the house, it had a weird feeling, as if someone had died in it. My nerves were beginning to act up, and I felt as if I had no control over my life. I began seeing the psychiatrist on a more frequent basis. He told me that I was suffering from depression, and that I'd need to see a doctor also for clarity. For the next while I was encouraged to continue to see him, so that I could cope with whatever, she threw at me.

Esther was away from the house for at least two weeks and would call and accuse me of all kind of things. She believed that Austin's behaviour, not to see her was my fault, and that I was corrupting him against her. That was a blatant lie, because I always encouraged Austin to see his mother. He was hurt and I felt that she just didn't only leave me, but also left him as well. Austin was building a wall up around him, when it came to talking to him about his mother. One morning while Austin and I were sitting in the basement of Uncle Fitzroy's home, I was asked to answer the phone. On the other end of the phone was Esther. I couldn't believe that she was actually calling to speak with me. By the sound of my voice, it was obvious that I was happy to hear from her. She told me that she was calling to give me some good news. I assumed that she was calling to say that she had decided to come back. She said that she had moved back into the house; however, the bad news was that I was no longer welcome at home, because the locks had been changed. At first I thought that she was kidding. I had to ask her again to verify if she was indeed telling the truth. She told me that if I ever come around the house again, she would have no choice but to call the police. I hung up the phone and warned my family of what Esther had said to me.

My Uncle Fitzroy, Uncle Walter and my Aunty Winifred and Austin accompanied me to the house. We arrived at the house and rang the doorbell. We rang the doorbell a few times before anyone would approach the door. Esther and her father had come to the door to address the situation. He informed us that Esther has taken possession of the home until all the other formalities have been worked out. I disagreed, and told her that I had as much right to the home as she did until the home was sold. She suggested that we leave the property, or she'd have to call the police. I agreed that she would call the police to put an end to this nonsense. Within minutes a police officer attended the house. He had a discussion with Esther and her father and informed her that I had as much right to the property as she did, until the lawyers have settled. He made her aware that if I choose to smash the door down, there was nothing that either of them could do. Realizing that I wasn't in the mood to play games, he offered to return the keys back to me.

In the meantime, her father threatened me by letting me know about his intentions. He told me that he intended on breaking me, and that I'd only have until the end of August to be out of the home. He suggested that if I couldn't come up with Esther's share of the money, he'd make sure that I was out. He wanted to see me walk the streets like a "lost puppy," he said. He believed that I took advantage of his daughter, and that his daughter would never have married me if I wasn't so clever. He never did answer me when I asked him to answer what he meant by "clever."

I realized right then that this was going to be a David and Goliath fight. When we had purchased the house, although I was totally against it, Esther's father had made us sign a clause that said that, for whatever reason, if Esther and myself were to separate, the house would not be sold. At the time of signing, I didn't read over what I was signing because I had so much faith in my ex-wife. I never thought that she would trick me to take over our asset. I believed that this was a plot from the beginning to cover them so that I'd receive nothing in case we ever broke up. Esther had packed her car and was all ready to move out for the third time. She reversed out of the garage with a look of the devil on her face, as she pierced her eyes on me. In my entire time with her, I had never seen her look at me like that. Her father had a few ignorant words with my uncle, but got nowhere with his childish threats. The officer saw to it that the key was handed back to me, and that we had left the property at the same time with him.

On our way back to my uncle's home, I received a phone call from my bank agent. She insisted that it was urgent that I came into the branch to see her as soon as possible. My antenna was up and I started to wonder what kind of problem I'd be faced with. I dropped off my aunt and uncles and had Austin stay with them until I returned. I had a great relationship with the financial advisor at the branch. Christine called me to the branch to explain to me what had happened. She told me that my account was emptied. She said that my ex-wife had been to a few other branches and had withdrawn sums of money from each bank. She explained that Esther knew what she was doing because she had realized that if she had attempted to withdraw all the money from one branch; it might have resulted in raising a red flag. So she decided to withdraw a little at a time from the other branches, and saved her final withdrawal because she knew the staff had known her and wouldn't have thought of anything about it. She withdrew the money and walked out of the branch like a robber making his last heist. I asked Christine if there were anything that could be done. She explained that because Esther and I had shared an account, she had as much right to the account as I did. I had no money in my savings at all and the little money I had in my chequing account was just enough to pay for my car loan. The branch offered me a five hundred dollar extension on my checking account. My life was an absolute fiasco, and I didn't know what to do.

I now had the challenge of finding a place to live, and I found it so heartless for someone to place their anger in front of their child's life. My life with my ex-wife began to remind me of *The War of the Roses* with Michael Douglas and Danny

De Vito. I knew that if I had any chance of my son with me on a permanent basis, I had to do everything in my power to stay a step ahead of Esther. One morning while I was sitting in my therapist's office, he received a very disturbing phone call. Esther had called to make the therapist aware of my insanity. She suggested to him that I was a danger to society, and she believed that I was planning on killing her. The therapist wanted to know the reason for her call, rather than informing the police of her feelings. She explained that she would like him to diagnose me first and help me with whatever problems I may have. She also wanted him to be aware that she mentioned that she was afraid of me. After the conversation with her, he realized how manipulative she was and the length that she would go to. I was advised to be careful of her and to do my best to stay away from her.

Although Esther and I were apart, she continued to maintain her membership at the Y.M.C.A. I found it to be very unreasonable, seeing that I paid for her membership, and she knew that we were very uneasy with being around each other, but she would continue to come there. Esther wanted to tarnish my reputation at the gym and anywhere else she felt would harm me. On this particular Friday, I attended the gym to play my usual squash games with my friends. There wasn't a great turnout that evening, so I only played a few games and decided to leave. As I was making my way up the stairs, I saw Esther at the top of the stairs with a phony smile on her face. I kept to the right side of the stair case as she was coming down the left side. For whatever reason, Esther decided to encroach on my side of the stair case. She purposely bumped me with her elbow as she was making her way down the stairs to the workout area. Her action had me stumped for a brief moment. I couldn't believe that she did that, and she didn't even say a word. I stood at the top of the stairs and stared at her as she sat on the stretching mat. I wasn't about to let her get away with, thinking that she could intimidate me. So I walked back down the stairs and approached her on the mats. She denied elbowing me while waking down the stairs. I decided to lean over, and quietly advice her of my intention. I told her that I would approach one of her clients and let him know all the things that she used to talk about with me. As I rose from the bent position, she struck me with her foot, stating that I threatened her, and then I struck her with my bag. She paraded around to everyone canvassing on whether they over heard me threatening her. She played the game to the hill by crying and acting as if she was terrified of leaving the facility. I left the Y and made my way home to tend to Austin.

I mentioned what had happened to my aunt and uncle so that they would be aware of any trouble that may land on their front door. The following morning while I was sitting in the lunchroom at work, my supervisor asked if I could see him in his office. I thought nothing of it, until I walked into his office. In his office stood two plain clothes officers and a uniform police officer. Curious why I was there, I decided to ask them a question. The officer indicated to me that the reason for them being there was because my ex-wife filled a complaint on me. He asked if I could tell him about the events that took place at the Y.M.C.A on Friday afternoon. I explained my version of what took place, but they felt as a result of her complaint, they had no choice but to place me under arrest. It took a fairly long time in his office to convince me to agree to attend the division.

I felt utterly embarrassed as I made my way through the hallway with handcuffs on my wrists. The only thing on my mind at that moment was disposing of Esther. I figured if

216

I was going to be convicted for an act that I didn't commit, then I might as well do something that justifies the arrest. As the police vehicle pulled up to the division, I could see the custody entrance within an eye distance. It reminded me of the times I delivered custodies to the Don Jail and various divisions.

They had me walk up to the booking desk and report my name. Nothing was different from the way I treated the custodies from the way they treated me. One of the officers gave me a quick pat down and removed my belt from my uniform. The reason for taking my belt was to prevent me from trying to hang myself. I was placed in a single cell that smelled of stale blood and other body secretions. As I sat in the cell with no one else around me, my focus was drawn to the destruction of Esther. I sat in the cell from approximately 10am until 4:30 pm.

My uncle Fitzroy had posted bail for me, and had me released in his care. I contacted my friend Adam that worked at Forty-two Division and informed him about my situation. I asked him to do some investigation for me, because I was unable to make any contact with anyone at the gym. He looked into the matter for me and by the following day, I had a positive answer in my favor. The prosecutors had no idea that I had someone working on the case also. I was asked to attend the division and notified that they had completed the investigation, and found my statement to be true. They informed me that they would be preparing a crown brief to charge my ex-wife with deceit and falsely charging someone with a crime that they didn't commit. The following morning a friend of mine had called to tell me that Esther had received a phone call from the division officer. She told me that Esther had gone plain mad when she found out that I had been cleared of all charges. She went on to explain that Esther even went as far as to break a few items in her bedroom. She said that she could hear her screaming and crying from the kitchen. It went to show that her initial intent was to harm me at any cost.

After a few weeks had gone by, I returned to work. The idea of being arrested at work was shameful because of the world that I lived in. If a person is charged with a crime in our society, depending on the degree of the offence, you may not be forgiven. In my case, because it involved a domestic, it automatically placed a bitter taste in their mouth. Although I may have been cleared of all charges, the public still had the rumour circling. At approximately a month and a half into the separation, Esther visited Austin at my Uncle Fitzroy's home to tell him that she's traveling to Portugal. I couldn't believe what I was hearing. Why would someone decide to travel out of the country when you're going through a separation, and you know that your son was extremely hurt? It's evident to me that the man that she was traveling with was the man whom her mother used to speak of. Her mother always felt that this man was the perfect person for her, not counting that he was a Jewish. Austin said to her that we also needed a break, but we didn't have the money to travel because she had stolen all of my money and that her father was doing everything to harm me.

After she returned from her trip, I made an attempt to try and mend our relationship back together. I approached her father early one Saturday morning at his home and tried my best to see if he would be willing to assist by speaking with his daughter. We stood in his driveway and discussed the situation, and the negative impact that it could have as a result of us not being a family. He told me that he was happy with whatever decision his daughter made, so I realized quickly that I wasn't dealing with an ordinary family. A normal family would never approve of a marriage being ripped apart.

I was just about to say my goodbyes when Esther's mother came walking down the driveway from inside her home. Without saying a word or any sign of provocation, she attacked me verbally. Her eyes were red and misty, as if she wanted to cry. Her voice was loud and harsh. She stood about four feet from me as she pointed her finger at me, and as she was telling me how much she hated me.

She said that it was my entire fault why her daughter was back at home with them, not that they're uncomfortable with it, but she shouldn't have left in the first place. She went on to tell me that she never liked me, and that she didn't care for blacks in her life. It was extremely difficult for her to pretend every single day for all those years. She pointed out to me that whenever her daughter was prepared to leave, she'd make sure that she left with a Jew and not with a black like me. At this point, I realized that it would be best that I leave and never return. Unknown to her at the moment, while she was releasing her wrath on me, Austin was sitting in the car the entire time. I got into the car and told Austin that everything was going to be alright and not to worry, I told him that he didn't need to be around such hate. As the tears flowed from Austin's eyes, his grandmother ran beside the car while the car was reversing, she was trying to explain to Austin why she acted in such an evil manner. She began to tell him that it's not him that she didn't love. I stopped briefly to look for traffic, and at that moment Austin said to her, "If you don't care about my daddy, then how can you say that you love me?" Her mouth was left wide open as we drove away.

As soon as we arrived home, the phone rang. Esther had heard about what had taken place and was trying to butter everything over with Austin. She told Austin that her mother only acted that way because of what I said. She felt that as a result of me being on her property and what I had said to her husband, it provoked his grandmother to say the things that she may not have said otherwise. Austin said to his mother that his grandmother was totally lying about what had happened in their driveway because he was in the car the entire time, and I never said anything upsetting to neither his grandfather nor her.

Esther felt that I created the environment for her mother to react in that manner. Uncle Fitzroy and some of my other family members believed that it was time that I tried being on my own to teach Austin that regardless of what happened, we had to continue and to never give up. I found an apartment on Neilson Road, approximately ten minutes away from my uncle's home. The apartment wasn't the greatest, but I knew that I had to make it work. We moved into the apartment building with an old waterbed without the lining. We didn't have a television set or a dining set to eat on. I had purchased Austin a new bedroom suite before we had separated, but his mother felt that the bed would serve better if it stayed with her. Esther's father decided that he would prefer to deliver whatever furniture Esther decided to settle over the separation and would have it delivered to the apartment free of charge. I received an old couch and an old television that I kept in the basement for Austin to play on and hang out with his little friends. One piece of art from my collection of paintings was delivered. Out of all the art that I used to purchase at art auctions, the art was delivered with a huge crack on the glass. A few boxes had some old cutlery and linen that we were going to throw away before we separated. My Aunt Monica and Uncle Stanley were placed as the family negotiator to mediate on my behalf for a settlement.

They met with Mr. Hardenberg on my behalf for an out of court financial settlement to avoid any unnecessary arguments and possible altercation. His initial intention was for me to leave without being compensated and to fight her in court. I felt that by going to court, I would have been able to convince the court of all the ill treatment that I received and how I had put my life on hold to give her a better life. So for those reasons, I believed that I should be compensated for the years I lost. Both my aunt and uncle urged me to settle and walk away with whatever had been agreed on. Although I was reluctant, I went along with what they felt was right and agreed to their settlement. They settled on a figure that I felt was totally unfair but being in the financial situation that I was in; I had no other choice at the time but to take his charitable donation. Esther and I had our hearing in court, and the decision was in favor of me having custody of Austin and Esther having visitation rights. The court battle was extremely expensive and grueling. Her lawyer advocated on her behalf and listed a trail of awful things about me that could not be proven at all. Esther tried to make me look like the type of husband who was emotional, abusive and envious of her career. She felt that I created an atmosphere that was unhealthy for her son to live in. She spoke about me asking her to approach her family for funds so that we could have a better life. This was the thing that I spoke about earlier on in our relationship. My lawyer suggested that we allowed her lawyer to make all the scandal remarks that they wished, because there was no proof for them to stand on.

From the first day I realized that Esther had the intention to leave me, I began taking notes of everything that transpired between us. I kept notes on her dress code and her relationship with other men behind my back. I also kept an agenda on the fabricated lies that she made up to have me arrested. I spoke about some of the ill treatment that she did to our son Austin. The incriminating evidence was when she told me that she wanted to have her parents executed and how she used to steel from her father's safe. Knowing full well that I may be asked to produce proof of how I came into such information. I had it all written down on the area of where her father's safe was kept. I was willing to even describe exactly where it was, because she had shown me one evening when they were away. My lawyer was fully prepared for anything that her lawyer was going to make knowledge in the court. The Judge had some very harsh words for Esther and suggested that she took control of her life and stop trying to ruin her son's life. Before making her decision, she had a few harsh words for my ex. She spoke about her behavior in court and the lack of respect she had for her family. The judge pointed out to Esther that it was totally disrespectful to think of her father as a cash cow and that one day those words might come back and haunt her. Her decision was in, and she awarded Austin to me, with Esther having visitation access.

Esther swore to me at the end of the trial, (away from the judge) that I hadn't heard or seen the worst of her. I took it as a threat, so started to wonder if I had to protect myself by carrying a gun. In a subtle way, I welcomed her hate towards me and was awaiting the moment to show her and her family what type of animal I could be.

After that comment, I can remember seeing her and her sugar daddy one day at a stoplight. He had lots of tough words for me at the light. So I followed them to the park where we all got out of our cars and confronted each other. Esther wasn't as tough as she was in the car when stopped at the light. I had no time for biting, I just wanted to get right down to the barking. I wanted to get the show on, so I kicked him on his knee sending him to the ground. As he knelt on his knee and looked up at me I slapped him like a punk that he was. Before leaving, I grabbed him by his throat and tried to choke him out until I decided that he wasn't the one that I had to destroy.

Austin was involved in hockey and other sporting activities that we once shared together. Esther would appear at his hockey games in hope that she would have an opportunity to talk with him. By this time so many things had transpired, including a dislike that Austin had built up towards her. Esther couldn't get to him if she was the world's best mountain climber. Regardless of how much she tried to speak with him, he ignored her and kept on walking away.

Austin was attending the Montessori school system before we separated. I enquired if Esther would be willing to split the tuition fee with me, seeing that I had to pay for so many other school related things. At the time the year's tuition was $6,700.00 for the year. That didn't include his uniform, gym attire, and bus transportation, to and from school. The answer that I received from her was: "Remember what my father said about breaking you? Well we're about to sit back and watch you beg." I used that comment as a fire to fuel me to stay strong. In the summer time when school was out, Austin usually went to the Bay View summer camp in the west end. This camp was approximately $ 1,000.00 for the entire summer, with room and board included. Again, Esther refused to assist me with this bill, causing me to use up the money that I received from the settlement.

One afternoon, I was running a bit late from work, so I arrived at the camp a few minutes late to pick up Austin. The staff informed me that his mother had arrived a bit early to pick him up and had a difficult time getting him to go with her. They told me that Esther had twisted his hand behind his back and dragged him along in the hallway to her vehicle because he was unwilling to go with her. From what I gathered, Esther seemed to be pressed for time, fearing that I might show up. I wanted to call the police and have her charged with kidnapping, but I decided to go home and wait for her call. She did call after a few hours, sounding frustrated and crying on the phone, accusing me of tainting her child against her. I suggested to Esther that she took a close look at herself and to see the real reason for Austin's behavior. Esther didn't realize that by everything she said or did to me, made her that much more of a devil in Austin's eye. She continued to do selfish things and would have her family and friends believe that I was actually preventing Austin from seeing her. Esther became so believable that even a few of my family members had started to accuse me of not letting Austin see his mother. I used the word "letting" for a simple reason; because that was the word I had to listen to for many years. I made a pledge to myself that at no time would I prevent Austin from being with his mother. I was not saying that I liked the idea of him seeing her, but I wouldn't stand in his way if he wanted to visit with her.

One day while I was at the laundry mart when I received a phone call from Austin. Austin was hysterical on the phone, so I had to get him to settle down so that he could explain to me what was wrong. He finally settled enough to tell me that his mother was on the television talking about us. I threw everything back into the hamper and rushed home. I couldn't believe that Esther was indeed on the television and would go that far to tarnish my name. She had a documentary made about her life as a wife and mother and what it's like to be free. She spoke about her feelings for Austin and what it was doing to her, by not having an opportunity to see him. She spoke about her life with me as her husband. She told the world that she was trapped and feared for her safety on many occasions. She also advised the media that I was a sly person, and that I knew how to manipulate anyone. This documentary showed at least four times a day for years. When asked if she could have it stopped, she said that it was out of her hands, because they sold the right to the documentary company. Everywhere I went, I felt as if eyes were fixed on me. The phone was constantly ringing to inform me that my ex-wife was on the television. It seemed as if the entire world had seen her on the TV fabricating her lies.

I knew that I would have many people asking me about the show, but I had to hold my head up high. I believed that the friends that I had, if they were truly my friends, that they would know that the person that she's speaking about, was totally untrue. I lost some of the people that I thought were my friends, but in reality, they weren't my true friends anyway. This documentary didn't only destroy my relationship with some of my friends, but it also created a disturbance among our own family. Esther had found a way to turn my cousin against me. Knowing that one of my family members was now on the side with my ex-wife made me very upset, and I couldn't understand the reason for her doing so. My cousin felt that because Esther was a woman and a mother, she could understand how she felt. She supported Esther by being on the documentary and communicating with her at times with regard to Austin's well being. As a result of her action, it had a domino effect through the entire family, involving her family as well. The tension was so high within our family that it caused all of us to withdraw from the remainder of the family until everything was much calmer. I didn't speak to my cousin and their family except for my aunt, for quite some time. I couldn't bring myself to be around hypocrites.

So, for at least a year or two, I had no contact with the family and stayed away from any event that they had at their home. I started to talk with them after a few years because of the subtle attempts that my cousin would make to put the problem behind us. Knowing fully well that I was trying to have, the Lord blessed me and helped me to be a stronger and a forgiving person, I had to do what the Lord would want me to.

I believed as a result of what had happened, for whatever the reason may be, that no relative would entertain the idea of taking the side of an outsider again. As time passed, I realized that I had made an error in judgment, by scrutinizing my aunt and uncle for the actions of their daughter (my cousin). I never said sorry to either of them, but I was confident that they knew that I was regretful for what had occurred. Their daughter always had her own independence and felt that she should be free to make her own decisions regardless of how anyone else felt.

By blaming them for her poor judgment, it created an unsettling atmosphere within the entire family. I believed the family stood behind me as an honor of principal, not to bar them, but to show them how we needed to stick together at all times when one of us was in need. All was well now and I had placed the events that took place at the back of me and continued to look ahead, and hopefully, this had been a valuable lesson for all.

Chapter 6

The apartment that we lived in was small and cool depending on the temperature from outside. By the grace of God, I became friends with a beautiful young lady who lived two floors above us. We met in the elevator one evening as she was all dressed up for an occasion that she was attending. She gave me her home number and the apartment that she lived in. Because I left early in the mornings and worked the night shift, she was so wonderful to offer to look after Austin for me. She had children of her own, so it made it that much more convenient for Austin to stay there. Austin was beginning to come into his own, with regard to playing hockey. They named him the Tie Domi of his team. He protected his players from any unnecessary roughness by the opposing team. The other teams learned the hard way that this was one player who wasn't afraid of receiving a penalty. I believed Austin developed that attitude out of anger that he was storing inside of him. So by being aggressive, it gave him the outlet to vent his anger on the other players. We had an away game that meant everything to our team that was just around the corner. We were nearing the end of our regular season, so we needed to win all of our games to be in the play offs. Esther decided to attend this game to give Austin some extra support. As we stood outside of the boys change room, I observed a bright shinny engagement ring on Esther's ring finger. She obviously wanted me to see her ring, by the way, she placed her hand on the wall. I was shocked to see that we weren't fully divorced as yet, but she was already in a committed relationship to become married. I wondered to myself if this was the gentleman whom her mother used to speak about. I decided not to tell Austin, fearing that it may upset him even more. If Esther wished to tell him, then she could tell him when she was ready for.

The entire year was extremely difficult for me. There were many moments in my life where I had no milk or butter to put on the bread or in the cereal. I can remember saving one tea bag for at least two days at times, so that I could have something to drink at night. I had to rely on a friend of mine to pick me up to taking me to work because I didn't have sufficient money to buy gas for my car. I gave Austin whatever I had to make sure that he ate and was clothed, so that he wouldn't become sick. Many nights I fell asleep crying in my room. I prayed every night for God to take my pain away and to provide for my son. So many times I felt like killing myself, but because Austin was still so young I knew the effect it would have on him. I realized that the confidence he once displayed in himself wasn't as visible as it used to be. Esther and I agreed that Austin should see a children's doctor to assist him with any emotional problems that he was dealing with. Esther and her parents had chosen a doctor, who was recommended by a friend. I sat once with Austin in the meeting, and explained to the doctor the events that occurred. He saw the doctor approximately six or seven times and decided that he didn't want to see him any more.

Austin was convinced that he had nothing wrong and wasn't willing to talk anymore. The doctor spoke to me about Austin and felt that there was nothing wrong with him. He felt that Austin was upset at his mother and truly didn't want to talk to her. He believed that I wasn't doing anything to prevent a relationship from continuing between Austin and his mother. Esther's parents were totally upset and felt that the doctor didn't know what he was talking about. They were convinced that I was undermining Austin and poisoning his mind with hatred.

With all the tension and having to defend my character wherever I went, It started to wear on me. There were many people in my day to day life that I came into contact with that knew about the break up. Esther had done a masterful job of sighting me as the big, bad, and evil ex-husband. One day at work I just broke down and contacted my Uncle Fitzroy to have me see a doctor. They took me to Centennial Hospital and had me see a psychologist at the hospital.

Based on my mental condition at the time, I was admitted as a patient to the hospital, and I honestly say that, that was the lowest point in my life. Austin had come to visit me and during a discussion, asked the doctor if it would be possible to replace him and have me leave so that I could return to work. He felt that he should stay and take the pain that I was in. Everyone was shocked by his comment and impressed by his love for me.

I spent a significant amount of time in the hospital (from what I was told). The reason I say this is because I had very little memory of what took place back then. I had lost my mind and from the comments that I heard afterward, the staff at the hospital was worried about my health.

Apparently, one afternoon I became extremely irritated

because I wanted to see my son; so that evening, due to my emotional breakdown, I started to show signs of another breakdown. The staff had called the security officers to assist by holding me while they were trying to medicate me. Unfortunately, for the staff, by the time the officers arrived, I was already in a violent state. Normally, I was a pretty strong person when not agitated. However; because I was upset and angered because my ex-wife was preventing my son from visiting me, I felt emotionless and was willing to harm anyone who came close to me.

The security officers attempted to restrain me, but I didn't think that they were prepared for me. I was told that I had the strength of a raging bull, and no one could have controlled me. The officers had entered my room with the nurses prepared to inject me, but on this evening that was not about to happen. One of the nurses said that I behaved and acted like a person that was out of his mind. I threw the officers, around as if they were dolls. One of the officers ended with a sprained arm while I almost choked out the other one. The nurse told me that at first glance I seemed to be in a trance, and that I started to pant as I relaxed for a moment. I seemed to be panting like an animal. After I had settled down, the officers had moved in quickly and restrained me. The nurse then approached me and injected me with a relaxant.

On that evening, they placed me in a straight jacket and left me like that for the remainder of the day and into the most part of the following day. They had become afraid of me, so for my protection and the safety of the other staff and patients, they felt it was best to straight jacket me until someone had made an appointment to speak with me.

The desire I had to live had left me, and I was willing to do almost anything to die. I had tried cutting my throat after they left the room with the knives I hid, but that did not work. I even tried running through the hospital windows, but that didn't work either. I wanted the hospital to call for the police so that I could create a scene, but that didn't work either. Every avenue I tried was uncovered and left me restless and angry.

I sunk into a pit, and whatever the reason, I didn't intend to come out any time soon. The doctor decided to put me on a few different types of medication. For a few days after the violent attack, he believed that it would be for my best interest to place me in isolation until I returned from wherever my mind had gone to. Unfortunately, the medication wasn't doing me any good, and it had caused me to feel even worse, so they tried another combination of pills and this time it seemed to have helped. A few days had passed, and I seemed to have been in a better place and more at peace. The following day the doctor approached me and told me that a meeting will be held the following morning.

I began to wonder what reason they would have to call for a meeting. I asked one of the nurses and she told me that my ex-wife insisted in having a meeting with the doctor. That night, I hardly slept even with all the medication they had given me. I found it strange that the doctor and head nurse were allowing Esther the opportunity to speak when we were no longer together. Esther arrived at the hospital bright and early. One would have thought that she was applying for a job, and she was here for her interview. Think about the problems that I would have if she worked at the hospital. We all gathered in the boardroom and we all sat rather spaciously away from each other. Esther had the entire floor for herself. She began by talking about our relationship while we were

232

together and had information to support her comments through notes that she had kept as a record. Everything that she spoke about was extremely private and personal. I couldn't understand what our past life had to do with me being in the hospital.

She spoke about the night I referred to her as a lesbian. Yes I agreed on this particular issue, because she started to act differently and my patience was growing thinner. She explained to the doctor that because she had asked me to assist her in cutting her hair, I felt that she would be looked at as a lesbian. She began to cry in front of the doctor and nurses as she told her stories. Esther was trying to pull the same stunt that she tried in court and failed; all she was looking for was sympathy.

It was funny that she didn't mention how much she really looked like a lesbian at the time. I felt that Esther was trying to change into someone else rather than the person I knew. Her sudden and bold actions were due to her new friends she had found, especially one of her old high school friend who was even more cunning than she was, coaching her all the way. I realized that she was already at that point in her life where nothing really mattered anymore because her mind had already been made up. I still couldn't understand the reason for her being at the hospital to discuss our past relationship.

Esther at one time began to speak about our love life until the doctor interrupted and stopped her. She wanted to explain to the doctor why she cried after having sex with me, and sometimes felt as if she was a stripper at home. At that point, I realized that the lies were going to increase.

I waited for Esther to spill her stomach. I had to explain, although I didn't have to, but felt it was best that they had a better understanding about the person that was sitting before us. Before everything got crazy, I decided to rectify the reason for her feelings. I explained that Esther had an extremely high sex drive and was very much interested in role playing. I explained to the staff that Esther would purchase sexual tools, and on a Saturday night, she would rent dirty movies and re-enact whatever her fantasy was.

Another issue that was brought the table was the situation with her parents. On numerous occasions, I asked her to speak with her father and mother with regard to the way they spoke to me and at also the way they treated me. Esther continued to justify them because of their old age, and that they would have accepted me if I were Jewish. She said that these factors caused a behaviour in me that affected our intimate moments.

I said that I believed Esther turned to her own inner fetishes to try and tease me by acting like a stripper or a lesbian who enjoyed creating her own fantasies for her partner. I agreed that I would become excited, due to some of the things she did to herself, and how she made love to me after. Maybe I shouldn't have called it love making, because based on our relationship back then, I think the average person would have seen this as something weird.

Esther continued to point at me in front of the staff and made them believe that I was a mean spirited person. After she embarrassed me in front of everyone, she felt that it would be beneficial for everybody if the doctor kept me inside for a proper evaluation. She tried her best to convince them that I was a danger to her and possibly to our son, so she was making all efforts to make sure that I would be locked in.

I had very little to say except trying to clarify some of my actions. We rose from our chairs, and I walked Esther to the elevator. "Why," you ask? I had no idea. As we stood waiting for the elevator, I asked Esther if she would be willing to put all of this hate behind us and start again. I reminded her, of how much I loved her, and the way we fell in love when we first met. I told her that I gave her everything I had and had done my best to reunite her again with her family. The nurses were close by and had a clear view of me as I cried my eyes out for her love and affection. The elevator arrived and as I tried my best to reach out to touch her, she looked at me as if I had leprosy. Before she entered the elevator she didn't realize that the doctor and a few of the nurse were watching her monstrous ways as she twirled her fingers towards her temple and said to me, "I hope you stay in here for life and rot." I couldn't bear the way she spoke to me as I tried my best to walk to my room. My heart was so crushed that I felt as if I had been buried alive. I kept on telling myself that no human being deserves to be treated like the way she did. For her, I was the scum of the earth. Within minutes of being in my bedroom, a nurse by the name of Jackie approached me and sat and spoke with me. She told me that the doctor and the majority of the nurses had seen what had happened to me and felt extremely bad.

She also told me that whatever nonsense Esther spoke about in the boardroom, was not going to go anywhere. She wanted me to know that she had also experienced pain and hardship in her life. As a nurse it was out of practice for her to sit and discuss her own private life with me. However, she did and she even expressed the hurt that she struggled with when she thought about the way her ex-husband had treated her and her children. I couldn't believe that I was in the hospital for treatment, and that I found myself consoling another human being. As she wiped her own tears away, I realized that Nurse Sweetheart was indeed a wonderful person. Every one of the staff wanted to see me succeed.

A few days later, I received a phone call early in the morning from Austin. He was very happy to speak with me. He wanted to know when I'd be well enough to leave the hospital, so that he could come back home with me. I told him that I was doing my best, and hopefully I'd be out within the next week or so. Suddenly, Austin started to scream and cry while on the phone with me. When asked what the problem was, he said that his mother was giving him exactly one minute to speak with me, and then she's going to hang the phone up. This really annoyed me to the point where I began screaming back at her on the phone. I realized that she couldn't hear me, so I told Austin to hang up, and that we would have enough time to share. As we came to the end our conversation, I could hear Esther counting from ten on backwards. Austin cried and screamed at her not to hang up, but she didn't listen. I walked away from the phone only with one thing in mind, and that was to become a smooth operator. At first I wanted to inflict pain on her, but as I remembered my mother's teaching, I realized that God would decide what is best for her.

I had to get my act in gear if I was to have any chance of Esther trying to reverse the judge's decision. The physician met with me the following morning and discussed with me the idea of giving me a few electric shock treatments. I had no idea what it was or the reason for applying it to me. He said that he felt that by giving me a few treatments, it would help me to feel more alert, vibrant, happier, and would keep me from feeling as low spirited as I was.

Within the two weeks while I was there, he gave me three electric shock treatments. After a few days, I was told that my face seemed more alive and bright. I felt better about myself, and my energy level was almost back to normal. I was released from the hospital and asked to do my best not to return to the ward again. It was almost immediate that I felt that something was not right with me.

On the way home, I found myself not being able to remember where I lived. I had difficulty remembering people's name and even things from my past. I remembered returning to work and
having to approach the supervisor to ask him to assist me with the whereabouts of my locker and the combination number. I felt extremely embarrassed when I had to ask to be retrained in my work, especially when I was the one that trained people. The electric shock treatment was positive in one way, but very negative in another.

Chapter 7

Esther insisted that Austin see another children's doctor, because she feared that Austin would grow with some type of anger towards women. I believe that she was trying to get a doctor to agree with her, so that she could use it against me. We saw a Jewish doctor this time in the downtown area. The doctor seemed to be a bit arrogant towards me, before we even explained the reason why we were there. After three visits to this doctor, Austin told me that he didn't want to continue the visits anymore, and instead he would go to please me. I asked him if he had mentioned any of his feelings to the doctor. He said no, but he's willing to tell the doctor and his mother at the same time. I didn't want to get involved to give them any reason to think that I was not trying to help in the situation. As usual, Esther wasn't satisfied and felt that he's only behaving that way because she felt that Austin was afraid of me. The doctor told Esther that she didn't believe Austin was afraid of me, but she did believe that I was preventing Austin from seeing his mother. I didn't expect anything else from her, seeing that they were both cut from the same piece of cloth. We sat and spoke briefly before I felt that I was being attacked by her and felt that as a professional, she wasn't being as objective as she should. I told her that they could both think whatever, they wanted, because I really didn't care a damn about either of them. What I really wanted to tell them was that they could both die and rot in hell, but I decided not to. Esther decided to become like an actress and started to play the girl who was so afraid of being killed by her ex-spouse.

As I walked out of the building, I had to release a big laugh to keep me from blowing up, so I laughed until even Austin started to laugh also. The story was being spread was that Esther believed that I'd been diagnosed with some sort of depression that made her believe her life might be in danger. The truth about what Esther claimed was that if I truly wanted her dead, I could have done it quite easily. Her parents continued to try to drain me financially by having me brought to court for every little thing. Having your lawyer attend court over little things, could be mighty costly over a period of time. Esther and her father gave them almost anything when it came to assisting with the needs of Austin. I said "needs" not wants. I was so thankful to my lawyer for requesting that the judge charged Esther and her father with the expenses for Austin's needs. Austin was given the same type of lifestyle as when the marriage was working properly. We asked for Esther's father to continue to pay for his school. She also had to assist with any cost related to his sports and activities.

I requested my lawyer to ask for financial support for him as long as he attended school. Knowing that she had to pay me alimony really bothered her to the point where she tried playing hard ball with me. I agreed that I was all over her finances and made sure I did to her what she would have done to me; however, the joy I felt for overcoming the barriers that were placed in my way, was very whelming.

I really didn't think that I could have survived without my son in my life. The love that I have for him, and the love that he maintained for me, was above and beyond. Personally,

I don't believe any child should be without their parents, however if for whatever the reason might be, I've always said from the beginning that I'd do whatever it took to have my child or children with me. So for this reason I strongly believe that a marriage is something both parties should consider carefully before any serious commitment.

Esther had called the house late one evening wishing to speak with Austin. He took the phone from my hand and answered it. Esther and Austin spoke for a brief moment. I don't even think the conversation had lasted more than a minute. My son told me that his mother wanted him to be a part of her wedding ceremony. Austin told her that he wouldn't be attending. The next time we saw each other, she seemed to be very upset about the idea that Austin had refused to be a part of her wedding. She introduced him to her potential husband, and Austin didn't even look at him, and did not shake his hand as her fiancé extended his. Austin told me that the guy would try to have a conversation about taking him to his games sometimes but Austin told him that he already had a father to do it. He said to me that his mother's face had looked like she wanted to cry.

Whenever Esther had asked to take Austin away with her, she felt extremely rejected, by the way her own son would look at her. Esther was beginning to feel what she never thought would happen to her. Esther was losing the love of her only son. For months, Esther's parents would try to have Austin accompany them on a trip to Israel. The answer continued to be "no" until they finally realized that Austin would require some time before he was willing to allow them to make small steps back into his life.

Esther got married, but our son was not a part of her precious day. For the next few years Esther and her father continued to do whatever they could to financially ruin me. Eventually, they ran out of reasons to take me to court, this was a financial burden for them as well. Austin was older now and he was at an age where he had the opportunity to present to the court his desire of choosing which parent he would want to stay with. Esther knew that, hence she didn't have a chance of having the decision over turned.

Two years later, her marriage was over, and she was back at home with her parents. I hoped that the public would have seen that I wasn't what she had said I was, especially when she couldn't hold on to a marriage that was created by her and her parents.

At the end of Austin's eighth grade, I decided to place him into the public school system. I didn't have any more money to continue, and besides, he was at an age where he could understand better. Austin was a fine young man with lots of friends and was heavily involved in his sports. Football still seemed to be the sport of choice, and even though he is much older today, he still sleeps and walks around with a football. Since his mother and I have parted from each other, I can't say that Austin has suffered being around me.

Austin still continues to visit with his grandparents. I believe he has a warm spot towards his grandfather and wishes to keep the relationship going. Nevertheless, when it comes to his mother, he has voiced his feelings on numerous occasions about his willingness to be with her. Austin maintains that he only goes to see her because he feels that it is the right thing to do. He's also stated that he doesn't love her but sees her only as his mother. Whenever he spends time with her, he says that it is usually for an hour or so because he doesn't have a true mother and son relationship. He feels as if he was robed, and that he shouldn't have had to go through what he did. He recognizes I loved his mother very much, and that I may have had my own issues that required some attention, but not to the point where the family had to suffer. He missed the times when we all played and chatted together.

Austin asked if he could have a tattoo because he wanted to show his own creativity. He had a tattoo done with him sitting on my shoulders when he was about four years old. He said that he wanted to show me how much he loved me and that no matter where he goes, he'll always have me near. He told me that his mother had seen it and that her eyes started to become teary but she tried her best to hold it back. He knew that she felt it, and he wanted her to know how he really felt about her by putting him on my shoulder. He continues to visit her, but it isn't as much as it should be when it comes to a mother.

I devoted all my time and energy towards Austin being cared for properly. I decided that I'd give the dating scene a chance again, and started going out with my friends. I believed I must have been approached by more than two or three dozen women once I started back dating. I broke a lot of hearts and enjoyed myself along the way. I sought vengeance by allowing the women I met to believe that I would share my heart with them and love and care for them an they poured their soul into me I wanted to make sure that I was well prepared for anything that the women came at me with. I had women asking if I'd be interested in moving in with them. I had some women willing to pay off my debts if I were to promise to marry them. For the first time in a longtime I felt as if I was in control. I looked at the women whom I dated as being the fruit of all evil, and that I was sent to destroy them. I guess I was trying to seek revenge on every woman because of what my ex-wife had done to me.

For a short period of time, I looked at all of the women whom I came into contact with, as shoes that I wore until I needed another pair. I enjoyed telling them whatever, they wanted to hear, as long as I kept them at a safe distance. No one was about to break this heart of mine ever again as long as I lived. I can recall one woman, in particular, falling so deep in love with me that she made the decision to leave her family and move in with me if I would let her. She approached me one evening after we had gone out for a drink and showed me the title of her house. She was willing to take me the following day to her lawyer and have my name added to her house without any clause.

She even opened her wallet and told me that she was going to add me to her saving account so that I could have whatever. I wanted when a situation arose. This was the first time that I had to change my way of thinking and do what I felt was right. For her to move out of her family's home and to give her tenant notice that she would be moving in would be a dangerous thing to do in God's eyes.

I met an old friend whom I used to talk to when I was single. She was very beautiful with skin that shined like smooth peanut butter that hadn't been touched. Her eyes pierced right through me as I stood on the opposite side of the club. She swayed back and forth to the music like a snake crawling down a tree branch. Her lips were moist from the lip gloss that she was wearing as she drank from her glass. At times I would wish that I was the glass that she was drinking from. Knowing that I was probably looking at her, she would spin around so slowly as the light caught her skirt, presenting an image of her core, from her ankles to just below her fruit of the loom.

Finally, after rehearsing every line in my head, I decided to approach her. We both stood there and stared at each other as the music played before embracing each other. She hugged me so tightly that I had to ask her to give me a moment to breathe. She was so happy to see me again after so many years. I quickly glimpsed at her fingers to see if she was taken. She had no ring on her finger or any markings from a ring. We stepped away from her friends, and casually danced our way to the dance floor. Every time I touched her. I could feel the moistness that lay on her skin.

We stood in one spot just moving from right to left holding each other's pinkie finger. Without any notice, she pulled me into her and kissed me with her moist shinny lips. Her lips felt warm and tingly. All the nerves in my body were now on alert and ready to get busy. I knew that I had to have her that night, and nothing was about to step in my way. Thankfully, she asked if I could take her home instead of her friends. I was more than pleased to do such a gesture as a citizen of Toronto. As we drove, all I could think of was what I should do. I knew that I had hurt her once, and I didn't want to do the same thing all over again.

I pulled up to her apartment, which seemed more like a condo. She said "thank you," placed her skirt between her legs and got out of my car. Once she was out of the car, she removed her slippers and walked towards her door. Before opening her door, she turned around with a smile and said thanks for the evening, but "are you going to park your car and meet me in my apartment or not?." I couldn't believe that my night was about to be a night from heaven. I made my way up to her floor. Her door was left slightly open, with a note at the shoes mat that said, "Meet me in the shower." I removed my clothes and quietly made my way into the shower. Her body was like a coke bottle that hadn't been changed over time. We kissed and kissed and I gently placed her on the floor with a towel under her. We made passionate love in the shower that left us both exhausted. After such an amazing encounter, she dried herself off and made her way to the kitchen where she prepared a tea for the both of us. Unfortunately, we couldn't last long enough to drink the tea. We made love to each other in the kitchen. It seemed as if we could have gone all night. She looked at me and said that she's never experienced love making like this ever.

She sat on the counter top shivering. I asked if she would like me to carry her into the shower, but she said "no." She explained that she was shaking because of how her body felt. Her body was out of control, and she couldn't move for a while. Finally, after showering again, we finally had our tea. My sweet heart and I stayed together for a very long time, until realizing that I wasn't willing to get married, she moved to the Dominican Republic. She moved back to her home in hope of finding herself a man that was would want to settle and have children.

She wanted that from me, but at the time, there were so many things going on in my life that it would have been unfair to her. She wrote me a few times after she moved back, in hope that I might have changed my mind. My baby was willing to return to Toronto only if I was willing to settle with her in the near future. I couldn't make that promise because of how I was feeling and with what was happening in my home life. She eventually got married to a doctor and had a child. She wrote to me and said that she would never feel for anyone again the way she felt for me. She even went as far as to ask if it would be alright to name her next child after me. I said that she should think about it, or perhaps mix match my name so it's not my entire name. We ended our conversation by saying "I love you always," and to live in peace.

Chapter 8

The apartment building that we were living in was uncomfortable to be in. I had problems doing my laundry, whenever I went down to the basement. The laundry area was always over flooding due to the kids playing games with the machines. The basement required pest control's visits. The number of mice that I came into contact with was intolerable. I had to park my car outside because there weren't any parking spots left in the basement. Some of the vehicles that were parked outside were vandalized, and I couldn't afford to have that done to my car.

I discussed moving back into the apartment with my Uncle Fitzroy that he had for rent. He agreed to rent me his apartment for a reasonable price. After a while, at the apartment, I started to feel very low about how my life had turned out. I was struggling on a day-to-day basis. I became very antisocial for some time where I stayed away from my friends and just wanted to be alone. One evening after work, when I couldn't have taken it any more, I approached my uncle and told him that I was going for a drive to the beaches. He couldn't understand why I was leaving my home at that time of the night to go to the beaches. I asked him if he could look after Austin from time to time.

I made my way down to Queen Street and Woodbine Avenue, parked my car and made my way into the park. If my memory serves me right, I believe my uncle called me on my cell phone wanting to know when I'd be returning home. Based on how I may have sounded, I believe he alerted the police to seek for me. After being there for at least an hour, I decided to make my way to the lake. Not realizing that I had company, my intention was to dive into the murky dark water. Suddenly lights went on and I could hear the voices of officers on their speakers. They wanted me to come towards them so that they could have a discussion with me. That wasn't about to happen so I decided to make a run for it. I started to run in the direction of the lake just hoping that I'd make it there before the cruiser. The officer who was running beside me seemed as if he was running in reverse. He had no running ability and should probably need some type of training exercise. The park was swamped with police cruisers, and I felt as if I was about to be taken out. This became a cat and mouse game. All I had on my mind was making my way to the lake before they could stop me.

I decided to make a run for it. I had most of the cars beat, because of the trees they had to maneuver around them. I couldn't believe that I was within meters of diving into the water when a police car struck me down. I didn't see the hidden vehicle that was behind some of the trees. After being knocked over by the car, I lay on the ground and looked at the many officers that were needed to take me down.

As I lay on the ground, I thought for a second that I was about to have a re-enactment of the Rodney King episode. One of the officers reached out and assisted me to my feet. He asked why I would run, when we're all on the same team. I had no response. After talking for a while, they informed me that they had to place me on a form 9 because they believed that I was a risk to myself and possibly to others. They trusted me enough to drive my own vehicle to the hospital with an escort behind me. Once at the hospital, I was interviewed by a doctor. The doctor felt that I had some emotional problems that I was dealing with, but wasn't ready to release me yet.

He had me stay at the hospital for some time, although I tried to reassure him that I wouldn't hurt myself. Obviously knowing that I had to stay in the hospital again had upset me. I had to call my uncle and made him aware of my situation. Once again, I found myself being in an altercation with the staff at the hospital. After injuring one of the security officers, they injected me with a medication that had me calmed and out for a while.

I woke up only to realize that I'd been straight jacketed on my bed. They were concerned that once the medication wore out of my system, I'd become violent again. The staff at the hospital didn't want me at the hospital anymore, and had enquired if any other hospital was willing to take me. The doctor suggested that while I was in the hospital, I should consider being a part of the classes that they had daily. I enrolled in a class that spoke about hidden anger and abuse. The class was enlightening and served me well. I realized a few things after listening to the speaker and decided to try and make it a part of my life. Being in the hospital caused me more stress than ever, so I had difficulty relaxing.

Having to deal with the people who also suffered from a form of mental illness, eventually started to drive me crazy because of their uncontrollable antics that probably wasn't intentional, but it irritated me. To sit at a table and see them drool as you tried to have your own meal, prevented me from eating around them and caused me to lose whatever appetite I had.

So many times I had to speak to a nurse and have her speak to some of the patients about being in my room. One of the mornings I woke up only to see that my tooth paste had been used, and urine was on the floor. My last day at the hospital, I decided that I would boycott eating anything at all. I decided that I wasn't going to use their shower or be a part of any topic where any of the individuals that annoyed me, were there.

After the class, the speaker decided to pay me a visit. She felt that I truly needed her assistance, so she felt that she was willing to sit with me for a half an hour. I really appreciated her for thinking of me. We spoke about my life as a child and a bit about my marriage. She said that someone told her about the incident that took place when I was last there. She totally understood how I felt because she had a family member that went through the same thing.

She wanted to let me know that she believed that I was no ordinary person. She believed that I had something different than a lot of the other men she had had contact with in her life. She wanted me to know that by taking my life would solve nothing, except God being upset with me. As she looked at me, I could see the glitter in her eyes. I could feel that she was emotional when she was speaking, only to prove that she truly cared. I promised her that I'd do my best to stay strong and to persevere through everything that I encountered. After she left my room, I asked God to bless her for being so humane towards me.

My uncle came to the hospital and assisted me with my belongings as we made our way out. I was still having difficulty remembering my whereabouts. On our way home, my uncle gave me a long lecture about being strong. He felt that regardless of whatever medication the doctor gave me. The medicine could only work if my mind wanted it to work. He wanted me to show Austin the strength that I had so that he could feel secure around me. He said to me that if I didn't teach Austin about the struggles of life, then he'd grow as a weak man. Those words penetrated right through my heart, so I decided to try my best. I returned back to work, and my life was up and running again. I had an opportunity to be placed on a day shift only platoon. My Staff Sergeant offered me the position to accommodate me with my son and some of the issues that I was going through. I stayed away from dating, but I decided that I'd go out with women only on a casual occasion. Austin played football for Scarborough Thunder Football League. He still enjoyed playing football, and I enjoyed going to his games, because I loved to see him play, and at the same time, I would make new friends. One of Austin's teammates was having a birthday party after the game for her daughter and asked if I would like to join them. I declined, but I allowed Austin to attend the party. From what I gathered, there were a few single ladies who were at the party. The host of the party had known the women, because their children had attended the same school. During the evening, the host decided to ask the women if any of the ladies were available to date. All the women were single and not against dating. Later that evening, I received a phone call from Theresa, she said that she browsed through the room and found two women that were interesting in meeting with me.

She gave me the names of the ladies along with their phone numbers. I waited for a day or so before I called. I decided to call a
young lady whose first name was KK. I called her around

11pm in the evening and spoke with her over the phone for a while. The conversation was comfortable yet stimulating. I felt an instant connection towards her. Please don't get me wrong; it wasn't at the level where I was seeing marriage and children and all the other fantasies that come along with being in a relationship. I knew that I saw her as someone that I could possibly enjoy being with. Life with KK was full of fun and filled with excitement. We spent a lot of time with each other, and even spoke about going away with each other. We were approximately three to four weeks into our relationship, when out of nowhere KK suggested that I give the other person a call.

She explained to me that it was only fair that I called her and asked her out on a date. I couldn't believe what I was hearing, so I asked her if she was feeling well. For some reason, I had no chance of convincing her about leaving the idea alone. Finally, I decided that if she was that confident that nothing could separate us, then I'd call Candy and asked her if she was still interested in meeting me.

The following afternoon after work I called and spoke with Candy. She agreed to meet for a brunch at her favorite restaurant. We met on a rainy Saturday and had a fantastic brunch at Lime Stones. She used her feminine asset to the best of her ability. Her lower part of her body swayed from side to side like a flag in the wind. Her lips were moist and her eyes pierced right through my entire body. I knew that there was a connection when she started to touch my hand during her conversation.

At the end of the brunch, I asked for her opinion on whether she felt there was a connection or not. There was no doubt that she was seriously interested in having a wholesome relationship. I took her back to her home and asked for her to call whenever she felt like seeing me again. That same evening, just before I turned in for the night, the phone rang. Candy had called to tell me that she had a great time with me and the entire time at the table, she felt incredibly nervous, but she felt as if we were meant to be together. She went on to tell me that she couldn't stop thinking about me the entire day. She believed that for the first time in her life, she might have met her knight on a beautiful black horse. I had to inform her that I was still talking to KK, whom she had met at the birthday party. I could hear the thump on her chest as I told her that I was still trying to decide. She agreed to give me two weeks to make my decision before I chose the person that might be right for me. During the week, I met with KK and informed her about my date with Candy. Although KK portrayed herself as being strong, I could see right through her invisible shield.

As I stood and looked at her, I saw a beautiful woman that had her own beauty that made her shine. Every time I kissed her or touched her intimately I wowed myself. KK had the whole package to capture any man out there. However, even as we spoke and looked at each other with passion in our eyes, my thoughts were with Candy. I had the feeling that as much as I enjoyed being with KK, something told me that I had a connection with Candy.

The weekend was upon us, and my uncle was having a barbecue party at his home. I decided to take Candy to the barbecue so that it would give me an indication, of how she interacted around family. She got along rather well, for the most part, with the majority of my relatives. Because everyone was practically doing their own thing, it gave me an opportunity to give Candy a quick tour of the house. After the tour, we decided to sit in one of the rooms in the dark. We sat on the floor and talked for a while, but couldn't help touching each other. I believed if we weren't at the party, the possibility of us having sex, was a definite yes. As the evening came to a close, we said our good bye and headed for my home. It was quite late in the evening, so I didn't think that there was any chance of us making out. Well, who am I to try and figure out what's in a woman's head. She elected to come on up to my room for a minute. "Right." As I walked through the footpath, all I could think about was, "Are we really going to get it on tonight?" Before I could get too comfortable, Candy wasted no time in getting right down to the funky business.

She had a body like a little brick house. Her breasts were firm and looked like soft baseballs. Her booty was shapely with pretty nice skin. She moaned with passion as we touched each other all through the night. Her eyes showed excitement in them and without hesitation, she pushed me onto my back and proceeded to make sweet love to me. This time it was love making and not like the sex, my ex-wife and I had.

At the end of our lovemaking, she seemed a bit shy and shameful. After she freshened up, she approached me and sat on my lap. She told me that she had never experienced love making like that before, and she was hoping that we could be together. Just before she left, Candy broke down and cried like a little baby in my room. I couldn't believe what was happening. It wasn't in her to share a man with another woman, so she was hoping that I would put a stop to the other relationship. She felt that if I felt anything for her, even after

254

our night, then I'd give her a chance. Trying to envision myself telling KK that I made my decision to be with Candy, was going to put me in a place of mercy. I needed the strength and mercy from above because I knew what was going to happen when I told her.

We met at about 9pm and sat in a cafe and talked. As I looked into her eyes, I could see the tears preparing to pour as I told her that I've decided to stay with Candy. All I could have thought about, was why she would push me to date someone else, when I was perfectly OK being with her. The truth was, if I was fulfilled with her, I wouldn't have seen anything in Candy. I went on to tell her my decision, and with every word I said, I could see her tears and pain.

I felt like staying away from both, for the sake of not hurting her. However, I believed the real reason for me choosing Candy over KK was only because Candy had one child and a better job. KK had two children and had a mother who also lived with her, and she had issues with her daughter.

KK continued visit me every morning on her way to work for at least a week in hopes that I would change my mind by teasing me with sex and her body. She would come by in the early hours in the evening so that we could talk and make love. Many times I felt like saying yes to her, but I always feared that her mother might be a problem in our relationship. KK even mentioned that she would be willing to be with me regardless of whom she may be with.

Candy and I were officially dating each other without any distraction from any outside source. Every moment we spent with each other was enjoyable and neither one of us wished for it to end. One afternoon Candy and her daughter decided to make dinner for Austin and myself. Making dinner seemed like a simple enough task to do for us back then; however, I had no idea at the time that there was a catch for her gesture. It was like fattening the cow before you prepared him for slaughtering. After dinner, she approached me with the big question. Candy wanted to know how I would feel if she wanted to move in with me. She had caught me completely of the guard. To look at her and tell her that I didn't think it was a good idea, could be hazardous to our relationship, so basically I had no other choice but to say yes.

The joy that beamed through her eyes and body was out of this world. Looking from the outside, one might have seen her as winning the lottery. In my case, I looked at it as the beginning of stresses to come. It's always easier to date someone and at the end of the day return to your own little haven, but to live with me, is when you truly get to know me. After a week or so she moved in with her daughter and with a few of her belongings. Life was still moving along kind of smoothly, and Austin now had a stepsister to play with. Actually, Austin and BB got along rather well. Candy started talking about the future, and if at any point in my life, would I be willing to have a child with her. My response at the time was favorable, but not in the immediate future. I explained that having a child was of a serious nature, so we needed to know each other a bit longer. Candy seemed happy with my answer and felt that her future with me looked extremely positive.

From time to time, she would mention the baby story, hoping to get a change in my attitude. I reiterated that we're becoming familiar with each other and if everything continued to go well, then most definitely we could talk about

256

it at that time. Her eyes lit up like a flashlight in the dark. Her attitude was extremely exciting, and I almost felt as if she was ready to burst at her seam. To undertake the responsibility of having another person that quick in my life, was certainly a challenge.

The feeling of being by myself since my divorce was certainly refreshing, but I was unprepared for such a sudden change. One evening when the kids had turned in for the night, Candy approached me in the bedroom in a very timid way. She seemed as if she had done something terrible and was afraid to tell me. She stood beside me as I lay on the bed. She stood there with a slight smile on her face as her cheek twitched nervously.

As I looked up at her with great anticipation of what it might be for her to be so nervous, she began to speak. The last thought that would have crossed my mind was what she told me. Candy was pregnant, and she was awaiting my reaction to her comment. I looked at her with a smile on my face also and asked her not to worry and to go to bed.

That night I went to bed with a heavy heart. I couldn't believe that she would go ahead and get pregnant without even discussing it with me. I felt betrayed and undermined. The audacity of her to choose to get pregnant without my consent had caught my attention. I couldn't show my anger because of the condition that she was in. I didn't want to cause any stress on her that could create a domino effect on the baby.

Candy had an unexpected emergency to tend to in Jamaica. Her grandfather had passed away, so she had to attend the funeral. While in Jamaica, I had the task of preparing our new home to move into. I wanted the house to look fantastic when she returned. I did everything humanly possible by having the contractors put as much emphasis on our moving date. Thanks to the contractor and his team of workers, the house was ready on time. My family and a few of my friends assisted me in moving in on the date agreed on. The house looked fantastic, and it truly was a beautiful home. Austin had his own bedroom with sufficient room for him to do his homework and other activities. BB had her own bedroom, and she also had her privacy as a young lady. Candy and I had a beautiful master bedroom with a large suite. When she arrived from Jamaica that evening, without any hesitation we had a wonderful time blessing, the bedroom and the suite. Candy's stomach had grown significantly in the past weeks while she was away. She had a beautiful tan that shined on her skin like honey.

Her eyes glittered with joy as she looked at me, as happiness poured from her pours. As much as she looked captivating, I couldn't let go of the thought of being betrayed or trapped into a situation that I was unprepared for. Although I was happy in one sense for having another child that I always wanted, I couldn't let go of the idea of being manipulated. The next morning we got into an argument that probably wasn't anything to argue about, but because of my vexation towards her, I felt like punishing her emotionally.

I said a few hurtful things to her that had her crying and didn't confess to her until later in the evening that I had made it up. For the remainder of the week, I continued to vent my frustration on her. Knowing that it was totally wrong, I couldn't help myself. Candy began to think that I might be having an affair, but she didn't have an idea with whom it might be with. Realizing that I was hurting her and at the same time, as much as I was angry at her, I knew that I wanted her to have a strong and healthy child. I owned up to my boyish ways and agreed to act like the man, she felt in love with. I believe she understood how I felt, and the reason for my unorthodox behavior.

Things had settled down around our home, but something was wrong with the baby. There wasn't any movement from the baby, since she had been back from Jamaica. This was extremely odd to us, seeing that the baby moved a fair amount. We decided to pay a visit to our doctor to determine the reason for the lack of movement. The news wasn't very good. Candy had lost the baby. The baby had passed away while she was on vacation in Jamaica. The reason given to us for such a devastating blow was the result of her fibroids. Candy's stomach was congested with fibroids, so the baby had very little room to breathe and to grow. Candy was devastated and rightly so. I couldn't say I understood how she felt, but I could say that I knew that I was overwhelmed with sadness. The only thing that I could have done was to hold her and to let her know that I loved her. I promised her that once she removed her fibroids, we'd be in a much better position to have another child. The weeks ahead were extremely hard for both of us.

Austin took the news extremely poorly and didn't want to talk at all for a couple of days. The loss of little John was incredibly tough on everyone. After a couple of weeks had passed, a whole new Candy appeared out of nowhere. She began to attack me on not wanting her child. She felt that I must have been happy for not having her baby. I allowed her to say whatever she wanted, because I believed she was venting due to the loss of our child.

In the following weeks, I went through a barrage of verbal attacks by her. Her friends and her mother were placing stupid ideas into her head by making her think that I might be having an affair on her. Regardless of what I said to her, she continued to question every move I made. I couldn't even go to the gym, fearing the questions when I returned. On one occasion when I played golf with my friends, she would call an interrupt my game constantly just to make sure that I was where I said I was. She wanted to know if any women were playing with us and at what time would I be finished. Her constant intruding into everything that I did began to get on my nerves. However, I continued to answer all of her questions and did my best not to become angry with her. Candy's mother continued to be the central part of our breakdown in our relationship. She had full control over Candy's mind, and knew how to use it. Candy's mother was manipulating the situation into something larger than it really was. Regardless of whatever I said to her about my friends and my whereabouts, it was never convincing enough.

There were moments when Candy would be on her way home and would see my car going by our home, so she would take it upon herself to follow me. When asked about her intrusiveness, she would say, that she blinked her lights at me to stop, and tried honking her horn, so she had no other choice to follow me until I stopped. The feeling that I once held for her was beginning to diminish. I found it harder each day to come home, for I knew that all I would be doing was arguing.

There were times when I would either visit with my family or pay an unexpected visit to an ex-girl friend to sit and talk. Candy's daughter was becoming rude and defiant with my decision towards her behaviour in our home. At one point, she wrote a letter to her mother accusing me of physical abuse and a verbal attack on her. There were times when I had been anything but understanding and reassuring to her, and to reroute her misconceptions towards her mother. Little by little I started gaining her trust. BB then would reveal to me all of her secrets, rather than approaching her mother, because she felt she could trust me. She said that she felt more comfortable talking to me, than speaking with her own mother. She spoke about wishing to be older so that she could date and go to the clubs. She also spoke about how she felt when her mother would pick on her for little things. My role was to get her to see herself in the mirror as she spoke about her mother. I wanted her to understand the role of a mother and a parent.

I reassured her that her mother loved her, but she had to be a bit cautious, because of the world that we live in now. I told her that one day she'd look back and realize that her mother loved her dearly, so that's why she did what she did. I realized that I had to put a stop to this nonsense immediately, so I ran upstairs to her room and confronted her. I looked at her directly in her eyes, and asked her if at any time I had ever abused her in any manner. I knew that she couldn't lie at that moment, because she knew that I was terribly angry at her.

I had her follow me downstairs and repeat to her mother what she had said to me. Looking at her mother with tears in her eyes, she retracted her statement and apologized to her mother for concocting her story. Eventually, during that week she wrote a letter to me, apologizing for her action. To this day, I'm still in possession of her letter; but as for Candy, that was the beginning of the end for us. I realized that I couldn't win this war, so I started to prepare myself for a breakup.

Chapter 9

My ex-wife was still slandering my name and continuing to make my life difficult. At every chance, she would challenge my decision with regard to Austin by way of court. Her father had a discussion with my uncle one afternoon. My uncle suggested that the grandfather would continue to try his best to continue to support Austin as he'd done in the past. However, his response to my uncle was, "if Everard thinks for a second he'll ever see a cent of my money, then he better think twice." He went on to say that, "he wishes to see me poor and living on the street, and he'll never do anything to make my life better."

A few days later I had a short conversation with Mr. Hard Heart about Austin's university decision. During the conversation, I found his tone to be very abusive and compelling. I felt that l owed him, nothing and neither did he, so I expressed my desire to ban him from calling my home.

I asked that he contact Austin directly at his cell phone. I couldn't believe that he had the audacity to call me on my phone and expressed how much he hated me. I had to remind him that his feeling towards me wasn't as shocking as he thought. I refreshed his memory by reminding him of their behavior when they first found out that I was dating their daughter. I reminded him that if it wasn't for me, the likely hood of having a relationship with their daughter would have been impossible. Before I hung up, reminded him to check with his maker about his hatred. One evening after I returned from the gym, I found myself answering to Candy about my whereabouts. She wanted to know again why it took me that long to work out and to play a few games of squash.

She also questioned me about my female friends whom I had a platonic relationship with. I couldn't believe that she started answering my phone and even recalling the numbers. That evening, we had words with each other, and as a result of our anger, we both went to bed angry. During that night, I found myself being up most of the night. My head began to hurt as my chest rose up and down quickly. I didn't want to alarm Candy, so I made my way out of the room quietly. I had a glass of wine and completed the remainder of bottled wine in the basement.

As I sat in the basement, I started to think of my past. I thought of all the horrible things that had happened to me, and that I had done. I searched for an answer to why these things had happened. I looked deep within my soul for an answer to why my ex-wife had treated me the way she did. I looked up into the ceiling and asked for freedom and peace. I wanted all of my pain and misery to be removed from within me. So the only thing I could have thought of was to do the unthinkable.

I decided to take my own life that night. I took an electrical cord and tied it into a noose. I took a piece of wood and made it into a cross. I knew that there was a Bible in the basement, so I read a few pages of it, and prepared myself for the end. The feeling felt right, but I feared the feeling of pain that my son would feel. I placed a stool under my feet and threw the cord around the beams. As I stood there with the noose around my neck, the tears poured from my eyes, but I knew that what I was about to do, was the best for everyone. Just as I was about to make my entry into the world beyond us, Candy came into the basement. She had a look on her face, as if she had seen the devil. I realized that I was the devil at that point. Every second that I took to carry through with my descent to hell was terminated by her entry. She walked over to me with tears in her eyes, while asking for me to step down. I hated her for a short second, because I now had to stay around and harbor my pain even longer. We sat on the ground and cuddled each other while she cried for me. I couldn't cry, because I didn't know how to anymore. With all the alcohol in my system, I began to feel very tired and agitated. I believed she went upstairs and made an emergency phone call to one of my family members. I really didn't care very much for anything or anyone at that moment.

All I knew was that I had an opportunity to meet with either my maker or with my destroyer and Candy came back downstairs and ruined a perfectly one on one moment. The following morning, from what I can remember, my family along with Candy readmitted me into the hospital. My memory of being admitted was vague. However, I do remember being in an altercation with the security staff. The following day the nurse mentioned to me that I had injured two security officers and hurt an elderly.

The doctors felt that I was suffering from a severe depression that was dormant for many, many years. I missed approximately one month of work while being treated in the hospital. The doctor who was assigned to me felt that it was in my best interest if I considered having a few more Electric Shock Therapy treatments again. After careful consideration,

I decided that I'd have a few E.S.T treatments. The best thing about the treatment was that it had me smiling once again, and it also had me looking healthier in my face. The down side to the treatment was that I'd lost a good portion of my memory. Apparently, the treatment tends to cause a loss of memory. The doctors tend to believe that, for the most part, the part of your memory that tends to disappear is your short term memory. So basically, anything that I'd experienced in the past few years, I'd have problems remembering. The prognosis had been truthful, because I'd had some difficulty remembering names, places, and even my work. I recall returning to work and having to be retrained all over again. That was one of my most embarrassing moments in my life. Every time I'd undergone a treatment, I'd forgotten almost everything. I guessed by now my job place had come to understand what I was going through.

Having to represent yourself, based on your current condition was incredibly embarrassing and upsetting. For weeks, I had to undergo the jokes and their stupid remarks. Many times I felt like lashing out at my so-called peers, but I realized that was just the chemical imbalance of some North American people. I'd found that some people from North America are inconsiderate of other people's deficiency. The news had spread like vines on the side of a house. Esther had found out that I was admitted into the hospital, so this created a whole new court battle for me all over again. Thankfully, I had a great lawyer, and Austin was approaching the age of thirteen. Esther realized that Austin was within months of his thirteenth birthday where it would make him legal to decide on which parent he would prefer to live with, so she ended her ridiculous idea of going to court again.

A few months had passed, and Candy had become pregnant again. This time she agreed that she wanted to try to have another child because of the loss she felt for the first child. The prognoses would be the same, so she would have to abort the baby.

Candy's fibroids would be too much for her to carry a child safely, unless she had her fibroids removed. Having to abort yet another child brought a great deal of stress on her. I realized that regardless of whatever, we did, unless she was prepared to have an operation to remove her fibroids, the result would always be the same. For her to have the operation, some time off was needed from her work and no income received at all, since she worked as an independent employee, she wouldn't be paid for any time away from work.

After six or so months had passed, we finally agreed to go our separate ways. She had mentioned it in a conversation while we were having a discussion, and one thing escalated to another. My uncle Jude tried his best to encourage us to stay together, but as a result of multiple interference from her mother and her envious friends; she felt that it would be in our best interest to go in separate ways. Candy agreed to buy me out of my mortgage, and I began my search for an apartment.

Having to return to an apartment was a reminder to me that I had reached my lowest point again. Another relationship had failed again due to the interference of a family member. Two weeks before I moved out, Candy began to beg for me to change my mind. She felt that she had made her decision in anger and realized that she was allowing her family and friends to ruin her life. By this time, it was a little too late for sorrows; I had run out of patience. I had already deposited my first and last month rent on an apartment, and truthfully I had run out of mercy.

Candy couldn't bear the idea of me leaving, so she decided to stay at her mom's that day until I had moved out. The move was hurtful but at the same time I realized that she needed to grow up. Austin was extremely hurt, because he took it as another rejection. The apartment we moved into was not of the best quality. We lived on the seventh floor, next to some neighbors who owned two dogs. The apartment was small and had an extremely tiny kitchen and some of the windows and doorframes had holes that required filling.

My bedroom was extremely small, so I gave Austin the larger room so that he could complete his studies in comfort. One of his widows in his bedroom had a crack, so in the wintertime, the temperature would be extremely cold in his room. The balcony door didn't close properly, so again in the wintertime we found it rather freeze. Regardless of how many times, I approached the superintendent to have the window, door and shower repaired; it was never done properly.

After a while, we decided that we were going to have to make the best of it. The laundry room was in the basement of the apartment, where the lighting wasn't at its best. The laundry equipment constantly malfunctioned and in any occasion, you could find that you're face to face with a mouse or two. The most annoying part of the entire building was the elevator system. The building only had two elevators, and if at any time one of them was out of order, you were prepared for a lot of chaos.

The children who resided in the building had no respect for the property. Many times I would enter the elevator only to be surprised with urine on the floor or mucus on the elevator door. This was extremely disgusting and upsetting. Regularly, the fire department would have to attend for multiple reasons; either the alarm had been pulled or there was violence in the building. The police would arrive shortly after the fire department, to arrest a handful of individuals for assault or for drug trafficking. The underground garage was poorly lit and constantly had a leek. Water would be pouring from either end of the building at any time of the day. The bottom line, this was the best of the worst that we could have found that was within my budget.

The entire two years that we spent at the apartment, no one ever visited us. The choice was mainly ours because of the state of the building we decided that we wouldn't have any visitors. I spent a fair amount of time by myself while away from Candy. I focused mainly on Austin and his education. I wanted to be the best father possible for him, so that he could do his best at school. After a year or so, I started dating for the joy of it. I felt like I needed to be around people so that I could escape from all my frustrations. I met a variety of women, from all parts of the world. Some of the women were extremely caring, and some were just plain evil. Sadly, at that time of my life, I wasn't interested in having a serious relationship. I did meet one woman whom I had known from my past. We had met many years before while I was involved with my wife.

One evening while out with my friend, I had a wonderful opportunity to sit and talk with her. She was attending the jazz festival on the beaches. We enjoyed each other's conversation, and ultimately we ended up spending the summer with each other. She had been married but the marriage had fallen apart. At the time she was suffering from a medical condition, and I felt that it would be comforting for her to know she had a friend that she could lean on. Our friendship grew and as a result of being there for her, and I believe she fell in love with me. During the summer, I attended a family barbecue at my Uncle Winston's home. All of my cousins wanted to see what my motorcycle looked like, so I decided to ride to the barbecue on it. On my way, something came over me and directed me to the motorcycle store. The helmet that I was wearing was in poor condition, but still road certified. Something was telling me to purchase a helmet, so I tried a few of them on and found one that I really liked. Although I spent all my time trying on helmets, I still left the store without purchasing a helmet. After a quarter of the way into my route, I felt an urge to return to the store to by the helmet. As much as I fought with the idea of returning, I couldn't ignore the temptation. I turned around and made my way back to the store, narrowly arriving before they closed. I purchased the helmet and it fit perfect on my head. What a difference it made with my riding.

I arrived at the gathering that evening and gave a few of my cousins a bike ride. Unfortunately; my cousin Lynda burnt her calf on the muffler of the bike. I felt really bad about it, but every rider tends to have a mark on the body to be remembered by. It was just after midnight when I decided to leave. The temperature was cool and unfortunately for me, I only wore a sweater that day.

I recall pulling over to put my gloves on, and to zip my

sweater up as high as possible. I pulled up to the lights at Dufferin Street and waited for the lights to turn green. Just before the lights turned green, a white Honda Accord with the license plates that was placed in an abnormal spot stopped and tried to have a conversation with me. I did my best to ignore the two individuals in the car, because of their somewhat intoxicated behavior. I knew that they were hoping for a drag race, but I wasn't about to put myself at risk and possibly other drivers on the road. We stopped at the light at Bathurst Street and again they continued to annoy me to race. I allowed them to drive ahead of me, while I cruised at a comfortable pace. The speed limit in the area was 70kh with an island that separated the traffic from East to West. Suddenly, without any notice, the car slowed to a halt and positioned on an angle, obstructing the entire passing lane and half of the curb lane. The two individuals looked over their shoulders with a cunning smile on their faces. I had very little time to brake, so I tried to maneuver around the car but there wasn't sufficient room, so I ended up spilling the bike. I can recall sliding towards the vehicle as my head slammed along the asphalt multiple times. I kept myself as relaxed as possible to prevent myself from any serious injuries. I can recall hearing the sound of the vehicle accelerating as my bike came to a stop.

A few family members in the area had overheard the accident and called the ambulance to attend. The last thing that I remembered was a lady placing a blanket over me to prevent me from freezing. For a brief moment, I thought to myself that this could be the end. I felt myself going under, and I knew that my body was in severe pain. The ambulance arrived and escorted me to the hospital. I spent the entire night in the hospital and most of the morning.

The doctors examined me with great care and had me x-rayed at many points of my body. The doctor told me when I awoke that I was a very lucky man. He felt that if it wasn't for my helmet and being in good physical condition, it's highly possible that my injuries could have been far worse. I walked away with two of my fingers being severely sprained. I had gouges to various parts of my hands. My legs were scraped from the fall, and I had a large cut on my shoulder and back area.

Aside from a major headache and my bike being ruined, all was well. Baby girl arrived at the hospital the following day to take me home. Under normal conditions; I would have had my son pick me up, but at the time he was on a trip in Alabama with his aunt and uncle. I spent approximately three days at Brooke's home and was released by her to return to my own home. The short time that I spent at her home wasn't very hospitable.

My birthday was approaching, and I surely didn't want to spend it in the condition that I was in, however, I knew that it was unlikely for me to recover in such a short span of time. I couldn't understand her thinking at all, I knew she suffered from depression, but I didn't think that she would behave in the way she did. My birthday had come and gone like a cloud in the sky. I spent my birthday wrapped up in bandages, and terribly unhappy in the environment that I was in while I was pushing for recovery.

I had an appointment at the hospital the following day to follow up on my improvement and to have my bandages removed and cleaned. On my way back from the hospital, I decided that it might be best if I tried to take care of myself, so I suggested that she dropped me off at my apartment.

To my amazement, she agreed. I asked about my clothing, and she told me that she had packed it and left it in her trunk. Her reasoning for doing so was in case I had an urge to be taken home. If only you could picture the look that I had in my mind towards her. Once upstairs in my apartment, my only request from her, was to be kind enough to open my medication bottles, but to leave the lid lose so that nothing got into the bottles. I asked her to do the same with the orange juice and the parcel of bread.

After a few days, Austin had arrived home, and I was never so happy to see him. Having someone around who truly loves you and is willing to take care of you is sometimes difficult to put into words. I had never been so happy to see my son's face as he walked through the front door. Knowing that Austin was finally home gave me some comfort. It was good to know that I had someone whom I knew that I could count on. Once I was able to manage for myself, and I was well enough to ride my bike again, I decided to pay Baby girl an unexpected visit one evening after 9pm. I pulled up to the driveway and saw a vehicle that I had never seen parked in her driveway.

At first I thought that it might be her mother's vehicle or one of her girl friends. I was about to knock on the door when I realized that the lights were completely off in the entire house. I found that to be odd seeing that she had a visitor. So I peaked through the glass of the front door and was surprised of what I saw. I couldn't believe my eyes! I watched for awhile as Brooke and her male whore were

273

expressing their lust for one another. This individual had his leg spread eagle as he lay on his back with Baby girl in between his legs while Baby girl caressed his lips with her own lips.

They jostled like two kittens for a while before Baby girl decided to lie in a vertical position on him. I watched as he touched her on her breast and as the temperature rose between her private area. They continued to smother each other by locking their lips together as they survived only as a result from each other's breath. My eyes were fixed on them as I laughed to myself in disbelief. At first I wanted to kick the door open like Jet Li would in his movies, but I decided not to, instead I rang the door bell. Within seconds of the bell being rung, Baby girl did a fifty foot dash to the lights, hoping that she could make the home look as if no one was at there. I rang the doorbell a few times before leaving her property as she wasn't prepared to answer her door. As I made my way down the street, I refused to allow her to think she had got one over me. So I made a u-turn with my bike and went back to her home. This time I rang the doorbell along with knocking on the door a few times in a more police like manner. Baby girl finally answered the door with a nervous look on her face, alluding to the fact that if she was ever to be interrogated, she would be seen as being guilty. I asked why she took so long to answer the door; she blamed it on the television and not being close enough to hear the bell. As she welcomed me in with her body twitching out of control, she introduced me to her friend who claimed to be visiting from Florida. He stretched his hand out to shake mine, as though we were friends, while all I could think of was that we weren't family, so there was no reason for him to call me brother. I couldn't remember seeing this fool anywhere in my photo albums as a sibling or even as an adopted chump. I looked at his hand and told him that I already had a brother and walked on up the stairs with Baby girl. One of the reasons why I originally came to her home was for her to complete something on the computer; a task that she had started to work on a while back. The other reason was just to pay her a surprise visit. As Baby girl tried her best to remember how to do what she had started, it amazed me of how uncomfortable she was at that moment. She couldn't concentrate or even remember her own notes that she had made. Her hands were trembling and her nose was sweaty as her voice cracked while trying to speak. I loved every moment of it while she tried her best to stay calm and focused. With a great deal of nervousness along with a little self-control, Brooke tried her best not to fall apart and completed the task that I came for.

We made our way back down stairs where I had the nauseous moment of being in the presence of the swine. As I walked to the door, I thought to myself, why should I be upset at the fool, he had no idea that she was being intimate with me, so I decided to just nod my head as I approached the door. The thing that bothered me the most was when he said, "nice to meet you" I began to wonder if Baby girl had mentioned my name in their conversation. I asked Baby girl if she would be kind enough to step out on to the porch for a second so that I could have a word with her. She seemed very nervous but went with me to me to the porch.

This was the moment when I told her what type of person that I felt she was. I told her that I had seen some of her staring roles, as she was not aware that I had been standing at her front door. I told her that I was sorry that I was late so I missed the opening act, but if it was anything like I saw, then she's done a great job. I told her she was a neighbourhood's rug, and that I was not interested in lying on this rug any more. I suggested that she'd better hope that her sugar daddy sticks around and wasn't on his way back to Florida.

Baby girl felt embarrassed and ashamed as some of her neighbors were outside at the time. She began to cry and asked if I would grant her a second chance, and that it wasn't what I thought. I looked at her like a chalk mark on the ground as I made my way backwards down the stairs. For some reason, I wasn't terribly upset, but I was disappointed because I didn't see her as the type of person that would entertain such deception. I did receive a phone call from her that night expressing her sorrow.

As much as I felt bad for her, I'd always maintained that I would never continue with a relationship once it's being tarnished. Although we weren't in a full-blown relationship, I still felt a form of trust to one another. She continued to call me as she tried her best to convince me that she had made a terrible mistake. She told me that she had asked her friend to leave and not to ever return. Baby girl seemed genuinely regretful about what had happened. Even if I had decided to entertain the idea of becoming an item, I would have too many questions about what had happened on that steamy night.

I was happy about what had happened at the right time. I asked her to stop calling me for a while, because I felt it was the best thing for the both of us; plus I had lost the feeling that I had for her due to how she treated me at her place when I was injured. I believed that Baby girl was genuine and good spirited person with lots of love in her heart. Moreover, I do believe that given a fair opportunity with no interference from her past relationships, the possibility of trying to have a relationship might have been possible. However, because of the events that took place, it caused me to develop a form of resentfulness and mistrust towards her. So seeing how my mother was treated, I swore to never tolerate that type of treatment as long as I lived.

Chapter 10

Austin is the most sensitive boy whom I know; and he's extremely caring and loyal to me. He has a heart filled with love and joy, and appreciates every little thing that I'd done, and I would continue to do. I know that Austin's wish was to see me with someone that truly loved me, and who was willing to play a strong devoted role in our lives. Knowing full well what had happened in the past to us, neither one of us was willing to settle for just anyone. A couple of months had gone by, and I was almost on my way to a full recovery. I had decided that I'd devote myself to spend time with Austin and making sure that his school grades were always up. I dated a few people along the way and really never had a true match. There were times when I believed that I had met my soul mate, but as time passed by, it would tell the truth. The next couple of years I dated a few women and nothing real came out of it with anyone. I decided that I was going to hand my wish over to God because He's the only one that knew who the right person was for me. Then, I got more involved with my church and reading the Bible.

For whatever reason, some people tend to go to church to convince themselves that they're actually participating by entering the church doors, while others go because they're seeking a true relationship with God. After being in that despicable apartment for that long, I decided that it would be

good for us if I purchased a home. I found out that by living in that apartment, it had taken away Austin's freedom and self-confidence. To have a child and for him not to become comfortable to invite some of his friends over to play or even to complete a school task, could cause the
him to develop a lack of confidence causing other feelings to surface.

I'm not saying that he never invited anyone over, but it wasn't at the level where he did when we lived in a house as a family. One afternoon after work when I arrived home, I was slapped in the face with a bit of reality. I found myself standing in the hallway with a bunch of rowdy children going into the elevator, and once inside, the smell was really hard to bear even for a pig farmer. The elevator was slow in moving and would stop in between the floors or even miss your floor entirely. I realized that for me to keep my sanity, I would have to do something drastic and quick. Later that evening, I went out looking for a home that would be reasonable on the pocket, and pleasing to our eyes.

I wanted to keep this as quiet as possible so that I could surprise my son. I knew that once he found out that we were moving, he would be ecstatic. I decided that I'd search for a home that would be smaller in size, yet big enough to have that warm feeling. I contacted my uncle Jude and asked him to be my agent and to help me in finding the right house. After a month of searching, I found a house in Ajax, just about five minutes from where I originally lived. The house stood out like a rose among the plants. I couldn't stop looking at it, and I had to see what the inside of the house looked like. I had a strong feeling that I'd like what I would see inside, because of the positive feeling I got from being so attached and the good feeling I had to have that home. As we approached the door to view the house, I knew already that the house was going to be mine. We walked into the house, and the light had shunned in a manner as if this house, was chosen for me. The overwhelming feeling I felt was strong enough to know that God had brought me to this house. The house was about to have a new owner.

Austin and I moved into our new home on the thirty-first of October, Halloween night. As we pulled up to the driveway, I could see the joy on his face as he realized that we were about to own our own home. Austin exited the car like a man on a mission as he ran into the house to see his new home. He now had a bedroom that was large enough to do his homework, and a home where he could entertain his friends.

Just to see the joy on his face was satisfying enough for me, and also to feel that whatever the amount, it was well worth it. The joy I felt by owning my own home without any assistance from anyone was the best feeling ever. I couldn't rest, unless all the furniture had been mounted together and placed in their assigned spots. I believed I had the entire place unpacked and cleaned by the end of the following day. Austin and I were enjoying our home and felt so at peace to be in a home without any drama and filled with only fun and happiness. While e was moving along with his happy go-lucky life, I was struggling with a demon within me. I had no idea what I was fighting, but I knew that I was afraid of something, and it was driving me mad. At nighttime when the house was quiet and everyone was asleep, the big green multicolored demon would appear. Sometimes while I was sleeping, my entire body would become as cold as ice. My body would be so cold that I didn't know if it would be better for me to get up and put on a second set of clothing or to stay under the blanket and curl up until I became warmer. Many times while I was sleeping, I would have my feet touched or dragged across the bed, causing me to jump out of my sleep. At this point, I would sit upright for many minutes looking around the room. Sometimes I would cover my entire head, just leaving sufficient room to see and breathe.

This is when I would see something zoom by, faster than you can blink. I know this may sound a bit out there, but I was sure the demon knows that I had had a short glimpse of him. Even if I were to see the monster, it would be impossible for me to harm him. The mammoth size of the paranormal thing would destroy me in mere seconds. I took the advice of some of my aunts and uncles to pray and to play gospel music. I started seeing the demon in the back seat of my vehicle. I decided that since it hadn't killed me yet, so then I'd just have to ignore it until it left on its own.

After many nights of not being able to sleep, I started to sit and watch television until I finally fell asleep in the chair that I sat in. My doctor and some family members felt that the reason for me not being able to sleep was due to my brain not being able to shut down. They felt that whatever stresses I was dealing with at the time, I would go to my bed thinking about it. So as a result of my thoughts, I would act out whatever was on my mind. My dreams were so realistic that I would end up damaging my furniture and hurting myself. Many times during the night I would wake myself up, because I was punching at a piece of furniture or banging on the wall. I'd even gone as far as to hit my son by mistake. For some reason, I would have the sense to react quickly enough, so that I would not hurt the other person. I have survived having only three to four hours sleep for the passed six or so years. My body usually felt as if a vehicle had struck me in the mornings. I despised the thought of nighttime, due to the fear I had for what I believed to be a demon, and for the lack of sleep I got regularly.

One night when I couldn't have taken it any longer, I decided that I'd put an end to it, due to the money problems that I had to go through with Esther's family. It placed me in a situation where I needed someone to assist me. Sometimes I would sit and wondered how people could be so thoughtless and selfish with their wealth. In the past whenever, I knew that a friend of mine was in danger, I would offer my hand, hoping that whatever help I could give, would be of great help in cleaning of one or more of his wounds.

One day, which I chose not to mention, I decided that I would do something I never thought I would have done. I guess sometimes when you're down on your luck; you would do almost anything to survive. On this night, I decided to wear a black outfit that covered my entire body from face to feet. I parked my vehicle a block away from a spot I had chosen, with a change of clothes in it, and walked to the building that I intended to rob. As I walked along the sidewalk, every person looked at me like they wanted to stop me or to call for the police. The sweat ran down my forehead and along my back into the crease of my butt.

Once inside of the store I looked to see how many security officers were there. I guessed by now, you would figure out that it was Halloween night. I thought to myself

282

that this would be the perfect night to pull this heist off. I walked up and down the aisles, trying to determine when to make my move to the office. I had walked with a wooden stick that was covered with copper piping to strengthen it from breaking. I had a pair of plastic Swiss ties to ensure their safety, in case something went wrong.

My adrenalin was running so high that I knew that I had to get it over with quickly. Just as I was preparing myself to approach the office, a police officer stood beside me and asked me who I was supposed to be that night. Well, that just made me feel like blowing in my pants. I spoke to him with my head down and asked him what he was supposed to be that night. As he laughed, I walked towards the door and made my way to the car quickly. My butt was as wet as a brand new baby. I couldn't believe my luck. God was certainly watching over me on this night. Imagine the outcome if I had followed through with my plan. Today I would have been without a job or probably dead from some altercation that may have taken place. The dead part might have been a good thing, seeing that it might have been an easy way to put an end to my stresses. I took my crazy ass home and sat and had a strong drink as I laughed at myself.

I mentioned how much I dreaded the thought of knowing that nighttime was approaching. One night, I decided that I'd take matters into my own hand, and put an end to all my misery. I took a razor blade and began to shave my head until little chunks of flesh would fall off. The blood would flow down the side of my face as I bared the pain. After a while, I sat on the couch and began to clip my toe nails and cut the bottom of my feet. Many times I would try cutting around my testicles between my legs because I figured that would be the area that would give me the most pain, so I would make small incisions and watch it drip for a while as I endured the pain and stood in the shower moaning. I would clip them to the point where I was clipping off the fleshy part of my skin. I soon realized that I was enjoying the pain and the taste of my blood was sweet. I continued with this act almost nightly, just re injuring the wound. The following week when I ran out of things to do to keep me occupied, I decided that I would play a game. I went into the kitchen and got myself a bit of cooking oil and placed it on my neck. I found myself a rope that I used to tie things together or to keep the trunk of the car as closed as possible. I made myself a knot on both ends so that I could pull on it. I swung the rope around my neck and began to pull as tight as possible. I pulled and pulled until I could feel my neck burning from the friction. My eyes were feeling like they were about to pop from their sockets. The saliva in my mouth became very dry and my heart was beating strangely. However; as much as I tried, it was evident that I couldn't take my life like that. It had the same effect as trying to bite your own tongue off. You just couldn't do it. The following week after my neck had healed from the bruises, I decided that I'd tie the same rope around my neck and see how long it would take me to run out of breath if I tried hanging myself from the stair railings. I figured I would have a drink or two then I would climb over and gently place the rope around my neck and release myself slowly hoping to test it. Before I would try the act, I would drink from the bottle of Bacardi many mouthfuls until the inside of my cheeks would feel like they were on fire. For some reason, as much as I wanted to see what the effect would be, something kept on stopping me from going further.

I became so angry that started to have a conversation

with myself, and also with whatever spirit or mystic force that was in the hallway with me. Seeing that I couldn't get my other leg to climb over the railing, I placed myself on the floor and laid across the floor as I tested myself by hanging my legs down the stairs with the rope tightening around my neck. The feeling was almost the same as being hung. As I placed the rope around my neck and slid my legs down the stairs, it created the effect of being hung. By having your entire body hanging down the stairs, the only benefit to this is that I had the option of stopping whenever I felt that I was about to pass out. Your eyes would bulge and your head would feel as if it was about to explode. I was sure that you've heard of kids or junkies sniffing on glue for an extended period of time, and the effect of sniffing the glue, was an incredible high. Well, the experience was similar but painful and for some reason joyful.

My nights were still eventful and scary as a result of being in the house by myself with a demon that had all the time in the world. He decided at nighttime, whether he was going to bother me or not. So many times I'd been in my basement by myself and felt as if someone was watching me. To this day every time I walk up the stairs from the basement or to my bedroom, I'll stop at the top and look back. It's very difficult when you know that something is out there, but you haven't been able to see it.

I developed a pattern in my every day movement to glance at the upstairs windows from within my car before driving off to see if anyone was hiding behind the blinds. I believed that there was someone watching me, but I was not able to see them. At this particular time in my life, I'd learned how to live with it and I was comfortable with that.

Chapter 11

For years my aunt and uncle had been trying to get me to visit their church. I decided that based on everything that had been happening in my life, I'd give it a chance. The decision to visit the church had been my best investment ever. I believed that the feelings that I had, weren't as intense as before. The other point to being involved in the church was that I had an opportunity to read and learn all about the Bible. So many times when the preacher would preach and quote sections from the Bible, I had no idea what he was talking about. Well, I could safely say that, as a result of participating, I'd gained a fair amount of knowledge, and I looked forward to continuing on my guaranteed investment.

This investment has brought dividends that none other could have brought me. Sometimes when you least expect it, there's a little angel guiding you towards a friend. That friend had turned out to be my Uncle Jude and Aunt Eileen. The holidays were upon us, and it was around that time when we looked for a gift for my sister and father. Austin really liked his grandfather. My father would sit and talk to him about life and what he would like to see for him in the future.

I usually sat in the living room or spent my time speaking with my sister Maureen while my father told him about his life. He explained to him how he began working at a young age, and that he was one the best contractors back in Trinidad. He also told him about him being one of the few contractors who received a certificate from Pierre Trudeau (the Canadian Prime Minister in the early eighties). My father explained to Austin that he wouldn't become as successful as he was by not educating himself and working hard.

The majority of the time while they spoke, I sat with Maureen as she was in her bedroom every time we visited. The last Christmas I vowed that I would never return to my father's home at Christmas time again. Last Christmas when Austin and I visited with him and his wife; the evening turned into a mess. My father attacked me verbally, and if I didn't have some restraint in myself, it may have turned into something physical.

Austin and my father were having a conversation about cars and sports. He told Austin that his grandson from one of his daughters had a son, who was actively in soccer. He mentioned how good he was, and that he was one of the youngest players in the Trinitarian professional soccer team. My father was really proud of him. The conversation turned from his grandson to me regarding his mother Delta, who I did not know. Maybe I had forgotten about her, due probably of my depression.
I told my father that I didn't know him because I had lost part of my memory and still have difficulty remembering how to get to his own home. He continued to bother me so because I couldn't take it anymore, I said that the only Delta I knew of was the airline. This irritated him to the point where he started to bring up the past. I had forgotten that Delta was my sister, seeing that I haven't seen her in a long while, since she lived in Trinidad.

He mentioned to Austin that I created problems for

him when I told my mother about Delta being in Toronto and staying at his home. He felt that I should have kept my mouth shut and to add salt to the wound, I decided to take Delta to see my mother. Unknown to either of us, my mother had already known about Delta but chose not to talk about it because of the unnecessary heartache it my cost her. I should mention that my father had an affair on my mother in Trinidad with another woman and as a result Delta was born. The more I stood my ground on reaffirming that I didn't know Delta; it made him even angrier.

My father told Austin that I had been in jail as a child, and he had to have an act on my behalf to bail me out of jail. That was a total lie and nothing like that had ever happened. The truth of the matter was that I had to attend court for a speeding violation. The judge had found me guilty and decided to revoke my driving license. As a result of not being able to drive, I called my father and made him aware of the circumstances. Realizing how serious the situation was, he decided to place a call to his lawyer and had him attend the courthouse to have my matter dealt with properly. The judge put me in a waiting room until I received proper council, and that I'd be properly advised of what could happen.

During our conversation, my father went on to talk negative about my mother. I wasn't happy with the way he spoke about her, portraying her as a "nothing" to us. I reminded him that if it wasn't for my mother, the likelihood of him being alive today wouldn't have been possible, had not been for her faithfulness towards him. I told him that I knew that mom was the one who worked extra hard to assist him in having the wealth that he had obtained. I reminded him of how upset mom was when she found out that he had purchased two vehicles without discussing it with her. I told him that he should have looked back at the life he had before meeting this home wrecker, and he should sit quietly and thank his lucky stars to have found a woman as beautiful as my mother.

After I spoke to him about his ways, at this point he lost his cool and became verbally abusive. He started to call me names and to remind me of what a bum I was, and that I'd never rise to be anything in this world. He reminded me of how much he wanted me to be the one on the operating table that night when the doctor informed us about Maureen's prognosis in the hospital. He even went as far as to make me believe that I had been adopted, and that he wasn't my father. He told me that some bum had slept with my mother, and he had no choice but to adopt me when he started to date my mother. Technically, the way he said it, was much worse than I'm relaying it to you now. He went on to say that he felt that it was the right thing to do to adopt me. I couldn't sit there and let him abuse my mother without having her defend herself, so I acted on her behalf. I made him aware that if he felt that she was such a terrible person, then why he would have chased behind her, for all those years after she left him.

I guess I struck a nerve when I told him if he believed that, then the beached whale he was living with could never have held a candle to my mother. I believed this is when he lost his composure and became ignorant. He suggested that if I wanted to show him how much of a man I was. I would say one more thing about his wife again. He told me to say one more thing about anything about him or her and I'd see him stick the knife down my throat.

289

At this time, I was so hurt and embarrassed that I couldn't say anything else, even if I wanted to. Realizing that things were getting out of hand, Austin got up and went into the bedroom where Maureen was resting. After my father had got everything of his chest, he got up and went into the family room and talked with the red lobster. I spent the remainder of my time in the living room sitting and pondering on the events that had just taken place until we were ready to leave. Before leaving, I kissed my sister and made my way out the door to the car in the driveway. Austin spent a few minutes talking with his grandfather and Maureen and then left as well.

The drive home was extremely tough on me, and I had no idea, whether my son believed or not what he just had heard. After half an hour had passed, I asked Austin if he believed any of the things he heard. He looked at me with sorrow and sadness in his eyes and said "no." After a few minutes had passed, to bring laughter back into our day, he laughed out loud and said, "Daddy if you were ever to be placed in jail, I wouldn't want to see how angry you would become at some of the prisoners."

I told Austin that this was going to be the last time I visited with my father again around the Christmas holidays. He knew that I would be willing to drop him off at the house, and whenever he felt that he was ready to leave, I'd return to pick him up. This would be the last time I see my father alive. The Christmas of 2008 had arrived and Austin had bought a nice gift for his grandfather and was prepared to deliver it to him. I drove Austin out to the house on Christmas Eve night as we used to.

The snow had freshly fallen a few days ago, so the roofs of the homes looked beautiful. As we pulled up into the driveway, Austin saw that there were no movements of traffic on his grandpa's property. His footprints were the only prints that had made contact with the snow in days. He knocked at the door, and no one was available to answer. During the entire holiday season, we didn't hear anything from him regarding his whereabouts. Austin decided that he'd hold onto his gift and try to deliver it to him, whenever he returned from his disappearance.

Austin decided one day to pay his grandfather a visit near the end of March. He rang the doorbell and was greeted by Alice, my father's wife. She told Austin that he wasn't feeling very well. As much as Austin tried to convince her that he just wanted to see him for a second, she decided against it. Austin called me from his cell phone immediately after he had left the house. I immediately called my father's home, and Alice answered. I asked her why she wouldn't allow Austin to see his grandfather. She told me that my father was very ill, and that she didn't know if he would make it this time. She went on to say that he had good days and terrible days. I asked if she knew what the problem was, but all she said was that the doctors were trying to diagnose his problem. The problem I had was, if she really knew if my father wasn't going to make it, and that the doctors weren't sure of his problem yet.

I had a feeling that Alice was up to something, but I didn't know what it was. Alice wasn't God to make such a bold statement about our father. I asked Alice if she could keep me aware of his condition. She told me that they had a whole week of appointments already booked, and she'd let me know whatever she found out. The entire week came and went, and I hadn't received a phone call from Alice updating me on the condition of my father.

The following week I was lucky enough to get a hold of her. She told me that my father's condition had worsened. I decided that I'd pay him a visit. That day she told me that they wouldn't be at home because they'd be at the hospital for his tests, so she insisted that I come the following night after 7pm. I agreed to visit him with Austin and my cousin. We arrived at the house just after 7pm, and again, there were no footprints or tire tracks on the freshly fallen snow. We knocked on the door but there was no answer. As we were about to get into the car the phone rang. On the other end was Alice. She called to apologize for not being at home. She told us that the doctors decided to keep my father for further testing, so they'd be at home in the morning. The following day I showed up with my uncle Jude and Austin to see my father. We rang the doorbell again and again there was no answer at the door. I called Alice and told her that we're outside the door, and that no one was answering. The story that she gave was that as they were about to leave, my father fell ill and the doctors were opposed to letting him go. I asked her to tell me the name of the hospital he was in. She told me that it was the Princess Margaret Hospital. She also indicated that the doctors weren't prepared for him to have any visitors as yet. His condition was too serious, and they did not want him to catch any infections. I asked her to keep me notified with any changes and when we could visit him. I called and made arrangements to visit my father at the hospital on the Friday evening.

It was agreed that Friday would be a good time to see

him. That Friday I received a phone call again from Alice prohibiting me from visiting him. Her reason for me not seeing him was due to his condition. The doctors had placed him in an isolation room from visitors for a short period. My dad had caught a fever, so the doctors felt it was best for him not to be in contact with the public, due to any germs he may come in contact with. I told Alice that I'd become frustrated with all of her reasons to prevent me from seeing my father. I decided I would see him on the Saturday after 4pm. I made arrangements to visit him with my aunt and uncle along with Austin on Saturday after church. I'd always said that if it wasn't for bad luck I wouldn't have any luck. That Saturday and out of nowhere, a snowstorm came into the city. The roads were terrible and visibility was next to nothing. I felt extremely disappointed that I wouldn't be able to visit him. The snow didn't seem like it was about to let up, so I postponed it for Sunday after lunch.

That night I went to bed feeling very uneasy for not seeing him. I felt as if Alice was deliberately preventing me from seeing my father. For some reason, she had an excuse for every time I wanted to visit him, and I found it very suspicious. I decided that regardless of what happened, I was going to see him on Sunday where ever he was. At approximately 2:30am on Sunday morning, I received a terrible phone call from Alice. I answered the phone feeling a bit nervous. At the other end of the phone, Alice said, "Everard your father has just passed away." I had no words from my mouth for at least a minute. I asked if he was in any pain; she said, "No." Alice went on to say that he was prepared to leave this earth. He told her that he wasn't able to fight any more, and he wanted to say good-bye. He took two deep breaths and he was gone. I couldn't believe the audacity of her asking me if I wanted to see him now at the hospital. She prevented me from seeing him while he was alive, and now that he's no longer with us, I should rush out of my bed to see a stiff body that couldn't see or talk to me. Every question I had in my heart to ask him was robbed from me by Alice's insecurity and wickedness. I waited forty-eight years to find out why he treated me the way he did and in a split second …poof … it was gone. At around eight in the morning, I started contacting my family and those that cared that my father had passed away.

Alice suggested that I should be the one to break the news to Maureen my sister. I declined because they were the one that kept her isolated from everyone, so it would be better coming from her mouth. My brother and sisters were already on their way up to Canada. I was amazed that so many other people knew what was going on, and I lived here and knew nothing. I asked about the funeral arrangements, and she said that it's all being taken care off.

She had a whole house of family from both sides residing at my father's home. Some of the guests were from Alberta and Calgary. The remainder of the guests was from my father's side, which included his sister and my brother and sisters. The following night I paid a visit at the home and was introduced to her family. My Uncle Jude and Austin accompanied me that evening. We sat and spoke about his last moments and the reason for his death. It was obvious that Alice had known about his illness for at least a half a year. The reason for them traveling to Calgary was so that dad could see Alice's family for the last time. He felt that he needed to see them and to spend some time with one of Alice's sisters little daughter. After they returned, his illness took a turn for the worse. It's difficult for me to understand why she would keep his illness to herself and not inform the people that were close to him about his condition. I found this to be cruel and unjust towards his family.

I felt as being a sibling who had grown up my entire life around my father, that I should have been informed of the nature of his illness. After speaking with Alice and having an understanding of what had happened, I decided to take a walk around the house. His presence was all over the house as we sat and reminisced about his life. I walked into his bedroom where he had a variety of pictures placed all over the bedroom of himself in his younger days. As I stood and looked at the pictures, it was almost as if Alice could have read my mind. She offered to give me one of the pictures after the funeral. She said so in the presence of my uncle, that once the funeral was over, I could have the picture that was placed in the church near the casket. As I opened his walk-in closet door, I was amazed to see the amount of suits and hats that he had. There were so many hats that it wasn't worth counting. His suits were lined up in an orderly fashion with different types of dress shoes below to match. There was an assortment of belts that were hanging from the inside of the door on a hook. So I took one of the belts as a memory. I felt that I had been there long enough, so I decided that it was time for me to leave. The funeral arrangements were made, so all that was left was for me to be at the funeral home to thank the guests for coming. I must admit that I was surprisingly moved by the amount of people that turned out. My father always carried himself as a man who never had friends and didn't care to have any. As my eyes cast over the room and saw the amount of friends and family that turned out to respect his passing, I was certainly shocked. Even though he was my father, I never knew him. I had great difficulty approaching my father to say my good bye. The entire night I tried my best to avoid looking in the direction of the casket. For some reason, I couldn't look at him. I think I still had some kind of fear towards him, and being near the casket intimidated me even more.

His complexion was much darker than his normal skin color. This really bothered me and gave me the creeps. As I took subtle glimpses in the direction of the casket, I couldn't believe that he was actually in the coffin. I felt that, based on his attitude and behaviour; he would have lived almost forever. Looking at this carefree of a man in a wooden box all shined up for nothing, actually made me think even more about the value of life.

My sister Delta had a hard time dealing with the loss of our father. She spent a great portion of the time sitting in the lobby of the home. I knew that the evening couldn't have gone flawlessly without having a confrontation with Alice. Austin had left work a bit later than he wanted to, so he called for the direction on how to get to the funeral home. Because I wasn't as knowledgeable in the area as she was, I asked her to give Austin some direction on how to get to there.

Alice's attitude was totally uncalled for when I asked her to speak to Austin. She behaved as if Austin was asking for a favor that was out of this world. She spoke loudly so that everyone within her vicinity could hear her unhappiness by being disturbed. After she gave Austin a half answer, I asked my uncle to explain to him the route that he should take. Once Austin understood the direction, I thanked my uncle and told him that I was about to give Alice a tongue lashing that she'd never forget. My uncle felt that the time for such behaviour was not appropriate at this time. He wanted me to respect my father's time and to ignore Alice's behaviour, for the time being. It took all the animals inside of me from tearing into her. At that precise moment, I wanted to take every moment that she took away from my mother out onto her. I guessed a wise man always runs from a fight so that he can talk about it the following day.

The night had come to an end, and most of the guest had left to return for the ceremony the next day. At present, I had not spent any time with my father and as much as I wanted to, I still couldn't force myself to face him. For whatever the reason, I just couldn't find the strength to face him. I left the funeral home feeling a bit confused on the reason for my fear. The morning had arrived and we were ready to attend the funeral. The drive along the way to the church was cool and fresh. I felt as if I had a moment to rest with what has happened. I felt as if I could smell the air from which his soul had departed to. We arrived early enough to have a short conversation with some of the guests.

I had my emotion in check, and everything was flowing smoothly. We had a short moment to sit in a family room to pray and to talk as a group. As I sat in the chair and looked around the room, I had a moment to visualize everyone in my mind. It was almost as if I were replaying a short video of their pass. I saw each and everyone as if God was checking their hearts and motives. I saw some as being regretful about their misdoings and trying to change, and I saw some as being truthful in their ways and genuinely missing him.

As for the remainder of family and close friends, I saw them as a bunch of opportunists, grave-digging scoundrels. I looked at some of them out of the corner of my eye, like a cat deciding on the best pray. The priest was ready to start the service, so everyone had to take their places. As a family we lead the coffin into the church slowly as everyone stood. I guess my father would have been proud to see how much his friends and family admired him.

As I walked down the aisle, it almost felt as if I were driving down a street with trees shaped as umbrellas that were covering both sides of the street. Everyone stood and steered, as we walked on by. The casket was placed at the front of the church, with part of the windows open for a final viewing.

The pastor did his best to deliver a message that would paint an image of my father in the audience's mind. Strangely, enough; no one actually had a chance to speak about their time with my father. I guessed Alice took care of that to prevent anyone from saying something that might embarrass her. He read from some notes that were prepared by us before the service had started. The letters would speak about our time with my father. The letter that perked my attention the most was when Alice spoke about her life with her husband. She spoke as if she had met my father before my mother and how she felt in love with him.

Every word that came from the pastor's mouth had me purring like a cat, just waiting to attack. I am sure that everyone in the church could have detected my feelings towards Alice as the priest read from the podium. The service had come to an end with a few hymns that my father always loved.

We took our places once again and walked alongside the coffin as we stopped at the front of the church as the honor guard paid respect to the end of my father's life. We carried the casket down the stairs for the last time as we prepared to put the casket into the hurts. As much as I tried to compose myself; my heart over flowed with pain and sorrow. I couldn't hold my tears any longer. I fell over the casket; hugging it almost as if that was the first time I had hugged my father.

As I stopped thinking; it was the only time that I could think of, as being hugged or giving a hug. The tears had poured from my eyes like a fountain, and my heart ached out of regrets. I felt awful for not having had the opportunity to hug him before he had passed. In the short time, I spent with him, I never felt what it felt like to be hugged. I never knew what to do to make him proud of me. I spilled my sorrows out to him, asking him for his forgiveness for not being the son whom he would have been proud of.

After crying all over the casket, I removed myself from within the Hurst, and allowed the director to close the doors. I walked away by myself, and stood at the back of the church for a few minutes to gather myself. Once I felt strong enough, I took part by eating and drinking with the guests, to celebrate in the long life lived by my father. Every single one of the guests had a pleasant word to say about him, and what a great job we did in celebrating his final day on this earth.

As I walked around the room, I felt as if my father was watching me by way of the picture that sat in the auditorium. The feast was well prepared and for those that came with their stomach empty for an opportunity to eat for free, and to gather as much gossip as possible, I say bravo to them. I had an opportunity to meet with the guests who had stayed for lunch. I expressed my gratitude and how much it meant to my extended family and me.

The police had arrived a bit early and was ready to escort the vehicles to the cemetery. The officers did a fantastic job of getting us there in a timely fashion, and being courteous enough to salute as my father entered his place of rest. The service at the cemetery was pleasant and moving enough to understand that we all had a place on earth, and our reason for being here. As the cemetery officials prepared the casket to be lowered into the grave, I noticed that the date placed on the casket was incorrect. Alice had altered my father's birth date and replaced it with a date that would be more appealing to her and hopefully not to be seen as being extremely old.

Alice was at least forty plus years younger than my father. So to avoid not being scrutinized by the guests, she changed his true birth date to a date that made her look alright. I pointed out the error to my siblings and was prepared to make it be known publicly to how conniving Alice really was. My aunt and brother both felt that it would be a terrible mistake to make at this time. They wanted my father to be buried without any incidents. My purpose at the funeral was to see my father off, and to allow him to rest in peace.

As I looked over at Alice; I pictured her collapsing into the whole, as the operator filled the hole with dirt. By looking at her act, I figured that she was willing to lie for him and destroyed everything that my family had. It probably would have been proper to see her reside with him for the rest of her lousy life. Nothing would have made me happier than to strip her of her clothing and to stomp on her before kicking her into the grave.

Again, I was prevented from getting justice, as she so justly deserved it. We said our final goodbyes to the guests and made our way to the cars. As I followed the hearse back to the church, I realized that I had absolutely no idea where my father was buried. The air was crisp and the sky was as blue as the ocean. Looking at the hearse in front of me, I went into a deep trance in my mind. I realized that from the minute I heard that my father had passed, it never really struck me as it did with my mother. I asked myself many times why I couldn't bring myself to look at my father in the coffin. I wondered why it took me so long to finally fall apart. I wondered about the effect it had on me, when my mother passed, and the difference I felt when I first heard the news. The truth was that the only reason I could have come up with, was the result of all the mental and physical abuse I went through.

I drew a lead wall around me to protect me from being hurt by anyone again. My father never really tried to reach out to me, or even hinted on trying to apologize for his beastly behavior. The best thing ever happened out of this uncharacteristic relationship was; that I was so happy I always listened to my beloved mother. She always preached into my head that, a child should never raise his hand against his mother or father. There were so many times when my father would say and do certain things to me that I felt like lashing out. However, through all the verbal and physical abuse, I never retaliated. For this reason, I'm so happy that I have absolutely no regrets on my conscience.

As I drove behind the hearse, and the breeze blew over my shoulder, I had such an overwhelming feeling. I thought to myself, "how much I would have wished to be forgiven for my wrong doings if he had left this world without asking him for his forgiveness." I looked up to the sky with a slight smile on my face, and as I said to myself, "Mommy always knows best." The lessons that I have been taught as a child, I've done my absolute best to pass on to my son. God is great and He spared me a heartache that I don't think that I would have ever been able to over come. We arrived at the church and prepared to leave. As I made my way into the church to retrieve the picture, I realized that it had been taken away.

When asked about the whereabouts of the picture, Alice said she had no idea where it was and that she never stated it was alright for me to have my father's picture. I sensed a war was just about to begin in the parking lot of the church. As my luck would have it, my aunt would intervene again just when I was about to let loose on that ton of beast of a hippo. My brother and my aunt would stop me from taking the biggest bite out of Alice's face. I wanted to leave her with a scar on her face just as she did on my mother's heart.

She made her blubber self to her vehicle that my dad paid and bought, with his own money. She drove around in his vehicles, as if they were hers, made me so upset that I actually felt like scratching them all with my own knife. I realized that my father married her and there's absolutely nothing that I could do about that. However, my sister's destiny lied in her hands now and made me very uncomfortable as my father was no longer around to watch over her.

My brother and my sister wanted me to join them at my dad's home after the burial for some conversation time. I declined because I didn't think it was right of me to break bread and drink wine with a person of her qualities. I drove my aunt and uncle back to their residence and sat with them for an hour or two and spoke a little about my father and the situation that I was faced with.

My father had left a will to be read by Alice's lawyer after a period of grieving. Alice believed that because she was responsible for my father's estate, that she had all rights to take as long as she wanted to disclose the content of the will. I felt that she should have some time to grieve, but I certainly didn't intend for her to dictate when she would agree to have the will read.

After a month of grieving time, I contacted her through the assistance of my lawyer. This angered her because she felt that I was being pushy, and I didn't allow her sufficient time to grieve. If Alice wanted to grieve; I suggested that she took her wicked way to a priest and confess all of her sins that she had committed. We received her acknowledgment from her lawyer indicating that she'd notify us with the information about will within a week or two. My brother and sisters weren't as successful in having her inform them with the content of the will. I felt sorry for them but there wasn't much that I could have done because each person had to seek their own interest. They had to wait for a substantial amount of time to be given whatever our father had left for them. I received calls from various members of my family, seeking instructions on what they should do. I believed that it was in their best interest that they do nothing and sit back and wait until she approached them. The reason I felt that way was that my brother and sisters had a different relationship with Alice, and if they wanted to keep it in touch, it would be advisable for them not to rock the boat.

Robert and the others enjoyed visiting Alice at her home in the summer months. By creating a problem, she could become vindictive and prevent them of their rights from visiting our father's home. The truth of the matter was, even if you go to church every Saturday or Sunday, it doesn't really matter if you do not understand the truth of the Bible. We had the desire to want to feel the power of God's hands. I found myself believing and trusting in Him more and more. There were many times when I saw and felt His remarkable power in my life. For me to go through the many times that He'd protected me and assisted me, it would be another story all together. Whenever I believed all was gone, He always showed His mighty hands by solving the problem.

Chapter 12

My cousin Janice spoke to me about a co-worker of hers that she felt might be a good match for me. For almost an entire year she tried to get me to meet with her friend. My family organized a family reunion to Grenada during the summer for a little relaxing time, and to meet some of the other relatives whom we probably had never met before. We wanted to meet with all of our relatives; because we knew that they were all getting older. The time we spent in Grenada was one of the best vacations that I had ever spent. The women in Grenada were lovely and for the most part, if I wanted, I had my choice at many of the Grenadian honeys. They were forthcoming and willing to entertain me in almost any capacity. I did have an opportunity to speak with two young ladies who had my mind thinking "what if." These two individuals were pretty and seemed to be educated and spunky. They didn't seem as if they needed a man in their lives. One of them, in particular, took an interest in me, and wanted to have me over for dinner. I avoided the opportunity because I didn't want to start something that I felt that I wouldn't be able to continue.

As for the other woman, she made herself very visible to me daily. I found her to be very direct and wasn't afraid to show her intention. As my time came to an end, they found themselves to have an attachment towards me and were wondering if I would continue to stay in contact. On my last night on the Island, one of the ladies wanted to have an opportunity to take me out. As much as I wanted to, I declined fearing that I may be put in an awkward position, so I had to disappoint her.

The other lady wanted me to sit and have dinner with her on the patio near my building. As I stood toe to toe talking with her, it was evident in her eyes that she had a lot more planned on her mind than having a platonic dinner. As I looked at her as she "undressed" me with her eyes, I soon realized by the many attempts she had made to kiss me on my lips, that if I were to go off with her, that I would be placing myself into a no way out position, so I gave her a nice hug along with a peck on her lips and said my good-byes.

After I returned from Grenada, Janice approached me once again about her colleague. We spoke for a while about her mysterious friend and based on all the fantastic things that she had to say about her, I decided that I'd pursue based solely on the unknown. Misty had traveled to Grenada to pay her final respect to her father. Her father had passed away from prostate cancer. Ironically we had just returned from Grenada on a family reunion.

In the meantime, I had met a wonderful lady who had almost everything that I had been looking for. I said "almost." The one thing missing was that softness that I was looking for in a woman's soul. We saw each other for sometime as I tried to figure out if she was really the one for me. I believed that when God is ready, He will see to it that that special someone is standing beside you.

The relationship had its ups and downs, but there were more ups than downs. However, I still felt that there was something missing, and I couldn't help but want to see what this mysterious person was like. I sensed that Charlie was developing feelings for me, so I had to see Misty before I went further. Finally, I got word from my cousin whom Misty had returned from Grenada and was back at work.

My cousin and I had to put a plan together so that just in case I wasn't attracted to her, that neither of us would feel anything if it didn't work out. We decided that I would call and ask to speak with her, and that I would act as if I were interested in placing my sister in care of her hospital. I made an appointment with her and attended at the appointed time. From the minute, I got off the elevator on her floor, I knew that she was the person that I had to see on that date. She had a beautiful smile, and she seemed as if she had a wonderful personality. We greeted and were given a tour of the facility, and all questions and answers were explained. After the tour was finished, I shook her hand and felt as if we both liked each other. I joked a little with her and left. Before I got onto the elevator I told my cousin to call me because I think that I'd found my angel. I spoke to my cousin on the phone, and I told her to find out for me if Misty felt the same way before I made my move on her. The answer came back as being "yes" and it was a "go." All antennas were down and I had the ok to fly smoothly as I wanted.

Whatever happened in that interview, I couldn't call it a relationship yet, but I knew that the emotions were heavy, and I didn't want to hurt her. The sad thing was that someone always gets hurt either in at a short or long way. I found an avenue that I thought was going to work, so I used it and made it seem as if I was doing it for the benefit of us.

For a short period of time, I began to feel like a Fed-Ex Company, meaning that I couldn't wait to end the emotional deception that I was playing in. Finally, one afternoon we got into an argument about absolutely nothing, but this caused her to feel concerned about how things were going. That was the opportunity that I was waiting on. So I decided that it would probably be best if we gave each other some space. Needless to say that the space was still there, even though we hadn't been in contact with each other ever since. The opportunity that I was waiting on was finally here. Misty decided that she would like to choose the restaurant that we eat at for the first time. By now anything that she suggested would be more than adequate. I picked her up from her home and dined in a German restaurant. She looked ravishing as she walked toward the car and all I kept thinking was that "Everard you have to be proper but still be yourself." I anticipated that the night was going to be one that we would never forget. I sensed a bit of nervousness from her as she spoke to me.

That was completely alright with me, because I knew that by the end of the night, she'd be completely calm and elated with happiness by being with me. We spoke about a variety of subjects and of course our fellow Grenada. Grenada was a subject that we definitely had a lot in common.

As she spoke, I visualized myself kissing her and touching her all over her body. Her lips shined and her eyes glittered like a young girl on her first date. Before our meal, I decided that I'd get to her side of the table and gently place a kiss on her forehead. The kiss was subtle yet intriguing enough to let her know that I was more than satisfied with being with her. As I was about to sit, I observed a look that suggested that I was what she might be looking for, a big fat

308

smile.

Dinner was served, so I decided to thank God for the meal and for the opportunity, He had granted me by meeting Misty. Misty looked at me with a puzzled look on her face as I held her hand to give thank for the meal and the people around the world. Her comment to me was that she found this to be incredibly sweet and thoughtful of the Lord. She was pleased to see that there're men who still believe and carry the faith with them still. I thought that no matter where you were that I should never be afraid to mention His name or to stop and give thanks for what He has granted us. We held hands and I lead us in pray.

The meal was delicious and I could only say that based on her attitude, that she felt the same way. At the end of the meal we sat for a while before escorting her home. This was the beginning to a wonderful relationship and hopefully my lifetime partner. My goal was to fulfill whatever dreams she had.

As time passed, I realized that everything looked much clearer as we spent time with each other. One thing I could remember from the conversations that I shared with my mother was that she always preached that a woman is like a garden and if you don't take care of it, the beauty of the garden fades and a garden is much harder to rejuvenate.

The first time Misty and I became intimate was just amazing. As I said at the beginning, Misty was not the type of girl who had a whole lot of experience, but she made up for it with her emotional beauty. She stood at the side of my bed one evening after we came from having a nice dinner. As I exited the washroom from my bedroom, I was hypnotized by what I saw. As the light from outside shun through the crack of my blinds, it made her skin look like she had just showered with bee honey. She had skin that was as smooth as silk and shined like fresh smooth coco butter that had just been applied. Her arms were slim long and firm. She had broad shoulders that matched her physical appearance with a chest that only a picture could explain. Her breast was close to perfect with legs that were long slim and sexy. As she stood there with the light that shun through the window, her eyes were warm as her body was eager to become one with mine. She didn't have to say to me that her body was her temple, and she wanted me to be her permanent figure that enjoyed the temple. I knew that she was not one to have herself used like a neighbourhood rug. She climbed into bed first, and I followed like a worker pleasing his master. As we laid with each other in the bed with our legs wrapped around each other, It almost felt like our legs were wrapped around each other the way an anaconda would hold its pray.

That night neither one of us wanted to let the other one go because of the way we felt towards each other. Our affection for each other was touching some serious temperatures, so we both knew that if we weren't careful we could be facing a situation that we probably weren't ready for. After playing like two little kittens that had no care for anything around them, so we decided to give ourselves a justifiable amount of time to appreciate what was to come.

In our day-to-day conversations, I could gather that her upbringing wasn't filled with love and affection. Misty had difficulty expressing herself when confronted to do so. Simple things like giving little hugs and gentle kisses would make her feel as if the entire world was looking at her. The ability to express herself by expressing her love to her partner could be a challenging moment. Her belief was that she showed how she felt by the things that she did and not by what she said.

She understood that it was important to inform each other of their feelings by expressing to each other that they appreciated and love each other. Her spin on it is that because her father had never expressed his love for her, it didn't mean that her father didn't love her. One of Misty's weaknesses was that she had a problem with following through with whatever she started. From the day that I met Misty, I'd expressed my desire to be married. She knew that I wished to be with someone one day that I could share my life with. Numerous times I'd canvassed Misty's thoughts with regards to marriage and the possibility for us to give that step. I asked if she would like to settle down and become one in the spirit of God. Her answer had always been if I wanted to, then she would. Now being the type of person that I was, I couldn't see myself standing before a person of authority and being asked if I take this woman to be my wife for life and knowing that I had a problem with it.

Making a commitment meant that both parties were on board with the idea, and hopefully my partner would be happy and enthusiastic with being committed to each other. So for these reasons I'd decided that I wasn't going to ask Misty to marry me.

Misty still believed that just because she didn't wish to be married at this time, didn't mean she wouldn't in the near future. Misty still insisted on going through with it, because she believed that she would be happy being married to me, but the fear of the unknown was stopping her. One day I suggested to Misty that we separate and concentrate on building our own lives. I couldn't believe the reaction that I received. Misty was incredibly emotional and couldn't function. She was crying and insisting that was not what she wanted. She said that she loved me very much, and that she couldn't bear the thought of being without me.

At that uncomfortable moment, I realized that she loved me but suffered from something from her past. I understood that she was feeling unhappy at that time but needed some affection. I asked Misty if she would like me to help her find a specialist that would be able to help her with her fears and emotions. She agreed and was grateful that I was willing to be patient with her while she sorted herself out. In the meantime, I'd decided that if someone was to take an interest in me, and I felt the same about her, that I'll pursue it. I had also told Misty that I did care dearly about her, but I couldn't take the chance and be hurt by her choosing to stay disengaged, so I'd decided to date her, but if someone was truly interested in me, that I would notify her first to see if she had a change of heart.

So in the meantime, we continued to see each other and hopefully within a short period of time, things would change for the better. Misty and I had a discussion about her fears and decided that it might be in her best interest to speak with a professional. I wanted Misty to get the help that she needed to overcome some of the challenges that she has. I told her that even if we don't work out that I'm happy to see her make an attempt for change.

The councilor did meet with Misty and to the best of my knowledge, some skills were gained and that was a positive regardless of what happens. At the end of the sessions I sat with Misty and told her that I didn't think that it was healthy and fair to either of us to continue as we are. So I told her that she had a short period of time to decide on her future, or I'll be gone. I do love her, but I would like to have a life of joy, fun, love, affection, romance, respect, faithfulness and most of all, the faith and strength to believe in God.

Misty and I agreed that it would be unfair to the both of us to hold each other in limbo. So we decided to give each other or freedom to seek our happiness. Knowing that Misty wasn't going to leave her mother's home and wasn't strong enough to make a decision to marry or live with me, I felt that I had to begin to make a life for myself. The feelings we shared for each other were unlike any other but sometimes in life you're confronted with a situation that is unsolvable. This was one that I couldn't solve. We agreed to be friends and to be there for each other whenever required. The journey ahead will be difficult, but I believe with my whole heart that there is someone out there that God has waiting upon me. I hope my life would be filled with joy, love, sex, romance and the blessing of God and may the same blessings fall upon my dear friend Misty. All aboard.

CPSIA information can be obtained at www.ICGtesting.com
Printed in the USA
240019LV00005B/6/P